*Four Sociological
Traditions*

Four Sociological Traditions

RANDALL COLLINS

Revised and expanded edition
of *Three Sociological Traditions*

New York   Oxford
OXFORD UNIVERSITY PRESS
1994

Oxford University Press

Oxford   New York   Toronto
Delhi   Bombay   Calcutta   Madras   Karachi
Kuala Lumpur   Singapore   Hong Kong   Tokyo
Nairobi   Dar es Salaam   Cape Town
Melbourne   Auckland   Madrid

and associated companies in
Berlin   Ibadan

Published by Oxford University Press, Inc.
200 Madison Avenue, New York, New York 10016

Oxford is a registered trademark of Oxford University Press

Library of Congress Cataloging-in-Publication Data
Collins, Randall, 1941–
    Four sociological traditions / Randall Collins.
        p.   cm.   Rev. ed. of: Three sociological traditions. 1985.
    Includes bibliographical references and index.
    ISBN 0-19-508208-7
        1. Sociology.   2. Social conflict.   3. Solidarity.
    4. Microsociology.   I. Collins, Randall, 1941–
    Three sociological traditions.   II. Title.
    HM24.C652   1994   301–dc20   93-24249

9 8 7 6 5 4 3 2 1
Printed in the United States of America

Preface

The argument of this book is that sociology has made good progress in its knowledge of the social world. Though it is often claimed that sociology does not cumulate, and that the classic thinkers remain as important, or even more so, than current theorists and researchers, I will attempt to show that there are some significant lines of development from the classics through modern versions of sociology. That does not mean that modern sociology is without some basic cleavages among theoretical positions. The reality of today's intellectual world is that we are deeply divided among opposing points of view. But these disagreements are not infinite in number, and they do not rule out another important fact about our field: that several lines of thought have been acquiring increasingly sophisticated knowledge throughout the last hundred years.

In the first edition of this book, I focused on three great sociological traditions. The first I call the conflict tradition, which in my view derives alike from Karl Marx, Friedrich Engels, and Max Weber. The Marxian and the Weberian traditions are frequently regarded as opponents, but in fact, sociologically speaking, they have a good deal in common. Together, they have developed the theories of capitalism, social stratification, political conflict, and related macro/historical themes in sociology. Especially in recent years, many theorists and researchers in the Marxian and Weberian traditions have borrowed a good deal from each other. If we leave aside the political activism associated with Marxism, as well as the most conservative politics that have sometimes been associated with the Weberians, and concentrate on their purely intellectual contributions, we can see that a sophisticated view of the macrostructure of society is emerging based on both wings of a general conflict tradition.

The second tradition outlined here is called the Durkheimian tradition, after its greatest expositor. This is the self-consciously "sociological" tradition, since it includes Auguste Comte, who coined the term "sociology," as well as Emile Durkheim, who argued most forcefully for sociology as a unique level of analysis. Again, I have argued that the tradition is divided into two main wings. One wing has concentrated on the macrostructure of society, but in an organicist and evolutionist manner very far removed from the conflict approach of Marx, Engels, and Weber. This wing stretches from remote predecessors such as Montesquieu, Comte, and Herbert Spencer, through Durkheim himself, to more recent functionalists such as Robert Merton and Talcott Parsons. This side of the Durkheimian tradition has been sharply attacked in recent years for its tendency to idealize and reify the social structure. But a second wing, which I have called the lineage of social anthropology, has produced many realistic insights. This wing emphasizes the mechanisms by which social rituals taking place in face-to-face groups produce solidarity. Rituals also produce emotionally charged symbols that become the focus for moral beliefs, as well as boundaries between insiders and outsiders of the group. This line of analysis has made some important recent advances, including its application by Erving Goffman to the rituals of everyday life. Other sociologists have connected it to social classes and the cultural foundations of stratification, thus building a bridge between the Durkheimian tradition and the conflict tradition.

The third tradition examined in this book is the microinteractionist tradition. Again, there are various wings within this approach. There is a pragmatist version deriving from Charles Sanders Peirce and developed by George Herbert Mead; the symbolic interactionist line, with important imputs from Charles Horton Cooley, W.I. Thomas, and explicitly formulated by Herbert Blumer; as well as the phenomenological or "ethnomethodological" sociology produced by Alfred Schutz and Harold Garfinkel. Erving Goffman, too, enters this general arena. He was not a symbolic interactionist, as he is so often labeled, but originally a developer of the Durkheimian tradition of the analysis of social rituals. Later in his career, though, Goffman took on the new sociology of consciousness and produced what I would regard as a fruitful and interesting counterattack on its basic questions of the social construction of reality and the sociology of language. Like the other two traditions outlined in this book, the microinteractionist tradition continues to make important advances in our own days.

For this new edition, I have added the utilitarian tradition, which in recent decades has been variously known as exchange theory or rational choice. In the previous edition, the utilitarians figured largely as a foil for the other traditions. Durkheim set sociology off in a new direction by criticizing the rational theory of the social contract and denying that any theory of individual action would be able to explain the features of society. Conflict theory is closer to the utilitarians, since both traditions share a focus on self-interest and the importance of the material economy. The difference is that conflict theory has taken a much harsher view of social relationships, pointing to dominance and periodic outbreaks of violent struggle, whereas the utilitarians have tended towards a benign liberal view that rational individual interests work out for the best for everyone. This optimistic side of the rational/utilitarian tradition has changed in recent years, however, and modern utilitarians have become much more critical of today's society. In this respect modern rational choice theory has tended to blend into conflict theory, although in a politically ambiguous way; where classical conflict theory was usually on the Left, modern rational choice theory makes critiques both from the Left and from the Right.

The microinteractionist tradition, which represents the flow of idealist and pragmatist philosophies into sociology, has always been hostile to the rational/utilitarian approach. In a sense what we have here is a continuation, on the grounds of sociology, of the long-standing philosophical battle between Continental idealism and British empiricism. In the 1980s, the idealist and relativist side of this philosophical tradition has been enunciated in a highly polemical version under the label of Postmodernism. This movement is especially hostile towards the positivist approach; thus in a sense one can say that the intellectual battlegrounds of the late twentieth century have been shaped by yet another upsurge of old opponents: the growing movement of rational/utilitarian theory on one side, and the interpretative, culturally oriented philosophies that have descended from German idealism on the other. The ongoing debates among these traditions are very much part of "where the action is," intellectually speaking.

The four traditions I have selected here are not the only areas of sociology that have undergone cumulative development and made some progress toward theoretical sophistication. But I think they have a claim to be considered the core traditions of sociology. They have a continuity in time and a depth of thought matched by few others. My hope is that *Four Sociological Traditions* will give a picture of what progress sociology has made over the four or five generations it has been alive.

A companion volume is available, also from Oxford University Press, *Four Sociological Traditions: Selected Readings*. This contains major texts from each of the four traditions, from their classics up through their recent theoretical developments.

San Diego   R.C.
May, 1993

Contents

Four Sociological Traditions

Prologue: *The Rise of the Social Sciences**

Social science derives from a social base. In this statement there are two paradoxes. *Science* means knowledge about the objective world that is true because that is the way things are, not just because we have imagined it. Yet this science is now asserted to be socially based, determined by the society in which social scientists live. That is paradox one.

Paradox two is that the social base is nevertheless held to exist. It is an autonomous, objective world that exists independently of individuals and that determines what they think. If social science is successful, one might even someday write the objective laws of this social determination of ideas.

Paradoxical or not, the statement is nevertheless true—at least true enough so that one can write a whole book in this vein. In a sense that is what this book is about. The four sociological traditions have each played a part in uncovering the laws by which social ideas are determined.

From the *conflict tradition*, we discern the dynamics of ideology, legitimacy, the conditions of mobilization of self-interested groups, and the economics of culture. For the conflict tradition, ideas are weapons, and their dominance is determined by the distribution of social and economic resources.

*The prologue gives a sociological look backwards at the conditions in society that underlie the rise of the social sciences generally and of sociology in particular. It may be skipped if one wishes to proceed directly to the ideas of the four traditions.

3

From the *rational/utilitarian tradition*, we learn of the limited nature of human capacities for processing information, about bounded rationality and the paradoxes of cognitive choice.

From the *Durkheimian tradition*, we learn of social rituals that create not only solidarity, but also the symbols that we use for thinking. Our minds are made up of ideas infused with moral power by the groups to which we belong. Our social memberships determine what we believe is real, and they place a moral sanction on the necessity of believing it and a moral condemnation on doubting these accepted beliefs.

From the *microinteractionist tradition*, we learn that society is in the mind itself. Our conversations and practical encounters of everyday life construct our sense of social reality.

The four sociological traditions, then, are among other things sociologies of knowledge, and they turn a social determinism on their own foundations. The four traditions themselves are subject to each other's laws: knowledge founded on ideology, rational limits of rationality, truth coming from ritual, and the social construction of reality. How is this possible?

Ultimately the conundrum can be addressed, I think, by the methods of philosophy and mathematics (deriving from Bertrand Russell, Kurt Gödel, and Ludwig Wittgenstein) that distinguish various levels of referential statements. But this is not a work of philosophy. I make no effort to solve the paradoxes, only to illustrate them.

The chapters of this book serve up the contents of these four theoretical traditions as they have developed over the last century and a half. In the prologue, we turn the sociological eye on the conditions that have shaped their foundations.

Social Thought in the Agrarian Empires

Ideas always have their carriers. In the agrarian empires that make up most of world history from the third millennium B.C. up through medieval Europe, there is little in the way of distinct intellectual groups with their own communities. In the empires of Egypt, Mesopotamia, Persia, India, China, and Japan, there were literate classes: mostly priests, government officials, and some merchants. These classes developed some knowledge of astronomy, engineering, and mathematics, and some of them created elaborate religious philosophies. In general, however, these forms of thought were tied to practical or religious activities: knowledge, especially of the social world, was not sought as an interest in its own right. Here and there we find outstanding individual thinkers who touched on social matters—Confucius, or the Machiavellian statesman of ancient India, Kautilya—and no doubt there were worldly wise men and women whose names we have never heard because their thought was not passed on. But this is exactly the problem: social thought develops only if carried by a community that preserves earlier contributions and builds on them. Lacking communities dedicated to this purpose, little social science has come down to us from these civilizations. Only in a crude form of history—mainly chronicles of the reigns of kings compiled by government or religious officials—do we find the beginning of a cumulative investigation of society.

For any objective social knowledge to develop, two things had to happen. First, societies (or at least parts of them) had to become rationalized—in Max Weber's term, disenchanted. This began to occur in the large agrarian empires of antiquity in which the practical matters of commerce and government administration created a more matter-of-fact attitude towards the social world. But practical necessities by themselves are only a small aid to social thought because it is possible to develop practical know-how without any conscious understanding of general principles. Practical skills can coexist with all sorts of social myths and misconceptions. The second condition, therefore, was the rise of a group of intellectual specialists who could create a social community of their own—an intellectual community—within which the search for knowledge in its own right could receive support. We will be concerned, then, with tracing the rise of such intellectual communities and with looking at both their internal structures and their relations with the larger societies that surrounded them.

It has been difficult to create any social science: far more difficult than creating the natural sciences. Although the realms of physics, chemistry, astronomy, biology, and the rest of the natural world were at one time permeated by religious myths, *on the whole* it has been relatively uncontroversial to replace them with a technical science. It is true Galileo was condemned by the Catholic Church and Darwin's theory of evolution stirred up public controversy, but for the most part these sorts of incidents have been exceptional. Not so for social thinkers. For them the pressure of social orthodoxy has been so great that intellectual heresies have had a hard time being formulated or even entering intellectuals' minds. It is probably for this reason, not because the social sciences are "younger" or the subject matter intrinsically so much more difficult or indeterminate, that the natural sciences came first. Hence, the first fold of the twofold argument: how politics, religion, and educational institutions had to mesh in just the right way so that an intellectual community could arise with enough autonomy so that social science questions could be addressed at all.

The first systematic efforts at social thought were produced in the Greek city-states in the 500s B.C. Ancient Greek civilization occupies a prominent place in the history of Western thought because it was here that for the first time a fairly distinct intellectual community arose that was not subordinate to government or religion. Greek society arose out of relatively primitive tribes on the borders of the great Middle Eastern empires. Protected by the geopolitical conditions of the time, they were able to acquire the wealth and culture of their more advanced neighbors without their oppressively centralized governments and religions. The Greeks retained the crude democracy of tribal war coalitions and the myriad local religious cults that went along with them.

When Oriental literacy and its accompanying knowledge flooded into this situation of religious and political pluralism, there sprang up a number of Greek intellectual schools. Groups around such philosophers as Thales, Pythagoras, the Sophists, Socrates, and Plato were the most famous. In one sense they were innovative religious cults that added rationalized knowledge to the rituals of earlier forms of worship. But these schools were also political factions within the politics of the city-states; and they were a source of income for traveling teachers who taught the skills of argument to would-be politicians and citizen-lawyers (since everyone argued his own case before the assembly of the city-state). The key feature of this situation was the competition that resulted owing to the presence of many intellectuals selling their wares to the public. Because they were free intellectual entrepreneurs, not taking orders in a priestly or government hierarchy, there was no built-in bias towards maintaining tradition. Competition with others meant intellectuals had to develop new ideas and improve them against rivals' criticism. During the time when the city-states flourished, there was the unparalleled situation of a free intellectual community with many markets to exploit; the result was a period of intellectual vigor, which subsequent history has regarded as a Golden Age. The roots of modern philosophy and science are found in this period; here, too, we find the beginnings of social science.

The first systematic consideration of society is found in the philosophies of Plato and Aristotle. To be sure it is primarily concerned with the evaluative question of what form the best society should take rather than with an explanation of why things exist as they are; but this is what we might expect from an intellectual group that also aspired to play a role within Greek politics. At the same time their thought was more intellectual than that of other politicians. In the next generation after Plato, his pupil Aristotle provided the first example of empirical analysis when he collected the constitutions of dozens of Greek cities and attempted to state the conditions under which they were ruled by kings, aristocracies, or democracies. Aristotle was not only concerned with value questions, but also with developing a system of knowledge. The crucial factor may be in the structure of the school that he organized: whereas Plato's school was intended to train government leaders, Aristotle's was primarily intended to train other intellectuals. Aristotle's form of organization itself led him to systematize, and its internal insulation from immediate political goals led to a greater emphasis on knowledge for its own sake.

Aristotle's sociology and economics were promising but rudimentary. The finest achievement of Greek social science was the creation of history as we know it: that is to say, serious narrative history. In the same period when the Sophists and the other philosophical schools were engaged in their most vigorous debates, the same intellectual marketplace encouraged retired politicians and generals like Thucydides and Herodotus to write histories. These created a new standard by their efforts to gather historical facts objectively, free from religious interpretations (such as those with which we are familiar in the Hebrew Bible) and going beyond bare administrative chronicles to an analysis of the causes of events. Although the relatively autonomous intellectual marketplace of the Greek Golden Age was not to last, its tradition of history-writing was one legacy that did survive, to some extent at least, in the more religiously and politically top-heavy societies that were to follow. In Rome, politicians like Julius Caesar or out-of-favor aristocrats like Tacitus wrote informative and even somewhat analytical histories; a millennium later, Arab thinkers such as Ibn Miskawaih and Ibn Khaldun ventured into comparative sociology in the guise of historical reflections. During the long centuries when Aristotle and Plato, if remembered at all, were treated like sacred fossils to be venerated and commented on, history-writing kept the spark of social science alive in the West.

Medieval Universities Create the Modern Intellectual

Modern social thought begins to achieve a critical mass of intellectuals in the 1700s, and it is only after that date that the modern disciplines as we know them begin to form. But since we are pursuing the social foundations of social science, it is necessary to glance at least briefly five or six centuries further back. In the realm of social ideas, we find little more than isolated figures throughout that period: Thomas Hobbes in the 1600s, Niccolo Machiavelli around 1500, Thomas Aquinas in the 1200s, and others. But in the realm of intellectual institutions, some major foundations were laid. Without these, the later rise of sophisticated traditions in social thought could not have happened. Social thought in the Middle Ages was still trammeled by religious orthodoxy; the first breaches towards intellectual autonomy occurred in safer areas, first in philosophy and then in mathematics and natural science. But the institutions that pioneered these intellectual developments provided an anchor to which later social science could attach itself.

The major contribution of the Middle Ages to subsequent

thought was not an idea, but an institution: the rise of the university. Universities grew up in the 1100s and 1200s as teachers and students congregated in cities like Paris, Bologna, and Oxford. Eventually the teachers (or sometimes the students) acquired legal charters from the Church or state that gave them the right to govern themselves as autonomous corporations. The intellectual community for the first time had acquired its own citadel: for better or worse, it had a clear boundary between inside and out and, at least in principle, claimed the right to follow its own affairs.

This autonomy only came gradually. For the most part teachers and students were interested in theology, law, and to a lesser degree medicine: practical traditions of the outside world rather than intellectual subjects per se. University degrees at first were marginal for most careers because many priests were barely literate and church positions were frequently political sinecures; of course this was even more true of most government officials in the feudal-patrimonial states of the time. But the Papacy was beginning to bureaucratize, and university degrees in theology or canon (religious) law gave prestige to ambitious churchmen bent on higher office in Rome. At the same time the stirrings of commerce in the economy of Italy and elsewhere produced a market for lawyers, as did the property disputes and other administrative matters of the burgeoning secular states.

The universities were officially parts of the Church to which teachers of law and medicine became attached, thus piggybacking on the prestige of a religion with sacred scriptures. Persons of an intellectual bent soon found that their abilities counted for something within the university world itself; here they could pursue careers as professors. Most of the students, then as now, were mere place-seekers and carousers with no intellectual concerns. Nevertheless the autonomous university corporations were an expanding network spread out through the cities of Europe, places where intellectuals were brought physically into contact and insulated from the pressures of the rest of the world. It became possible to make one's career inside this community as a famous professor by making no other contributions than intellectual ones.

Over the centuries of the late Middle Ages, university credentials began a long process of inflation in their social value. As more people acquired degrees, educational requirements began to develop in the religious and political positions of the time, which in turn made longer years of study socially necessary for the same jobs. As students flocked in, the community of teachers expanded. Universities proliferated and competed among themselves to attract students and the most famous professors. As typically happens in a period of competition, intellectuals began to try to distinguish themselves from their rivals by creating new ideas. The long centuries of tradition and dogma began to give way to innovation—not because the surrounding society valued tradition any less, but because within its hard cocoon a dynamic intellectual marketplace had formed.

This innovativeness first occurred in the part of the university most insulated from the outside world, namely, the philosophical faculty. Originally this was the least important of the four faculties: the higher faculties—theology, law, medicine—trained practitioners for the worldly professions and placed a premium on the prestige of tradition and orthodoxy. Philosophy originally granted only the lower (Bachelors and Masters) degrees rather than the Doctorate; it was merely a preparatory faculty in which students learned logic, grammar, and similar subjects as a kind of undergraduate or secondary-school drill before going on to higher studies. For that reason, the teachers of philosophy were not subject to the same pressures for orthodoxy found in the higher faculties. Such men as Peter Abelard, Duns Scotus, and William of Occam began to develop philosophy less as an introduction to theology and more as an independent subject in its own right—moreover one in which innovation could take place.

From the point of view of the modern sociology of organizations, what took place was a "goal displacement"; a staff division struggled to raise itself from being a means to some other end into being an end in itself. Usually in the organizational literature, goal displacement is regarded as a pathology, for example, when the accounting department stops acting like a service to the organization and begins to elaborate accounting as an end in itself. In the history of intellectual institutions, however, this kind of transformation of means into ends was to be the beginning of a social interest in developing knowledge in its own right. With the rise of the universities and above all with the creativity of the philosophical faculty, intellectuals acquired their own "home" and their own sense of purpose. The history of human thought ever since has revolved around both the interaction between the intellectual community and the outside world and between the universities' insulation from ordinary practical issues and ideological orthodoxies as well as the ways in which these concerns seep in to provide intellectuals with new proddings and problems.

The philosophical upsurge of the medieval universities does not lead on a direct line into modern intellectual life, however. The universities went through several waves of expansion and contraction. Credential inflation peaked out in the 1300s and 1400s, and university prestige declined sharply. The supply of students dried up in many places. During this period, creative intellectuals tended to desert the universities and to find positions in the outside world under the patronage of princes and wealthy merchants. It was this shift that now goes by the name of the Renaissance.

THE RENAISSANCE: INTELLECTUAL LIFE GOES SECULAR

The glory of the Renaissance was primarily in the realm of art. But it had a structural significance for the intellectual community as well. For the first time since antiquity, there was a role for intellectuals to find their livelihood outside the Church (of which the medieval universities were a branch). The result of this break was the intellectual ideology known as humanism, a battle cry that emphasized secular culture over religion as the highest intellectual standard. Although at first the emphasis was entirely on reviving ancient Greek and Roman literature, the underlying theme that secular intellectuals should be independent of the Church was most important in the long run.

The typical humanist was an all-around entertainer at the court of some wealthy patron. He often served as private secretary; wrote poems, history, and essays; and perhaps dabbled in scientific experiments. For social science, this situation had mixed effects. The popularity of intellectual activity as a sort of spectator sport (because this was a time not only without the mass media, but also before the large-scale printing of books) meant that there was a ready market for ideas. On the other hand, the intellectual's role was primarily to be an entertainer, and emphasis was more on dramatic renditions and literary style than on accuracy or analytical penetration. The one social science that flourished was history-writing. But histories remained superficial; the few really good historians (Francesco Guicciardini, Flavius Blondus, and a few others) were not well received because their scholarship was too austere for current tastes.

The big intellectual event of the 1500s and 1600s was the takeoff of natural, not social, science. This came about by a combination of social roots. On one side, secular intellectuals of the Renaissance type developed science as a new entertainment. This interest was deepened by contact with practical artisans and also by government patronage. It was a time of technological innovation in warfare—the gunpowder revolution; of world exploration and, hence, interest in navigation; and of commercial expansion and slow improvements in manufacturing techniques that were building up towards the Industrial Revolution. Science was not only becoming amusing, but there was some inkling that it might be practical.

These influences were probably not enough to produce genuine breakthroughs in scientific theory, but they happened to coincide with another institutional change that provided the missing piece: the revival of the universities. The 1500s and 1600s saw the second great wave of university expansion after the first expansion of the Middle Ages and the following trough of the Renaissance. The influx of new practical ideas and Renaissance interests into the pure-theory realm of the university philosophies brought the pieces together to create modern science as we know it: a synthesis of empirical evidence with theoretical generalization. The same institutional combination revived philosophy, which had stagnated for centuries, and prodded it into new paths; it was precisely at the same time, in the 1600s, that modern philosophy was created by persons who were active in the scientific takeoff as well: Francis Bacon, René Descartes, Gottfried Leibniz.

For the social sciences, the path was not so easy. The ideological basis of society was in turmoil during this period, beginning with the Reformation and continuing through the religious wars that pitted Catholic against Protestant down through the end of the 1600s. If natural science could remain relatively nonideological, social science could not. (I say *relatively* nonideological: Galileo was condemned by the Inquisition, although fortunately only in his old age after he had done his work. But by and large science flourished in both Protestant and Catholic countries.) There was no independence for theorizing abstractly about the social world. The one established social science, history, was pressed into service to write propaganda for Protestant and Catholic sides in the religious wars.

RELIGIOUS WARS AND THE ENLIGHTENMENT

The religious wars did mark an institutional transition that would be important for subsequent intellectual developments. With the growing armies of the times, kings began to replace feudal aristocrats and churchly advisers with an administration of civilian bureaucrats. The Church had been the traditional source of civil servants because it was the only large-scale literate class in medieval society. But given the politics of the time, the Catholic Church with its loyalty to the Pope could no longer be relied on by kings who wished to build their own national states.

Just how the church-state conflict was resolved in various countries was to be crucial for the character of intellectual life in each place. In Protestant Germany, the church simply became part of the government bureaucracy. The universities, including theological and legal faculties, were absorbed as state offices. When a mass elementary-school system was later erected, this, too, would easily take its place as another branch of the central government administration. Thus, virtually all intellectual roles in Germany were to be those of bureaucratic state officials. One result of this was that social science when it appeared in Germany was part of the official interest in developing information and techniques for government purposes. Its first appearance there, called *Staatswissenschaft* (state science) was a combination of what we might call public administration and descriptive statistics. It was out of this German milieu that the major part of the conflict tradition in sociology was to grow, inspired perhaps by its tone of *Realpolitik*, the principles of hard-nosed realistic politics.

France, on the other hand, had a severe internal battle between its Protestant and Catholic factions but ended up remaining nominally Catholic. But the French government was just as eager as the Germans for independence from Rome. Accordingly, the French left the universities as a bastian of Catholic orthodoxy, but they left them to rot on the vine by cutting them off from official recruitment. Instead, the French made use of secular administrators and intellectuals. An entire new nobility, the *noblesse de robe*, appeared alongside the old warrior aristocrats. It was from this bureaucratic aristocracy that such social thinkers as the baron de Montesquieu, the baron de Turgot, the marquis de Condorcet, and Alexis de Tocqueville were to come. Because the loyalty of the universities was questionable, the government set up independent academies and training schools in Paris for engineers and other public servants. Later, after the French Revolution, Napoleon sealed the victory of this technical elite by abolishing the old universities entirely and putting these secular schools in their place. On the other hand, elementary and secondary schools remained in the hands of the Church until late in the 1800s.

The result was that French intellectuals were concentrated as an elite group in Paris, competing for a small number of high-status positions in the academies and the *grandes écoles* and congregating in the salons of aristocratic patrons. Whereas the typical German intellectual was a university professor in a middle-level civil service position, the French intellectual was a cultural elitist close to the corridors of power and potentially ready for a revolutionary takeover. Whereas the German intellectual was systematic, scholarly, even pedantic, the French intellectual tended to be oriented to science as well as to political controversy and to be lucid and brilliant as well as facile and flowery in exposition. One may call this national character if one likes, but that is only a metaphor; more accurately, it represents the influence of different social institutions on the structure of intellectual life. And this was to be the social milieu of that sociological lineage I have called the Durkheimian tradition.

England provides yet a third pattern. Of all the European societies, only there did the minor gentry succeed in arresting the bureaucratic development of the central state. The success of the Protestant Reformation in England made its universities independent of Rome and, hence, acceptable to the political elite. But the fact that the government had no extensive bureaucracy to speak of meant that the university had little function to fill. The higher faculties (theology, medicine, law) decayed completely; law was already largely taught outside the universities by the Common Law specialists at the London Inns of Court. English universities were reduced to little more than finishing schools and paths to church sinecures for younger sons of the gentry. The universities thus played a minor role in English intellectual life throughout the 1700s and up until the administrative reforms in the late 1800s.

Instead, intellectual roles were confined almost entirely to the private amusement of wealthy gentry. In itself this would not seem an auspicious basis for intellectual creativity. An occasional gentleman (women were almost entirely excluded from this realm by the sexist practices of the time) might happen to have intellectual interests, but there was no provision for training students or carrying on a cumulative line of research. If research equipment or funding for expeditions were needed, their presence depended entirely on the accident of whether the interested person happened to have the money. Even if new discoveries were made, there was no guarantee that someone else would be found to carry on where the innovator had left off. As a result English thinkers in natural science, philosophy, and social science alike have been notably individualistic. English intellectual history is full of idiosyncratic characters like parson Thomas Malthus, Francis Galton, or Charles Darwin, but it lacks sustained schools or movements such as those organized in France or Germany.

Countering this, though, was the fact that England was

in steady communication with the intellectual life of the Continent. English thinkers were able to provide creative new leads on lines of study begun abroad and to have their own ideas taken up by movements elsewhere. We will see a prime instance of this in the English-French interplay of ideas that Chapter 3 treats as the Durkheimian tradition. The social organization of the English intellectual world would not likely have sustained long-term growth if it had existed in isolation. But as part of an international network, it provided roles freed from the constraints of the dense intellectual environments of Paris or the German universities and, thus, was capable of some notable innovations. England also had the advantage of being the wealthiest country in Europe for several centuries, which meant that quite a few of the gentry and even some of the middle class had the means to devote themselves to intellectual pursuits.

A few other countries might be mentioned. Scotland is the most important of these, for its universities retained an importance in church and government more akin to Germany; hence, Scotland provided the systematic university basis lacking in British intellectual life. Once-proud Italy and Spain were in an economic decline, and their universities were in the grips of the Catholic reaction, a kind of cold war left over from the struggle against the Protestant Reformation. Intellectual creativity might still be found in Italy, especially among cosmopolitan intellectuals oriented towards Paris.

For the social sciences, the takeoff period was the 1700s. In a characteristic burst of self-confidence, the thinkers of the time referred to their era as the Enlightenment. A secular intellectual community had been building up in the wealthier countries of Europe ever since the Renaissance. It could be found partly in the universities of Germany and Scotland and in the great technical schools of France; partly among the intellectuals who entertained the most cultivated salons of the aristocracy, especially in Paris; and partly among the gentry—especially in England, France, and Italy—who used their personal culture as a mark of private distinction. The great era for this far-reaching community was in the 1700s. The religious wars had died down and secular tolerance was the mood of the day. Government bureaucracies and some of the new schools provided career opportunities for intellectuals, and the increasing level of wealth gave aristocratic patrons and gentry-intellectuals plenty of resources to support their hobbies. Conditions were uniquely favorable for intellectual activity.

The Enlightenment intellectual was an all-purpose thinker. Thus, we find individuals who contributed to wide-ranging areas: Turgot and Adam Smith wrote both economics and social philosophy; philosophers like Locke, Leibniz, Voltaire, Hume, and Kant contributed to areas ranging from science to politics, literature, and history; and the writings of Montesquieu, Vico, or Condorcet can as easily be called social philosophy, sociology, political science, anthropology, or universal history. Such disciplines did not yet exist because there were no separate intellectual communities to give them distinctive identities and standards. Instead, the intellectual role led simultaneously in all directions. Two things are notable about the kinds of ideas this situation produced. It was the first time that thinkers tried to provide *general explanations* of the social world. They were able to detach themselves, at least in principle, from expounding some existing ideology and to attempt to lay down general principles that explained social life. The principles were not necessarily sophisticated, but they marked the beginning of social science in the sense of clearly formulating the goal of what a social science might accomplish. Probably this was due to the influence of the natural sciences, which were riding a wave of explanatory successes and a good deal of public popularity. Isaac Newton was the hero of the age, and mathematicians, astronomers, and biologists were in vogue. Together with this, social thinkers acquired some freedom to try to make a science of society owing to a general exhaustion from the dogmatism and the slaughters of the religious wars. Also contributing was a relatively placid political climate in the era of the bureaucratic enlightened despots. In Naples, Giambattista Vico produced a system of world history, which he entitled *La Scienza Nuova*, the New Science.

Moreover social thinkers had some new and striking materials to ponder: the newly discovered tribal and non-Western societies of the Americas, Africa, and the Orient. Information had been brought back by ever-increasing numbers of explorers since the voyages of the late 1400s, and public interest was manifested in large numbers of popular books. From these accounts, social philosophers like Thomas Hobbes, John Locke, and Jean Jacques Rousseau derived their notion of a "state of nature" against which to theorize about how their own societies might have been constructed. The notion of an evolutionary sequence of stages was gradually built up by Turgot, Condorcet, and the comte de Saint-Simon, culminating in the explicit sociology of Auguste Comte.

In general it was not an age of empirical research. The tribes of the "Indies" and the ancient civilizations of Persia and China were known more by hearsay than by systematic study. Only historians, by the nature of their pursuits, were engaged in factual analysis. Their audiences were primarily popular, and literary standards were given the highest regard. The most prominent historians were individuals like Edward Gibbon who mainly retold early histories rather than uncovered new facts. The social role of the Enlightenment intellectual did not offer much room for sustained efforts at research. It was an immediately striking product that gave the greatest success— hence, speculative philosophy and literary flair characterized most of what was written.

But a beginning had been made. Already the specialized disciplines of the social sciences were beginning to create their own intellectual communities. Once these were in place, the popular interests of the public could be downplayed and internal intellectual competition would force each discipline into a higher level of sophistication.

Economics: The First Social Science

The first area in which factual information was systematically accumulated came in conjunction with the expanded administrative bureaucracies of the 1700s. The mercantilist state tried to regulate commerce, control currency, and engage in complex forms of taxation. Accordingly officials and intellectuals hoping for government consultation began to write practical tracts on economic policy. In Germany, where the government bureaucracies were closely tied to the universities, law professors developed a discipline variously called statistics or *Staatswissenschaft* that collected economic information. This growing literature contained a good deal of description but few general principles. One might say that the practical orientation was too strong to allow much intellectual detachment on this material.

This theoretical interest began to develop as economics became part of the concerns of the larger intellectual community. In England and France, political factions or rudimentary parties began to form. Commercial development created a business class independent of the government and the older aristocratic and religious factions. Intellectuals began to appeal to this new audience by writing partisan tracts on economic policy. But in the context of the intellectual life of the time, arguments on specific issues were generalized into a "philosophical" mode of discourse, and hence, into the beginnings of economic theory.

In France during the 1760s, the medical doctor François Quesnay formulated an economic philosophy called the physiocratic doctrine. It acquired quite a following in government and intellectual circles with its reasoned advocacy of commercial farming as the source of all wealth. This of course appealed to the agricultural interests. A parallel appeal to business interests was formulated shortly thereafter when in 1776 Adam Smith published *The Wealth of Nations*. This was perhaps the single most popular book of social science ever published; it went through numerous editions in England and was translated within a few years into French, German, Italian, and numerous other languages. Adam Smith had a pleasing literary style, but he was not entirely original as he systematized information and economic ideas that were already available. Politically his popularity was due to the way he gave succinct arguments and slogans supporting the political policy of laissez-faire in economic matters. Adam Smith was also more theoretical than his predecessors. He was a professor of moral philosophy at the University of Glasgow, hence, his writing did not rest merely on making a political argument but aimed at the generalizability of academic philosophy. Although others wrote about economics before him, one might say that Adam Smith gave economics an intellectual identity as a professional discipline. He occupied a favorable social position to do so. He was a professor who came from a family of Scottish civil servants and through his connections in the Scottish diplomatic service was acquainted with the circles of free-ranging intellectuals in Paris. Adam Smith was what one might call a role-hybrid, a situation often favorable to intellectual creativity. He had an insider's view of administrators' economic concerns as well as familiarity with politically popular economic publicists like Quesnay. His professorial role provided the systematizing bent that transformed this material into the basis of a science.

The Rise of Public Schools and the University Revolution

At the same time that the Enlightenment intellectuals held the center of the stage, a quiet revolution was taking place in Germany. In Prussia and elsewhere, free and compulsory elementary schools were established, the first anywhere in the world. Their purpose was to inculcate obedience to the state. They were staffed originally by low-ranking clerics from the bureaucracy of the state church. This meant a revival of the importance of the theological faculty at the universities and of the liberal arts faculty that prepared students for it. Teaching positions were generally filled by university graduates awaiting a post in the Church or at the universities. The number of teaching positions available was further increased as secondary schools were established, in Germany called *Gymnasium*. The number of university students in the late 1700s vastly increased; not surprisingly, they tended to fix their aim on the highest and best paid teaching posts, the university professorships, rather than on the elementary or secondary schools, and they tried to transfer out of the latter as much as possible. In the modern United States, such a transfer from public school to university teaching would not be possible because these are separate systems. But in Germany, these were parts of the same bureaucracy, and intellectuals regarded them as steps on the same ladder.

The result of this expansion and competition was consid-

erable pressure to increase the number of university professorships in the liberal arts faculty and to upgrade their status.
Especially in the newer universities of Prussia and later in the
newly founded University of Berlin, teachers began once again
to compete through intellectual creativity in a fashion not seen
since the High Middle Ages. They fastened onto such preparatory subjects as classical languages (Latin and Greek) and
turned them into the research science of philology (the science
of language), which was later to have revolutionary effects on
research in history and anthropology. At the height of this
period of university overcrowding and intellectual competition,
the years between 1780 and 1820, teachers of the *undergraduate*
subject of philosophy (which was supposed to be merely a
preparation for higher study in theology or law) underwent an
intellectual revolution. Immanual Kant, Johann Fichte, Friedrich Schelling, Georg Hegel, Arthur Schopenhauer, and others
created entirely new forms of philosophy, and in the process
claimed that their field was not only a "science" but a form of
knowledge superior to all others. In Kant's words, philosophy
was to undergo a "Copernican revolution" and become "the
Queen of the Sciences." The result of this intellectual agitation
was a structural change: in 1810, the philosophical (liberal arts)
faculty was raised to a graduate faculty on the same level with
law, theology, and medicine, and the arts degree (now culminating in the Ph.D. rather than M.A.) was accepted instead of
the theology degree for teaching posts in the public schools.

This innovation, first carried out at the new university at
the Prussian capital of Berlin, was quickly imitated by the rest
of the 20-odd German universities. (Germany at this time consisted of dozens of independent states, most of which had their
own university; Prussia was merely the strongest state among
the others and had not yet unified Germany militarily, an
event that did not take place until 1871). The result of this
reform was that the German universities soon took over world
leadership in virtually all branches of science and scholarship.
What happened can be explained once again, as in the case of
the medieval university, as organizational "goal displacement". The arts faculty merely prepared students for the
higher faculties, but as its function changed to training teachers

for the public school system, it had an opportunity to assert the independent importance of its own activities. There is no intrinsic limit to what knowledge teachers should have (unlike theologians, lawyers, and doctors), hence, no clear criterion of how they should be trained.

Moreover, the specialized teacher-training function now gave the arts faculty a legitimate claim to be a separate and equal division of the organization. With this independence, university teachers were free to develop their own subjects and were given the opportunity to raise their prestige. The necessity of competing among themselves for posts made scholarly productivity an important goal for the first time since Peter Abelard and his rivals attracted students with their debates in the Middle Ages. The result was the development of philosophical and humanistic subjects, including mathematics, which underwent a profound revolution at Göttingen and Berlin by discovering the realms of modern higher abstract mathematics. The teachers of the old higher faculties now emulated their upstart colleagues, and new sciences spun off as well from legal scholarship (the history of law, giving rise to various branches of social science) and from medicine (giving rise to the birth of the modern university-based laboratory sciences).

The German university revolution was to be imitated eventually around the world. France, which had its network of technical schools and academies in Paris, was not so hard pressed to compete, at least in the natural sciences. But France nevertheless gradually fell further and further behind German science, and by the latter part of the 1800s, French scholars were traveling to Germany as foreign students to find what they could bring home to revitalize their own system. Émile Durkheim in 1885–1886 was just one of many French intellectuals who made the trip to sit at the feet of German masters. After the French defeat in the Franco-Prussian War (1871), France was ready to reform its moribund universities along the German model and to establish the public secondary-school system that was its base.

In England, too, the universities had languished. Amateur intellectuals continued to dominate the scene and German university mathematicians, scientists, and scholars were read and followed everywhere. In the 1860s, the English government reformed its civil service to award positions by competitive examination, and the universities began to improve themselves by bringing in the newer German scholarship. As late at the 1890s, though, Englishmen like Bertrand Russell went to study in Germany to catch up on the latest intellectual developments. The pattern was strongest of all in the United States. Although there were hundreds of colleges in America, they followed the traditional pattern of religious-dominated instruction until Johns Hopkins University was founded in 1876 as an explicit imitation of the German graduate school. For several generations on down to the early 1900s, the typical academic career for an American after completing an American college degree was to go to Germany to acquire advanced training. But by the turn of the century, the Johns Hopkins model was spreading rapidly. It was made especially famous by curriculum reforms at Harvard, which established the elective system, and by the founding of the University of Chicago in 1892, which used John D. Rockefeller's millions to lure away from other universities the most distinguished faculty available in all fields. It is scarcely an exaggeration to say that American intellectual life began at this point; before then the United States had its novelists and poets, but its impact on the world scene of science and scholarship dates from the time it adopted the German university revolution.

The university as an organizational form had great advantages over the more informal communities of intellectuals that had prevailed in the salons of the French Enlightenment or in the world of the English gentry. The university developed knowledge systematically because it had to be taught in courses; it provided for continuous training of students so that lines of thought and research could be developed across several generations; and it offered greater insulation from the pressures of ideology or the demand for immediate practical payoff, thus it could pay more attention to pure theory. As a result university scholars eventually outdistanced most of their nonacademic counterparts and the advanced segments of intellectual life ended up almost exclusively in the universities, except for literary and artistic endeavors. This process was already visible in physics and mathematics in the late 1700s as the French engineering schools took over these subjects from the gentry amateurs. With the spread of university reform, the process went much further by universities taking over philosophy and the social sciences as well.

Though in some sense this may have been good for knowledge, it nevertheless was not necessarily felt as an improvement by many intellectuals. For the first time in its history, the intellectual community became split internally—not merely over political or religious loyalties that its members might happen to hold, but along a divide in the intellectual organization itself. The independent, nonuniversity intellectuals became hostile to the new professorial form of knowledge production. Because the academic revolution had its first noticeable impact in the natural sciences, the first sign of estrangement was between scientific and literary intellectuals. Already in the late 1700s and early 1800s, literary figures like William Blake, William Wordsworth, and Lord Byron were rejecting cold scientific calculation and the intellectual attitude that went along with it. This romanticist movement was a new thing in the internal politics of the intellectual world, as can be seen by remembering that the typical French Enlightenment intellectual (e.g., Voltaire) adulated both science and literature and saw no conflict whatsoever between them. Romanticism was particularly widespread in Germany, precisely at the time the university revolution was being carried out. A philosopher like Hegel condemned mathematics as a lower, superficial, and "nonspiritual" form of knowledge, and this is an attitude that has persisted—in one faction even within the university world itself—on down to the present. Here we catch a glimpse of what lies ahead in this book: a distinctively German "romanticist" line that has emphasized the subjective side of sociology in opposition to a more proscience line centered in the positivism of Comte and Durkheim.

The weakness of the university professors' version of the intellectual community was the obverse of its strength. Its methodical character and bureaucratic organization resulted in increasingly fine specialization along well-trodden paths; once lines of theory were laid down at the beginning, further creative innovations were discouraged. For this reason, new lines of thought in the social sciences have tended to come from interaction between the university and the outside world. Practical and ideological concerns have posed new issues and pointed to new bodies of facts that the university intellectuals were eventually to turn into systematic research. But as the universities expanded into steadily larger numbers of professors, specialization became unavoidable. The various social sciences now began to break up into separate disciplines, and the old all-purpose intellectual role disappeared.

The Development of the Disciplines

HISTORY BECOMES PROFESSIONALIZED

The first social science to undergo the academic revolution was history. Philological research, beginning with the ancient languages, had a predominantly historical bent. Johann Herder, Georg Hegel, and the German idealist philosophers received most of their erudition from these studies of classical Greek and Roman culture, and they developed out of it a predominantly historical view of human existence. At Berlin after 1810, the classical philologist Barthold Niebuhr extended his scholarly methods from language to the related field of Roman history; he began the systematic basis of historical scholarship by examining the authenticity of documents and analyzing the bias of sources—the so-called German textual criticism. Shortly thereafter the law professor Friedrich von Savigny began the critical study of legal history. In 1833, again at Berlin, Leopold von Ranke founded his research seminar in modern political history—and the enterprise of academic historical scholarship was firmly under way. Of course history was written widely, and even well, before this professional base was established. What the German professors added was both an emphasis on research in the original sources rather than a reliance on previous accounts and a specific concern to keep literary style or ideological values from influencing the presentation of the truth. Von Ranke formulated the slogan of academic historians to present things *"wie es eigentlich gewesen"*—"as it really happened," not as we want to see it. It was the ideology of a scholarly profession declaring its independence from laypeople's concerns.

The ideal has taken only partial effect. There are innumerable historical facts, and to tell a coherent story, the historian must select on some basis. The traditional purposes of history before the "academic revolution" were primarily to bolster (or undermine) the legitimacy of some political or religious faction or to tell an entertaining story with literary grace. Academic history has often applied its scholarly techniques in these well-worn grooves. It was primarily in the less ideological areas of economic, literary, and social history as well as in the political history of remote times that von Ranke's disinterested ideal was best realized. History has continued to be written outside the academic world, especially in the form of memoirs by retired politicians (Winston Churchill is a good example). And academic works on contemporary issues have been just as partisan as ever.

Nevertheless scholarly standards went up sharply during the 1800s, even though history was written in an atmosphere of growing nationalism. If national consciousness fostered self-glorifying biases in each country, it also motivated scholars in a kind of scholarly race to discover the past. The nineteenth century is the period when history came of age. At the beginning of that century, a highly educated individual like Hegel could have only a vague and distorted view of world history. By the end of the century, historical knowledge had arrived at a broad picture that has remained largely intact since that time, leaving twentieth-century historians to work on the finer details. This was to be important for sociology. Max Weber, writing in the early 1900s, was in a position to draw on a wealth of comparative evidence that earlier scholars like Karl Marx or Herbert Spencer had been born too early to know.

ECONOMISTS BECOME ACADEMICS

We have already seen that the crystalization of economics as a distinct intellectual community took place around the time of

Adam Smith. The leadership of economics remained in England for almost a century thereafter. For most of that time economists were outside the academic world. The leading figures, David Ricardo and John Stuart Mill, were both active in practical politics and employed in business, the former a stockbroker and investor, the latter an employee of the East India Company. So was the former parson Thomas Malthus, who was appointed to the East India Company's "college" in 1801 after pronouncing his famous doctrine that poverty was due to overbreeding by the lower class. There were a few academic positions, such as the one the theorist Nassau Senior acquired at Oxford in 1825, but these were neither well paying, prestigeful, nor secure.

Economics at the time was primarily viewed as a political doctrine. Adam Smith had given it a focus—the operation of the market system—that was simultaneously taken as an intellectual concept and a political ideal. The intellectual side of economics was used to bolster the doctrine of laissez-faire, hence, its primary support came from the pro-business faction. The long sojourn of economics in the world of practical politics did result in bodies of factual data being collected by government investigating commissions, although this material was not much used to develop and test theory in a scientific manner. Economic laws were simply deduced and pronounced, ready to be used for policy conclusions.

The most striking attempt to create a scientific economics under these conditions was made by Karl Marx. Although Marx lived in exile in England after his unsuccessful participation in the French and German revolutions in 1848, he was an outsider to the British economic establishment. But Marx was intellectually equipped for the task because he was trained as a German university philosopher and, hence, was much more oriented than the English economists towards the task of systematic theoretical generalization. Marx's radicalism cost him a career as a university professor, but it pointed him towards a new kind of theoretical system. Marx was another role-hybrid: he took bourgeois English economics and the factual investigations of the conditions of the laboring classes and plugged them into the generalizing role of a German philosopher to create a new theoretical-and-empirical economics. But Marx's system was also a political system, and a radical one at that; hence, it was scarcely noticed by the respectable intellectual world during his lifetime. It only surfaced and began its *intellectual career*—for Marx's Communist *politics* had already made its own way in a growing underground—after the German Social Democratic (i.e., socialist) party became a parliamentary force in the 1880s and 1890s. Marxism was the Social Democrats' official doctrine, and their party newspapers, journals, and schools made it possible for Marxist intellectuals to hold positions as editors and teachers. Out of this material base came the upsurge of Marxian economics that caught the attention of the official intellectual world at the turn of the century.

Meanwhile respectable economics underwent its own revolution. Around 1870, it threw over the traditional "classical" concepts and substituted a more technical and mathematical analysis of marginal utility and general equilibrium in the market. This so-called marginalist or neoclassical economics was created by academics: William Jevons, Francis Edgeworth, and Alfred Marshall in England; Léon Walras in France; Carl Menger in Austria. At the beginning of this development, economics was still basically a political doctrine. Accordingly economics could get into the universities and undergo a transformation into a technical, academic field only if the Liberal (laissez-faire, pro-business) position was acceptable in universities. England was the main place where this was the case, once its universities were revived by the Civil Service reforms in 1864. Hence England was especially prominent in carrying out the Neo-Classical (i.e., academic) revolution.

Germany provides a test case. The German universities were specialized scholarly institutions long before any others; from the 1700s, there were even positions for economists in the teaching of administrative science. But the political position of English-style Liberals was not acceptable in Germany with its aristocratic tradition and heavy-handed government bureaucracies. Hence, the German academic world, especially after 1850, was either conservative or welfare oriented (sometimes both); in either case, it was not inclined to give any autonomy to business and the free marketplace. The German economists did a great deal of scholarly research, but they focused on institutional history instead of on the laws of the pure market. The new developments of marginalist theory were attacked as unrealistic constructions and sometimes as capitalist ideology. Some of the German economics professors were even referred to as *Kathedersozialisten* (socialists of the chair) because of their advocacy of a conservative form of socialism. This, too, was part of the background of emerging sociology. Max Weber began his career as an economist and took part in the disputes between the rival schools: historical, Marxian, and marginalist. In the United States, Thorstein Veblen and John R. Commons were famous reformers and proponents of institutional economics; actually they were carrying on the German tradition across the Atlantic at just the time when the American universities were being reformed along German lines.

France provides an opposite sort of test case. There the pro-business ideologists were firmly in the saddle from the 1830s, and they held control of posts for teaching economics at the elite Collège de France and the administrative Écoles. These were not posts in research-oriented academic institutions, but rather sinecures for a political-intellectual elite more interested in public pronouncements than in technical economic theory. Hence, the advanced economic work done by the mathematician Antoine Cournot was not accepted nor was that of the former engineer Léon Walras, even though the latter, the inventor of the general equilibrium model, has subsequently been considered the greatest of all theoretical economists. Walras had to find a post in Switzerland, where he inspired another former engineer, the Italian, Vilfredo Pareto, to further developments in economic theory. In his old age, Pareto was to go on to develop a cyclical theory in sociology to accompany his theory of business cycles. The Italian universities, revived along German lines late in the century, became major centers of economic theory through Pareto's influence. Austria, which had German-style universities but a more liberal, pro-business influence in government, produced yet another of the pioneers of marginal utility, the law professor, Carl Menger. The Scandinavian universities with their combination of conditions similar to Austria also became centers of modern neoclassical economics.

The twentieth century provides further proof of this political formula. The improvement of government statistics collecting in the 1920s led to theoretical developments of national accounting models with its now-familiar measurements, such as the gross national product (GNP). The United States soon became prominent in economics by dint of the sheer number of its professorial positions as its universities expanded into a mass system that dwarfed any other in the world. Here business-centered economics was not only acceptable but taken for granted as the ideological center and, hence, only the British liberal tradition was considered normal. The importance of politics was also illustrated in Germany. With the downfall of the conservative German empire and the rise of the liberal Weimar Republic in the 1920s, Germany took its place in orthodox (British-style) economics. Interestingly enough the Nazi period in Germany and the Fascist period in Italy interfered little with academic economics. The marginalist model, especially in the policy form given to it by John Maynard Keynes, had become the practical tool for government management of a mildly welfare-oriented business system and, hence, fitted the policies of almost all twentieth-century states. The major exception was the Soviet bloc, where a rival form of economics meshed with political ideology: Marxism. Economics, as the most politicized social science, remains even today only as much of a general theory as is compatible with the dominant politics of the state within which it resides.

PSYCHOLOGY BECOMES INDEPENDENT

Psychology derives from three main lines: philosophy, medicine, and pedagogy. Speculative philosophy from Plato to Arthur Schopenhauer and Rudolf Lotze dealt with the mind and the faculties of knowing and perception. With the rise of medical research in the early nineteenth century, the subject came to be approached by means of research on the nervous system. The German universities were the leading centers of such research by the mid-1800s. Experimental psychology arose through a combination of these two traditions; overcrowding of positions in physiology after a first period of expansion brought an influx of physiologists and their methods into the large but stagnant field of philosophy. A former physiologist, Wilhelm Wundt, set up the first European laboratory to study the philosophical data of human consciousness by experimental methods at the very time that an American medical researcher, William James, was doing the same thing. Wundt's innovation was widely successful in the academic world. Wundt and his fellow experimental psychologists attracted large numbers of students, both from Germany and abroad, and it was from this group that psychological research flowed around the world. Several decades later, German psychology came to fruition in the Gestalt school of perceptual psychology and its offshoot in social psychology led by Kurt Lewin.

Psychology in Germany, though, remained a specialty within philosophy departments and continued to be tied to the study of a traditional philosophical subject, consciousness. In the United States, psychology (largely carried on by former students of Wundt, despite William James's early laboratory work) also began as a part of philosophy departments. But U.S. universities were rapidly expanding in student enrollments and, hence, in faculty; then in the early 1900s, it became possible for psychology to split off in a separate department. It was during the period when American psychology was attempting to gain its independence that the program of behaviorism was crystalized. The American behaviorists declared that the subject of scientific psychology should be the laws of overt behavior, not introspective efforts to get at that illusive and prescientific concept, the mind. Sociologically one might see these attacks as the ideology of an academic faction that was trying to distinguish itself as sharply as possible from philosophy to justify separate professorships. The battle left American psychology with a distinctively behaviorist legacy that took 50 years to settle down and admit that cognition, too, could be a legitimate subject for psychological investigation.

The German and American routes were not the only directions psychology was to take. In the French and English universities, philosophy was viewed as little more than a medieval anachronism at the time of Wundt's movement in Germany. British and French medical-oriented psychologists had no real incentive to take over the philosophical territory and transform it into a science of consciousness. Instead, psychology was directly attacked as a part of science. But without an anchor in the philosophical role, there was little emphasis on creating theory, and the British and French psychologists concerned themselves mainly with practical applications. A former biologist, Alfred Binet, developed intelligence tests in France; the British gentleman-explorer, Francis Galton, worked on statistical measures that were designed to separate out the genetically superior from the inferior. The elitist biases involved in these sorts of measures have been the subject of much controversy in recent years, but for decades they were an acceptable "scientific" version of practical psychology.

A quite different psychological tradition developed in Russia. There the universities were heavily under German influence, but with less scope for philosophy. The physiologists Ivan Pavlov and V. Bechterev attacked Wundt's problems in a more radical fashion, investigating conditioned reflexes in animals. This began a tradition of psychological research that expanded outwards from the nervous system to what the Russians referred to as the "second signal system" of language. Its materialism kept it in favor after the Communist Revolution, and its connection with pedagogy gave it a fruitful field for research on the development of children. Another striking offshoot of the Wundt school is found in Switzerland, where a direct line of students deriving from Wundt led to the research by Jean Piaget on children's cognitive development. Piaget combined the German emphasis on a generalized theory of mind with new empirical materials: instead of investigating adults, he used first his own children and then the pedagogical institutions of Geneva to model the successive stages of mental operations. In recent years this "cognitive revolution" finally overcame the behaviorist prejudices of American psychologists and has become a flourishing enterprise on both sides of the Atlantic.

Yet another branch of psychology is the clinical. The most important figure in this development was the Viennese doctor,

Sigmund Freud. Before Freud, psychiatry fruitlessly pursued the search for physiological determinants of psychological disorders. Like Wundt, Marx, Adam Smith, and several other major theorists, Freud was a role-hybrid. Trained in medical research, academic failures and anti-Semitism forced him out of the high-status academic world into the role of practicing physician. Practical roles of this sort held little esteem in the Germanic world of the time, and Freud was motivated to create a new science out of the strange empirical materials his patients provided for him. Once again, the practical world provided the factual materials, the academic world the theoretical orientation. Freud and his followers never succeeded in cracking the academic world of German psychology, but his influence was more powerful in the United States and Britain where psychology (or at least one part of it) had a more practical bent. Freudian theory, although perhaps suffering somewhat from a lack of the systematic research tradition emphasized in the academic world, nevertheless has kept alive a concern for the dynamic elements of human personality and motivation that were left out by the emphasis of academic psychology on pure cognition or behaviorist experiments on laboratory animals.

ANTHROPOLOGY GETS ITS NICHE

The impetus for developing anthropology came initially from the discovery of tribal societies in the Americas, Africa, and the Pacific. This material inspired social philosophers from Hobbes and Locke through Turgot and Condorcet. It was no longer possible to explain European society as simply a God-given order, after the fashion of the medieval philosophers; and various theories were proposed as to how society changed, by social contract or by evolution, away from a primal state of nature. The explorations also had an effect on biology. Carolus Linnaeus and Georges Buffon were just then creating taxonomies of species, and slots were created for "man in the state of nature" as well as for "civilized man." This was a significant precurser of Darwin because human beings were now being put in the same table with apes and other animals, if not yet regarded as related to them. The term "anthropology" was coined in the 1700s, meaning the science of *human* biology, and it was used in titles of books on anatomy.

The main line of development of anthropology in the next century was as part of biology and the related natural sciences, with a second main line coming from cultural history, especially through philology (the history of language) and the history of art. The social forms of non-Western societies were little studied per se. Although social thinkers from Auguste Comte through Herbert Spencer and William Graham Sumner used this material in their theories, they were outside the circle of anthropological researchers themselves and had little effect on guiding such research until the rise of social anthropology in the twentieth century. The main theoretical interests of the anthropologists came from medical scientists and biologists—such as Georg Waitz and Rudolf Virchow in Germany, Paul Broca in France, and James Prichard in England—who began to measure and classify living peoples into physical types and to investigate bones of ancient people being unearthed by geologists or by accidental excavations. Such "accidents" were not entirely accidental, of course, because they occurred precisely at the time when interest was growing, making it possible for old bones to be noticed instead of simply being discarded by their finders. Neanderthal man, for example, was discovered by some workmen in a cave in southwest Germany in 1857; they brought the bones to the attention of the town doctor, who in turn reported it to his local scientific club. This kind of amateur-scientist role hung on throughout the nineteenth century in both biology and anthropology. This was particularly so in England, where wealthy gentry like Charles Darwin could devote their lives on their country estates to an investigation of fossils and the collection of travelers' reports. At the same time British anthropologists tended to have a relatively atheoretical collector's mentality as compared to the more systematic and encyclopedic researchers in Germany.

By midcentury anthropology had enough researchers to found organized societies (England in 1843, France in 1859, Germany in 1869), and anthropological discoveries were regularly reported to biological, geological, and geographical congresses. The mass of anthropologists had grown, and "accidental" discoveries were giving way to organized expeditions like the ones that discovered Troy in 1875 and Mycenae in 1876. By the 1920s discoveries were *almost* predictable, as a Chinese expedition turned up Peking man and rival British, American, and French expeditions raced each other for finds in the Middle East.

It is not possible to carry out deliberate searches for new "finds" or even to label accidental discoveries as meaningful materials without a general notion of what is wanted. The necessary theoretical framework to guide research was provided by the question of "origins": to trace the sequence by which humanity evolved and, thus, fill the void left by the decline of the Biblical account of creation. Darwin's theory of natural selection gave a more elegant theoretical formulation that was applicable to cultural as well as physical development; from the 1860s onward, the evolutionary model provided the framework for research. It also gave rise to a number of theories of racial or other (e.g., family) hereditary superiority, meshing with political programs of nationalism or eugenics. These theories were put forward mostly by nonacademic intellectuals oriented towards political audiences. As a result they were less interested in the standards of careful research than in bolstering their political program. Hence, academics like Georg Waitz, P. W. A. Bastian, and Franz Boas attacked the racist anthropologies, not necessarily out of political differences but because of loyalty to the standards of the research community. It is interesting in view of the later rise of the Nazis that it was *German* anthropologists who first scientifically disputed racist theories, because it was in Germany that anthropology was most especially an academic science. By the standards of the German universities, the racist theories simply ignored the evidence that there was continuous racial mixing throughout history and considerable cross-cutting among racial groups and language and other cultural traits—in short race was not a useful scientific concept.

Another contributory stream to anthropology came from the study of cultural history. The development of philology in the German universities had culminated in the early 1800s not only in the discipline of scholarly history led by Niebuhr and von Ranke, but also in research on the histories of language, art, law, and other fields of human creativity. The Grimm brothers collected Germanic fairy tales, marking the beginning of a *Kulturgeschichte* (cultural history) that led further and further afield into the European, Middle Eastern, and Oriental past. This intellectual movement spread naturally to the classics scholars of the more traditional British and French universities, where it brought forth some of the first breakthroughs into "modern" scholarship. Among these were the work of Numa Denis Fustel de Coulanges (Durkheim's teacher) on Greek and Roman religion; Henry Sumner Maine on ancient law, which formulated the famous sociological law that societies moved from "status" to "contract"; and James Frazer on the fertility rituals of ancient preclassical times. It is not too much to say that German-style scholarship penetrated England mainly through the classics, which was the key field of the traditional education when every student was primarily expected to study Latin and Greek. Conversely, classics gave anthropology a home in the British universities, making it respectable long before sociology could get in (which took until the 1960s in most places in Britain).

Anthropology thus arose from the dual roles of the cultural historian and the scientific field researcher. The two strands finally came together in the persons of the founder of German anthropology, P. W. A. Bastian, and his English counterpart, Edward Tylor. Both were world travelers, the former as a ship's doctor, the latter as a touring gentleman; both interested themselves in the religions, languages, art, and archeology of many lands, on which they periodically reported back to Berlin or Oxford. They finally settled down in various museum and academic positions and systematized their work. By the end of the nineteenth century, the cultural and biological interests had joined up around the role of field researcher, and anthropology crystalized its scientific identity under the rubric, "the study of man."

Entering the twentieth century, anthropology had firmly established itself within the universities of England, France, and Germany, although under varying rubrics: some were positioned as a part of the classics or philology departments, others were found in biology and medicine, but there were also independent chairs in archeology, art history, history of religion, or *Völkerpsychologie* (folk psychology). In the United States, the Bureau of Indian affairs was established in 1879 and provided posts for professional anthropologists to catalogue Indian cultures, and anthropologists began to find university posts in museums and joint departments of anthropology and sociology. Under the leadership of the German Franz Boas (a former assistant of Bastian), American anthropologists tended to reject evolutionist theory in favor of detailed cultural descriptions and a belief in historically specific patterns of cultural diffusion. In the German tradition, they emphasized the unique configurations of a culture, a doctrine that was raised into an ethical position of "cultural relativism" by Boas's student Ruth Benedict, in whose eyes all cultures must be judged by their own standards of right and wrong.

But in its period of academic success, anthropology faced a mild crisis. The questions that had effectively guided research—the origins of human beings and their culture—had resulted in ever-more detailed accounts and widespread evidence of diffusion that messed up the neat evolutionary model. The issues of the field turned into increasingly minute studies of the interaction of many different influences. The old agitation over the Biblical view of creation had long since died down, the popular doctrine of racial differences was discredited, and new discoveries of humanity's ancestral connection with the apes no longer carried much shock value. The field was in danger of falling into a hyperempiricism that left no prominent intellectual landmarks and no prominent thinkers or theories.

It was this situation that opened the way for modern social anthropology. In France, Émile Durkheim was casting about in the early years of the twentieth century for a scholarly community to carry his newly invented sociology. He hit on anthropology as a likely choice. The result was that Durkheim's theoretical tradition became the basis for synthesizing empirical research by anthropologists, an alliance between fields that has continued in France through Durkheim's nephew Marcel Mauss and subsequent anthropological/sociological thinkers such as Claude

Lévi-Strauss and Pierre Bourdieu. Somewhat analogously Freud and many of his followers seized on anthropology as a source of systematic evidence when the field of psychology remained closed to them in Germany. In Britain, these theoretical traditions were imported into anthropology by Bronislaw Malinowski and A. R. Radcliffe-Brown, who did field research in the British colonies as well as manning academic posts. The result of this combination of fieldwork and theory was the movement known as the British school of social anthropology, with its focus on rituals, symbols, and their relations to social structure. In America, the functionalist school of Durkheim made less of a dent in the essentially German tradition of *Kulturgeschichte* promulgated by Boas's followers. But the popular reception of Freudian psychology in America opened the way for a vigorous tradition in psychological anthropology that emphasized cultural socialization and the social effects of child-rearing practices.

And Finally Sociology

Sociology, as the general science of social phenomena, has the most diverse roots of all. It derives from the materials of history and from the generalizing attempts of philosophers of history, from the concerns of institutional and historical economists and from the fact-gathering of public administrators and social reformers, from socially minded psychologists, and from the interests of anthropologists in primitive culture and human evolution. But each of these areas of research has crystalized into a scholarly community with its own focus (history, economics, psychology, anthropology) rather than a concern for the generalizations about society itself. Sociology got its independent identity primarily through movements of political ideology and reform. Accordingly it was able to move towards a generalizing science only where an academic system existed in which left-liberal reformers were allowed. In this respect, the social conditions for the establishment of sociology were similar to those for economics, although economics classically reflected Liberals (with a capital "L") in the old sense—the business interest striving to be free from the domination of conservative aristocrats—

whereas sociology has depended on liberals (with a small "l") interested in welfare-style reforms, although sometimes with an appreciative eye for tradition. Sociology has had a harder time getting political support or toleration because its constituency, although large, has never been powerful.

Sociology and political science were largely indistinguishable in the 1700s when they made up segments of the amorphous intellectual scene: on the one hand, there were the social philosophers such as Hobbes, Locke, Montesquieu, Rousseau, Turgot, and Condorcet; on the other hand, there were the German professors of administrative science with their legal philosophies and descriptive "statistics". For most of the 1800s, these traditions were to continue, but then the intellectual world became increasingly specialized and organized into distinct groups. History, economics, psychology, and anthropology gradually split off. At the same time, the Industrial Revolution and the democratization of governments in Western Europe produced the beginnings of political movements and parties among the growing urban classes. This gave sociology a more strictly political focus than before. The first important sociologists/political scientists (for we cannot yet distinguish the two) are men like the comte de Saint-Simon, Auguste Comte, Alexis de Tocqueville, Karl Marx, John Stuart Mill, Frederic Le Play, and Herbert Spencer, all of whom were outside the academic world and addressed political audiences. We find in their thought the main formulations of most of the important ideologies that have since become popular: liberalism in both its laissez-faire ("L") and welfare-state ("l") forms, communism, and corporate conservatism. If we extend our focus to the second-rate thinkers, the group of nineteenth-century "sociologists" includes founders of utopian communities like Charles Fourier as well as early Fascist ideologues like Arthur de Gobineau.

Most important for the development of sociology were those individuals who combined a university orientation with their political and popular interests. One of these was Comte, who was trained in the natural sciences at the elite École Polytechnique in Paris. Auguste Comte hoped to take Saint-Simon's political ideology and build a social *science* out of it, for which he coined the term "sociology." At first, Comte

primarily aimed to have his new science accepted at the Polytechnique. Only after that failed did he turn to politics and
found his Positivist "church" as a political movement to re-
make society. Another role-hybrid, as we have already seen,
is Marx, who would likely have been a notable philosophy
professor if he had not been forced out of the university by
political circumstances. He made up for it by creating a comprehensive general theory out of his revolutionary ideas. A
third case of this sort is Le Play, the only field researcher in
this group. He combined engineering training with an interest
in conservative politics in launching his meticulous studies of
the European family. (The family, then as now, was a favorite
subject for conservatives.) Tocqueville stands apart from the
others; a nonacademic politician who was at one time a cabinet official, he nevertheless combined original observation
with a generalizing mind in his travels and in his historical
research. Tocqueville is really the last of the Enlightenment
philosophers, combining all the intellectual roles in the manner of a Turgot or a Montesquieu.

The institutional weakness of these sociological thinkers
was that their ideas appealed so directly to political movements
that they could not easily become the basis for a community of
scholarly researchers. This more strictly theoretical orientation
would depend on an academic setting. Factual research was
generated in the nineteenth century, but mostly from the practical administrators. A great deal of this kind of research was
carried out in Germany. In 1872, a group of German professors
and administrators organized the *Verein für Sozialpolitik* (Union
for Social Policy). Max Weber later belonged to this group but
found it was too narrowly focused on gathering detailed information and formulating welfare policies for it to create any
generalizable insight into society. In England, similar work was
carried out by government investigating commissions that
looked into the conditions of factory life. The nearest approach
to a theoretical role was made in the 1830s by the Belgian
astronomer Adolphe Quetelet, who immersed himself in government statistics on birth and death rates, suicides, crimes,
and so forth, and emerged with a proposed science of "social
physics." Unfortunately, Quetelet's laws amounted to little

more than the computation of a few simple probabilities and the demonstration that rates of population change or crime could be predicted from the data of previous years. There was a flurry of interest in Quetelet's statistics, which soon fell away as the statistics failed to live up to the claims either of their great practical usefulness or of their contribution to the advancement of theory.

Sociology began to enter the universities towards the end of the 1800s. In the United States, this happened at the time of the university revolution, a time when many new universities were founded and when others were upgraded by adding research-oriented graduate schools and by reforming their curricula to include modern subjects. The universities were remodeled along German lines but retained some distinctively American traits. They were controlled by a president instead of by the faculty, and they were oriented towards expanding student enrollments and attracting public support by any means possible. This meant the American universities were much more receptive to new subjects than the German ones because approval was needed only from the president without requiring the agreement of established faculty powers. American universities might be under the autocracy of their presidents, but they escaped the autocracy of traditionalist professors guarding control of their fields against newcomers. Although German universities were snobbishly hostile to practical subjects, American universities were highly receptive because administrative interests rather than scholarly factions dictated that the university should attract students by any means possible. Increasing numbers of students meant increased incomes through tuition, alumni donations, or state appropriations—vital matters to American university finances, but the sort of issues that German universities did not face. American universities were growth oriented, which meant that the number of faculty was continuously expandable, unlike the European situation where often a single full professor per field was the rule.

Because of these conditions, the new American universities soon incorporated all varieties of social science and achieved at least a quantitative leadership in sheer bulk of research. There had been numerous social reform movements in nineteenth-century America, including followers of Comte, Fourier, imitators of British liberal reform organizations, and many others. In 1865, the more respectable of these groups amalgamated into the American Association for the Promotion of Social Science, and it was from this organization that various subspecialities split off to form their own professional societies and to demand their own places within the universities. First history and economics in the 1880s and then sociology, anthropology, and political science in the 1890s got into the universities; it was in the American universities, too, that psychology first achieved positions separate from philosophy departments, an event that took place around 1910. The first department of sociology was set up at the new University of Chicago in 1892, others soon followed.

Sociology like the other social sciences got its academic home because its political and practical themes were in keeping with the prevailing atmosphere of liberalism and with the practical and popular emphasis of the expanding universities. Conversely, the least political and practical of the social sciences, anthropology, had the hardest time in the American universities, drawing much less interest and, hence, remaining much smaller than the others. In many places anthropology remained within sociology departments until the 1940s, even later at smaller schools. The opposite was the case in Europe, where anthropology was politically and intellectually respectable long before sociology could find an academic niche.

One result was that sociology in America was overridingly concerned with "social problems" rather than with developing and testing explanatory theory. Insofar as a theory was needed to give intellectual justification, early American sociologists picked it up from popular doctrines of evolutionism and from the social psychology found in philosophy departments. Because psychology had not yet broken free into its own departments, psychology was not yet so behaviorist as it would become and its emphasis on cognition was developed into a social psychology by Charles Horton Cooley, George Herbert Mead, W. I. Thomas, and others, which became known as symbolic interactionism. This social psychology also had political resonances. American sociologists were liberal reformers, not radicals nor conservative cynics; they wished to see America as a land of equality and opportunity, and social psychology was conveniently focused on the individual and the small group, and thus, away from embarassing questions about the larger structure of stratification, wealth, and power.

In Britain, sociology scarcely made it into the academic world at all. The intellectually and socially elite universities at Oxford and Cambridge would not admit a discipline they regarded as plebian and lacking in serious scholarly content. British sociology first found its home in the London School of Economics, founded by the Fabian socialist Sidney Webb, where it managed to pick up some theoretical clothing by associating itself with anthropology. A British sociological association was founded in 1908 under the leadership of city planners and philanthropists. Given its tiny resource base, British sociology made little impact until it began to acquire university positions in the expanding academic enrollments of the 1960s and 1970s.

The main theoretical breakthroughs in sociology came from the Continental universities. At the end of the nineteenth century, a number of sociologically oriented philosophers had reacted to the popular political doctrines of Herbert Spencer and Karl Marx. Some of these developed Spencer's biological analogies by producing models of society as an organism (Albert Schaeffle, P. von Lilienfeld, René Worms), whereas others incorporated bits of Marx (Ferdinand Tönnies) or neo-Kantian philosophy of social forms (Georg Simmel). But these theorists failed to gain a solid foothold in philosophy. Their sociology was tainted by association with liberalism and sometimes with positivism—the doctrine that the methods of science could be used to solve social problems. This was the slogan that had been used by reformers in England and radicals in France, hence, it was anathema in absolutist Germany. Sociology was excluded because it descended from an ideology alien to prevailing German politics. Simmel and Tönnies were kept from promotion to full professorships in philosophy for almost 30 years—even psychologists were reaching that status on an average of 15 years and more conventional academics in much less time.

The greatest German sociologist, Max Weber, began not in philosophy but in the research-oriented fields of legal and economic history. But he went beyond the narrow concerns of German historians by treating these materials from the more generalizing perspective derived from sociology, to which he had been introduced by participating in various liberal reform associations. Weber also had a half-sympathetic but cynical interest in Marx, whose followers were just then becoming politically important. Weber was instrumental in founding the German Sociological Association in 1908, and he spent much effort in trying to break the wall of political prejudice on behalf of his sociological and leftist friends such as Georg Simmel and Robert Michels. Weber's campaign against value judgments was an effort to break the hold of nationalist political standards that kept sociology from being recognized academically. He never succeeded, and the psychosomatic illness that kept him out of academic life for many years may have been at least partially the result of his crisis of conscience over compromising with this state of affairs. It was only during the short-lived Weimar Republic, when liberalism finally became respectable, that sociology found a place in the German universities. For a while there was an intellectual upsurge that included the liberal Karl Mannheim and such Marxists as György Lukács, Max Horkheimer, and Theodor Adorno before the crackdowns of the Nazi period wiped out sociology again.

Weber's sociology balanced between the particularistic emphasis of German historical scholarship and the generalizing theories of sociological positivism. Durkheim, sociology's classic proponent of general theory, had no such compromise to make in France. With the downfall of Napoleon III's Second Empire in 1870, the new Third Republic was favorably disposed to liberal politics. Durkheim was an ardent republican as well as a middle-of-the road social reformer, favoring both patriotism and social stability, social justice and labor peace. He also had an advantage in getting a new science of sociology accepted because the French educational system was just undergoing expansion and reform. The Republic had just created a new public school system that took education out of the hands of the conservative Church. The young Durkheim was a protégé of the Minister of Education, Louis Liard, who sent him to Germany to report on that country's successful university system. To staff the new public schools, the university system had to be reformed to train teachers, and Durkheim became a professor of Pedagogy and, thus, was entrusted with great influence in this process. The whole educational system underwent reform and there was a concomitant intellectual outpouring, comparable to that which had happened a century earlier at the time of the educational reforms in Prussia.

By adroit administrative maneuvering as well as intellectual brilliance, Durkheim was able to develop his chair of pedagogy into a professorship in sociology, the first ever on the Continent. An earlier position in sociology had been established in the United States. But the French university system was controlled by an intellectually snobbish elite, and interests in social reform and practicality that might be sufficient justification in America were not enough to legitimate a new field in France. Durkheim's task was to make sociology intellectually respectable by comparison with all other academic fields. He did this by combining his own training in philosophical generalization with new empirical materials, which he took from the kinds of researches turned up by previous unspecialized sociologists. From Quetelet he saw the usefulness of statistics on suicides, but handled with a more scientific method of systematic comparison to establish correlates and causes. From historians like his own teacher Fustel de Coulanges, he saw the usefulness of comparing legal codes, family structures, and looking for their connections with different forms of social organization. In the anthropologists' field data he discerned materials from which to build a general theory of ritual, symbolism, and morality. Throughout it all, Durkheim emphasized that sociology was to be a science that used the equivalent of the scientific method of experiment, that is, taking all theories as hypotheses to be tested by systematically controlled comparison.

Like other sociologists, Durkheim had his political biases and ideological blinders. Nevertheless, he stands out as sociology's most successful founder, not only because he established the field in the elite university system of France, but also because he gave it enough of method and intellectual content so that it could be built upon elsewhere. Because his most immediate academic rival was psychology, Durkheim took great pains to distinguish the sociological from the psychological level of analysis. Durkheim is the archetypal sociologist because institutionally he had to be most conscious of what would make sociology a distinctive science in its own right. Because of the highly centralized and elitist system in which he operated, Durkheim's sociological followers were a relatively small group, and these were badly hit by casualties in the World War I. Durkheimian theory survived in France mostly as an adjunct to anthropology; it was in the guise of social anthropology, too, that it made its way across the channel to England. But in the United States, with its much larger sociology departments and general eclecticism, Durkheimian sociology found a secure place, and its identity as an intellectual community was assured.

We end our analysis here in the early twentieth century. After these promising beginnings in Germany and France, the convulsions of world politics intervened to hand sociology over largely to the United States. The Nazis hated sociology, and between their coming to power in 1933 and the end of World War II, German sociologists were either dead or had fled abroad. The German occupation of France also caused many sociologists to flee; although unlike the Germans, many of whom remained in the United States, the French (including Claude Lévi-Strauss) usually returned home after the war. Britain, as we have seen, never did establish sociology in its core academic system until long after this time. The result was that the United States became a mélange of world sociology and experienced a mixture and development of different positions. Together the wealth and huge university system of the United States gave it a world leadership for a time in both theory and research. It also spelled the end of the distinctive national traditions, in that most of them had left their original homes and migrated elsewhere.

By the 1970s, the world pattern was shifting again. Vigorous expansion in the British and European academic systems put sociology on a new footing almost everywhere. But now it is time for us to turn back into the inner history of sociology—no longer to look at its institutional bases, but at four of its great traditions of ideas.

1: *The Conflict Tradition*

Strife is the father of all things.... Being at variance it agrees with itself: there is a back-stretched connection, as in the bow and the lyre.
Heraclitus, ca. 500 B.C.

A line of thought going back many centuries emphasizes social conflict. This sounds like it studies only certain dramatic events, but the perspective is much broader and includes all of what goes on in society. Its main argument is not simply that society consists of conflict, but the larger claim that what occurs when conflict is not openly taking place is a process of domination. Its vision of social order consists of groups and individuals trying to advance their own interests over others whether or not overt outbreaks take place in this struggle for advantage. Calling this approach the *conflict* perspective is a bit of a metaphor. The word focuses on the tip of an iceberg, the spectacular events of revolution, war, or social movements; but the viewpoint concerns equally the normal structure of dominant and subordinate interest groups that make up the larger part of the iceberg submerged below.

This conflict vision of society is rarely popular. Conflict sociologists have usually been an intellectual underground. Prevailing views of one's own society have usually stressed a much more benign picture, whether based on beliefs in religious beings underpinning the social world, or on secular beliefs in the goodness of one's rulers and the charitable inten-

47

tions of established elites. To conflict sociologists, these kinds
of justifications are ideologies cloaking real self-interests of
groups hiding beneath them. To point this out, obviously, does
not usually make one very welcome in mainstream society.

Nevertheless the conflict viewpoint has emerged over and
over again wherever there have been politically astute observers. We find it in Renaissance Italy, penned by Niccolo
Machiavelli in exile from a coup d'état in Florence; or we find it
2,000 years earlier with Thucydides, also in exile, writing from
the conflicts of his native Athens. More remotely, we know of
the conflict views of the machinating Hindu statesman Kautilya
and of the ancient Chinese philosopher Mo Ti. The conflict
viewpoint also emerges wherever intellectuals have seriously
tried to write history, whenever they have gone beyond chron-

SOME MAIN POINTS OF THE CONFLICT TRADITION

1800–1840	classical economics: Ricardo		Hegel
1840–1870	German historical economics *Realpolitic*		Marx and Engels
1870–1900		Nietzsche	Engels' dialectical materialism
1900–1920	Weber Michels		Marxist theories of imperialism	Simmel
1920–1940	Mannheim	Lukács Gramsci	Frankfurt School Marxist sociologists of science
1940–1960	Gerth; Mills organization theory stratification theory political sociology		functionalist conflict theory: Coser
1960–1990		conflict theory: Dahrendorf Lenski Collins sex-stratification theory	neo-Marxism and neo-Weberianism world systems theory; historical sociology of revolutions, social movements, and the state

icling the glorious exploits of kings to analyze what happened on the historical stage and why. For history has been largely the record of conflict, of war, political uprising, factional maneuver and change. And this is true even if one is writing the history not of the state but of an idealizing institution like religion. The history of every church—Christian, Moslem, Buddhist, or any other, no matter how loving or pacifist its doctrine—has nevertheless been the history of struggle, factions, persecutions, and conflicts, often entwined with economic and political factions in the larger society. Hence, conflict sociologists have tended to focus on historical materials and to be especially aware of long-term patterns of change. This intellectual tradition might just as well be called the "historical" or the "historical-conflict" tradition in sociology.

The Pivotal Position of Karl Marx

We could start our account of the conflict tradition with many different thinkers. But for our purposes it is useful to begin with Karl Marx. What is referred to as the thought of "Marx" is actually more of a symbol than the work of one individual. Marx is the center of a tradition that dramatized conflict more than any other. It also became the doctrine of a political movement—at one time revolutionary, but since the victory of the Communists in Russia in 1917 and subsequently elsewhere, Marxism has further had to serve as the statement of an official Establishment. As a result Marxism has gone through many splits and variations corresponding to political disputes within the camp of Communist regimes and of revolutionary movements elsewhere in the world. These political connections and applications are part of Marxism's appeal for some intellectuals, but they are responsible for considerable repulsion on the part of others. For all this, our concern here is with the *intellectual* contribution of Marxism to a realistic understanding of the world as a situation of domination and conflict. This means ignoring whatever is the orthodox or unorthodox socialist or Communist line and concentrating on whatever ideas prove to be most valuable in the lineage marked by the name of

"Marx." The very existence of the Communist regimes in the world today and the shape of their own internal conflicts cannot be understood if the Marxian tradition had not opened up a lineage of conflict sociology.

"Marx" is a symbol, among other reasons, because he pulled together the various ingredients of conflict analysis existing before his day. It is well known, for example, that he drew on the philosophy of Hegel. What is crucial about Hegel is that he gave more emphasis to conflict than any philosopher since Heraclitus. Hegel was the last of the great German idealist philosophers, and among the most dynamic. Kant had demonstrated that reality is never seen in itself but only through the screen of our subjective ideas, including the categories of time and space. Hegel had made these ideas less subjective as well as less static, explaining them as a gradual unfolding of the Spirit that makes up the world itself. In a sense Hegel (like Kant before him) was defending the religious world view in an era of growing science. The Spirit is God, but conceived in a heretical way and modified to encompass a changing historical and physical world whose secrets were increasingly being revealed by the viewpoint of science. Against the growing tide of chemistry, physics, and biology, Hegel placed his defense of the Spirit on the human realm of consciousness. Philosophy, religion, and law are not only subjective realities, but they also have a history and show the Spirit evolving from a lower to a higher form of enlightenment. In this light Hegel wished to show that the overemphasis on the material world, represented by science, was merely a passing stage in the development of the Spirit. Human consciousness inevitably went through a historical stage in which it took the external appearances for the essence of things; the Spirit, which is pure Idea, outwardly manifests itself at one stage as the idea of material things. This is because the Spirit is divided from itself; it is alienated and reified—terms that Marx and some of his followers were later to appropriate for their own world view. Eventually, though, the Spirit would come to full self-consciousness; humans would come to realize that they and the world were both God, both Spirit. The millennium would be achieved.

As in all religious or quasi-religious schemes, the endpoint of Hegel's system is hard to visualize in real terms. Hegel's earlier mysticism (formulated, to be sure, in the heady days of the German national reforms responding to the French Revolution) gave way to an ideological defense of the laws of the Prussian monarchy as representing some kind of historical and rational perfection. By the 1830s and 1840s, when Marx was a student, Hegel's system was fair ground for young liberals and radicals who wanted to take it much further. For Hegel, religion had been a progressive force, pointing the way to future history and the overcoming of human alienation. For the "Young Hegelians" of the 1830s and 1840s, religion was clearly the tool of Prussian authoritarianism and had to be exposed or drastically purified. Some, like David Strauss, used new critical scholarship to expose Jesus as merely a human historical figure; others, like Bruno Bauer (Marx's own teacher), expounded a religion based purely on love without supernatural sanctions or conservative dogmas. Still others, like Ludwig Feuerbach, attacked the entire basis of Hegel's idealism, turning it upside down and insisting that the world is thoroughly materialistic. The power of science, which Hegel had attempted to outflank and contain inside his idealistic progression, nevertheless had continued to grow and religion was no longer upheld by intellectuals but imposed by the brute force of the orthodox state.

The Young Hegelians were Marx's milieu. He shared their leading enthusiasms: atheism and materialism. But Marx was an ambitious intellectual driving to move beyond. Unlike his peers, he was much more politicized. The merely intellectual, apolitical stance of the others aroused only his scorn, as did the softhearted and utopian religion of love preached by Bauer and Feuerbach. In a time when Hegel was being criticized by his peers, Marx defended Hegel as superior to those who came after him precisely because he had seen all of history as having a long-term dynamic that moved through certain inevitable stages and did not depend on the utopian schemes and wishful thinking of the individuals of the time. Marx was also attracted by the explicit emphasis on conflict in Hegel's scheme. This was built into Hegel's logic, the technical driving force of his system. It is the logical contradictions, which Hegel uncovered in every philosophical concept, that produced a dialectic and, hence, change. For Hegel the history of philosophy was the key to the history of the world itself. Marx was later to regard this type of scheme as an ideology. But it needed only to be inverted to be put right: Hegel had the world standing on its head, Marx had only to turn it over upon its feet. Thus, unlike Feuerbach and other materialists, Marx's materialism retains Hegel's full historical vision—inevitable contradictions and changes, stages of development, and utopian outcome included.

Hegelianism was Marx's first intellectual acquisition, and it remained the basic framework of his thinking throughout his career. Already in the early years of the 1840s, Marx had fitted Hegelianism to his political radicalism. An inevitable contradiction existed in the material system of his own day, which would eventually bring about the system's downfall and the ushering in of a new stage. Logically of course it might be that many more stages would follow before the end, but like Hegel, Marx believed that he was living through (or near to) the final transition—the stage at which human alienation would finally be overcome. It remained only to find the mechanism by which this would come about.

The utopian and millennarian element in Marx was to prove to be a weakness in his intellectual system. But it did flow from two aspects of Hegel that gave a favorable impetus to the development of a conflict sociology. One of these was the emphasis on conflict itself as a driving force. Though Hegel drew primarily on philosophical and religious history, he nevertheless assimilated to his grand scheme of historical stages the realities of human domination. Ancient society (Hegel was thinking of the Greeks and Romans) he unsentimentally characterized as a world of masters and slaves, with medieval Christianity as a kind of lugubrious revenge of the slave mentality. It is only a step from here to class domination and conflict. History, said Hegel, is a "slaughterbench at which the happiness of peoples . . . have been victimized." Moreover he saw the conflicts and changes of world history as not random, but as logical and inevitable. No doubt Hegel's own theory of the pattern of these changes is overstated and erroneous, but the underlying message points directly to the creation of a sociological science. There is a general pattern, Hegel's theory asserts, and basic causal generalizations about social conflicts and transformations can be made. For this reason, however much the Marxian tradition has kept of Hegelian mystification (including the more recent fashion of emphasizing the uniqueness of each period of history), there is an underlying thrust in the direction of a general sociological science.

Historical inevitability for Karl Marx's own career came in the form of a crackdown by the Prussian government on radical antireligious professors like Bruno Bauer. Losing his mentor and his chance of an academic career, Marx went to Paris, the home of revolutions. He quickly went through and beyond the ideas of the French socialists, utopians like Charles Fourier (or his British counterpart Robert Owen) who advocated the dropout path of building one's own socialist communities: a path that could scarcely avoid the inevitable intervention of, and conflicts with, the surrounding society. More important, Marx read the French historians on their own revolutions, men like François Guizot who saw the actors on the stage as social classes, though they confined themselves to arguing for the triumph of the industrial bourgeoisie over the outdated landowning aristocracy. Marx's materialism began to take on a class content.

Most important of all, Marx discovered economics. This was not only the archetypal science of the material side of society, it also contained, in its own classics, a good many elements of the conflict perspective. The economics Marx learned was what we now call "classical" economics, to distinguish it from the "neoclassical" economics created by men like Jevons, Menger, and Walras in the 1860s and 1870s. In the "classical" form, economics still rested on the labor theory of value: the doctrine that the source of all value is the transformation of the natural world made by the application of human labor. This already implied a critical element, in that the worker was by implication entitled to the fruits of his or her efforts and was exploited if he or she did not receive them. (Neoclassical economics was to remove this radical implication by eliminating the labor theory of value in favor of the psychological conception of marginal utility: value became defined not in terms of what supplied goods and services, but in terms of the psychology of the relative demand for them.) Property, too, was seen as a key element in economic theory, especially in the classical form: owners of land and of capital confront workers who own nothing but their labor, which they are forced to sell to keep themselves alive. These "factors of production" were to become the major class actors in Marx's scheme. Marx even found a ready-made vision of harsh economic conflict in such writings as those of Thomas Malthus and David Ricardo—they argued that the interests of the different economic classes are inalterably opposed: for Malthus it was the overbreeding of the working classes that kept their wages down to near-starvation level, for Ricardo it was the inevitable shortage of land that favored the wealth of the landowners.

In such writings Marx found plenty of ingredients for his own vision of social conflict. To be sure, he criticized the bourgeois economists severely: for their inclination towards the stance of the capitalists and for failing to see that their economic "laws" merely represented the workings of one particular period in human history. Marx's Hegelian vision translated the conflicts of the capitalist economy into contradictions that would bring about its downfall and its transcendence by yet another type of system.

After much searching and synthesis of different positions, Marx produced the system for which he had been looking. He brought together his revolutionary political aims to found a socialism that would not be utopian but inevitable: His was a Hegelian vision of a series of historical stages that were driven by inner contradictions towards a final overcoming of human alienation. Marx's materialism was not merely static but resulted from a dynamics of the capitalist economy that produced crisis, class conflict, and eventually revolution. For sheer architecture of intellectual comprehensiveness, Marx's system is astounding. Its impressiveness is such as to compel admiration, quite apart from whether it works or not in the real world—no doubt one reason why Marx's ideas have always attracted followers.

Put briefly: Marx's system rests on the point that labor is

the source not only of economic value, but also of profit. In a pure market system, operating under the impulsion of supply and demand, everything exchanges for its own value. Hence arises the conundrum: Where does profit come from? Marx answers: from labor, which is the only factor of production from which can be squeezed more than the cost of reproducing it. This is, technically, the "exploitation of labor," which means working laborers longer than the number of hours it takes to reproduce their labor. But capitalist competition impels manufacturers to introduce labor-saving machinery, which in turn cuts their own throats. For profit still comes only from the exploitation of labor, and the more that labor is replaced by machines, the smaller the basis of profit becomes. The result, schematically, is a falling rate of profit and a series of business crises. Across these crises, capital becomes more monopolistically concentrated as weaker capitalists are driven out and into the ranks of the workers; simultaneously, productive capacity continually exceeds consumer demand among the displaced and increasingly unemployed workers. Eventually the productive technology of the system is completely at odds with the legal property forms of capitalism. The ideological and political superstructure falls apart; economic crisis is followed by class confrontation and political revolution.

For Marx, the economic mechanism is not the only reason for a materialist dynamic that produces Hegel's inevitable contradictions and transformations. History moves as a whole; Hegel's sequence of philosophies, religions, and laws are also part of the system, but in this case a dependent part rather than the driving source. Economics explains politics, law, and human culture. There is even a deep spiritual element in the whole process. The spiritual alienation built into Hegel's sequence of stages is completely taken up in Marx's economic series. Just as the Spirit is divided from itself in the form of reified ideas of the material world that seem to press on the individual consciousness from the outside, in Marx's vision humanity is oppressed by a material world that is itself created by humans. Workers create the social and economic world by their own labor and are then oppressed by their own products, which stand over against them. Thus, the overcoming of capitalism and the institution of socialism is not merely an economic change, but the historical overthrowing of alienation. The world created by humans finally comes back under their own control, ending the basic estrangement of the self.

Friedrich Engels, The Sociologist in the Shadows

Clearly there is much more in Marx than what we would call sociology. It is a technical economics and at the same time a kind of metaphysics—a philosophy that is both politically critical and activist and that also offers a quasi-religious hope of ultimate salvation of the human essence. All these features plus the fact that they fit together into the imposing architecture of one all-encompassing system have been the great attraction of Marx for intellectuals seeking something more than narrow and uninspiring specializations. At the same time I would have to say that these features are something of a snare and a temptation from the path towards a realistic sociology. Not that there is no worthwhile sociology incorporated within the Marxian scheme, but it has been so tightly entangled with the rest of the system that it has often been downgraded or overlooked and the whole system has been made to survive or fall on the strength of its philosophical and political vision. Yet the economics and the philosophy are actually on shakier ground than the sociology.

Marx is a symbolic figure in yet another sense. It is typical to refer to "Marx" or "Marxism" when what is actually meant is the work of Marx *and Engels*. Some of the most important "Marxian" works were written by the two men together, including the *Communist Manifesto* and *The German Ideology*. Friedrich Engels in fact is the more sociological thinker of the two. There is something of a myth about the relation between Marx and Engels: that Engels was intellectually inferior and no more than a loyal disciple and weak collaborator in the system belonging to Marx. In actuality Engels deserves to be treated in his own right. In many ways, what he contributed is the solider and more lasting in the "Marxian" contribution to a conflict sociology.

The myth about Marx and Engels is strongly entrenched, among other reasons because it was originated by Engels himself. After their early political agitation and their participation in the abortive revolutions of 1848, Marx went into exile in London, while Engels went to work as a clerk and later the manager of his family's British factory at Manchester. Shortly afterwards Engels all but ceased his intellectual work, while Marx kept alive the underground politics of Communist revolution and worked on his lengthy economic tomes, supported by what funds Engels could send him. Only in the 1870s did Engels reappear in the intellectual and political world, after a 20-year absence. By this time Marx was sick and little productive; Engels took up the slack, writing not only works of his own, but also representing Marx in political and intellectual affairs. Engels became the spokesman of "Marxism," coining its slogans and formulating its doctrines as well as editing and publishing posthumous volumes of Marx's *Das Kapital* after Marx's death in 1883. For all his own activity, Engels cloaked himself in Marx's intellectual identity.

Moreover the pattern was already set early in their career, during the revolutionary decade of the 1840s. In their joint publications, Marx's name always came first. Marx even published under his own name works that were actually written by Engels, such as Engels's analysis of the European upheavals, entitled *Germany: Revolution and Counter-revolution*, written for the *New York Tribune* during 1851–1852. Marx often asked Engels to edit or ghostwrite his manuscripts for him, but without printed acknowledgment; and Marx would arbitrarily change Engels's own writings and send them to the printer without consultation. Engels never protested, never raised an eyebrow. He was already totally loyal. His passivity has seemed to confirm the impression that he was merely the errandboy in the presence of a genius.

But this picture is hardly accurate. Engels in fact was a thinker of considerable originality and breadth: in some respects more so than Marx. Marx himself admitted this in a private letter to Engels late in his life: "You know that, first of all, I arrive at things slowly, and, secondly, I always follow in your footsteps." A strange revelation! Yet it was Engels in fact who first understood the importance of economics, properly critiqued and detached from its bourgeois ideological underpinnings. It was he who early in 1844 published in Marx's journal a "Critique of Political Economy," while Marx was still fighting the philosophical battles of the Young Hegelians. In this essay Engels argued that private property inevitably leads to ever-growing capitalist monopoly and simultaneously to the growth of its fatal enemy, the working class. Marx's reaction was to attempt to translate this economics into Hegelian terms, in the so-called "Economic and Philosophical Manuscripts of 1844." And it was Engels who showed, with the publication in 1845 of his own researches in the Manchester factories—*The Condition of the Working Class in England*—that the abstractions of philosophy meant nothing next to the concrete social conditions of a real social class caught in the throes of capitalism.

Engels, in short, led the way, although Marx was already predisposed to follow in this direction owing to the failed idealism of Hegel and the example of Feuerbach. But it is not so well appreciated how much Engels continued to lead, especially into sociology. Although Marx remained preoccupied with critiquing the German philosophers, Engels pushed for a more empirical and more scientifically generalizable conception of the real world. It is Engels who wrote the first draft of the *Communist Manifesto* and gave it a sociological slant, whereas Marx tacked on his usual critique of philosophical and political rivals and enhanced its vividness with his gift for literary phrase and biting invective. And while Marx demonstrated that his own genius could illuminate current political events such as in the brilliant analysis of the French counterrevolution in *The Eighteenth Brumaire of Louis Bonaparte* (1852), it was Engels who broadened the method to search for historical parallels and generalizations in *The Peasant War in Germany* (1850). Marx was always more the contemporary politician, Engels more the pure intellectual and the greater historical sociologist.

The extensive correspondence preserved between Marx and Engels certainly does not show Marx dominating the relationship intellectually. Instead, it shows Engels throwing out ideas and thinking on paper, while Marx tends to be more preoccupied with reporting personal and political news, detailing his adventures and escapes at the hands of hostile authorities, writing about his difficulties with publishers, and above all spelling out his financial scrapes, and appealing for funds. From the letters alone, one would probably conclude that Engels was more intellectual. This would not be strictly true. But Marx was narrowly focused as a political crusader, and his intellectual life was channeled into an almost monomanical obsession with building a system of political economy that would undergird his vision of the Communist future.

For sociology the crucial event in Marx's life was unquestionably his friendship with Engels. We see this from the kinds of writing they produced on their own as compared to what they did together. Before they met, Marx was a left-Hegelian, philosophically disposed to materialism and socialism, but lacking much of a sense of what the economic and social world is really about. After Engels converted him to an economic sociology, they wrote a series of works together. Some parts of these—*The Holy Family, The German Ideology,* the *Communist Manifesto*—contain a good deal of Marx's continuing polemic against the Young Hegelians and other rivals on the Left. But these are the pages that hold little interest for us today, whereas the enduring and famous contributions are the pages in which Marx and Engels together set forth their sociology in general terms. It is also in this period that Marx and Engels severally wrote out their analysis of particular revolutions, in a form ranging from analytical journalism to historical sociology. But after 1852 when Engels retired into the business grind at Manchester, Marx's sociology largely disappears, and he produces virtually nothing but technical economics and doctrinal or tactical statements for the maneuvers of Communist politics. Finally Engels returns, and in a series of books and articles from 1878 until his death in 1895 attempts to lift Marxism out of the realm of technical economics and to make it a general science of all questions—sociological, historical, and even encompassing the world of nature.

Marx without Engels would have the materialist-leaning left wing of the Young Hegelians, taken one step further in the direction explored by Strauss, Bauer, and Feuerbach. Perhaps he would have found his own way to economics. Certainly this became his preferred intellectual home, although he continued to rework Ricardo's economic system from the point of view not only of searching for the proletarian revolution, but also to make it consistent with Hegelian categories of contradition, alienation, and the dialectic of the individual and the universal. From the early 1850s onwards, Marx worked on a massive project in economics, of which *Capital* was to be merely one portion (along with volumes to come on *Landed Property, Wage Labour, The State, International Trade,* and *World Market*). The whole system was to be called *Critique of Political Economy,* the same title as Engels's brief work of 1844 that had started Marx upon this path. In his lifetime, Marx published various slices of this work, including an introductory *Contribution to the Critique of Political Economy* (1859), and volume I of *Capital* in 1867. Even this latter was only one third of the first sixth of the whole project, though Engels posthumously got the other two thirds of *Capital* through the press in 1885 and 1894. Almost 100 years later a fragmentary draft manuscript known as the *Grundrisse* was published, to the adulation of admirers. But even this 800-page segment was only a small part of the whole. Clearly Marx had set himself a large task, which receded steadily towards the horizon as he plunged in ever-more pedantic detail into the section before him. Engels was always pushing him to finish up and publish more quickly, but Marx lacked Engels's qualities of turning out a quick and rounded overview. If truth be told, the thousands of pages of Marxian economics, with their involutions through complex Hegelian abstractions, are a tedious maze. They would be sheer boredom to read if they were not enlivened by Marx's political crusade against capitalism and his intellectual opponents, which brings the prose to life by its invective tinged with moral outrage. It is this combination of emotion with endless intellectual abstraction that no doubt impressed Marx's contemporaries as a sign of his genius, and it continues to fascinate those who choose to fall within his orbit.

But to put the matter bluntly: Marx's own personal labyrinth is not a place that sociology should be trapped. It is Engels who breathed sociology into the vision, and it is Engels's own writings—and those of Marx that were collaborative with, or inspired by, joint work with Engels—that delivers what sociology can learn from this "Marxian" view.[1]

The question naturally arises: Why did Engels efface himself so deliberately before the intellectual persona of Marx? For one thing, Engels and Marx really did converge in some of their ideas, especially in the early part of their careers before Marx became all-absorbed in a Hegelianized economics. Both men were young and active revolutionaries; Engels actually led the military uprising in his own town of Barmen in Germany in 1848. After the eclipse of the revolution, it was Marx who kept up the underground political work, becoming head of the Communist International, while Engels contributed as he could by managing his factory and seeing to Marx's financial support. It was no doubt this political commitment, and Marx's much more forceful political personality, that conditioned their intellectual identities, at least in public. Moreover Marx was a difficult person to get along with. Engels was one of the few acquaintances with whom he did not break; in fact Engels was his one real friend. The terms of their friendship were simply the avoidance of any intellectual disagreement and any overt challenge by Engels to Marx's public preeminence in their collaboration. Perhaps this even appealed to Engels as a practical matter because he was, after all, outwardly a respectable business executive in Manchester society; whereas Marx put up not only with poverty, but with the dangers of the political police and endless struggles with censorship on the Continent. Engels may even have experienced an inner satisfaction on intellectual grounds. After all, it was *he* who had initiated the "critique of political economy" and the system of materialistic conflict sociology in the 1840s, and he must have had the satisfaction of seeing his own project worked out through all its tedious details by his friend's labor. Finally 25 years later, he was able to step back into the intellectual arena in his own right, bearing a more-or-less finished product in hand. With Marx sick and then dead, Engels was left on center stage as a popular and influential spokesperson with plenty of attention being paid to his own thoughts as he took the system on new tangents. One might say, at the price of not receiving his full credit, Engels was able to reap a pleasant and successful intellectual career—to a much greater degree than did Marx in his own lifetime.

If one wished to play with labels, one could say that the "Marxism" label is a myth and that for purposes of sociology Marx might better be called an "Engelsian." Marx wrote longer and more systematic works but in a narrow and somewhat monomaniacal vein; Engels was more wide ranging as well as more sociological. Engels was more willing to turn out rapid essays, trying out new ideas on paper—hence, the superficiality of some of his thoughts, such as on the dialectics of nature, or the somewhat facile evolutionism found in treatment of the origins of the family and the state. But Engels also was flexible enough to disavow his methodological mistakes and to foreshadow the progressive development of an ever-more empirically adequate conflict sociology. Of course what Marx and Engels did was an emergent property. Marx, who certainly had a giant's intellectual force and energy, absorbed Engels's early leads, amplified them, and made them his own—as one can see in the brilliance of the *Eighteenth Brumaire*. As he was left more on his own, apart from Engels's influence, the sociology faded before the monomaniac Hegelianized economist. In the final analysis, who contributed exactly what is a minor question. If I pull out themes that can be called "Engelsian", it is because intellectual works are not all of a piece and not of equal value in every part. At the risk of setting up a slightly mythical "Engels" in the place of an already heavily mythologized "Marx", let us focus on pulling out the threads of their thought that make the most enduring contribution to sociology.

THE THEORY OF SOCIAL CLASSES

Social classes are the center of Engels and Marx's conception of history. Social classes are economic and, thus, founded on a material base. But they are much more than the bare technology of economic production. Classes are defined by a crucial kind of *social* relationship that ties together the material, ideological, and political sides of society. This is *property*: the legal right, enforced by the state, over some material good. Every major type of society has not only its distinctive form of economic production, but also its distinctive form of property and, hence, of social classes. Engels and Marx only sketched out what these types of society and, therefore, types of class system might be; these should not be taken as absolutely fixed stages, but as illustrations of class systems. Thus, ancient societies of the Mediterranean world (Greece, Rome) based their production on property in slaves. Hence the major social classes were the patricians—the class of slave owners; the slaves themselves—the major producers in that society; and an intermediate class, the plebians—defined as those who neither owned slaves nor were slaves. We can see already that the scheme is not a simplistic one. The slaves sometimes rose in revolt, but the major form of class conflict in ancient society was that between the slave owners and the plebians, the intermediate class. These three-sided conflicts, as we will see, are extremely common in world history.

Similarly, "feudal" society (Engels and Marx's appellation for the agrarian states of the European Middle Ages) is based on productive property, consisting of the land with its laborers legally bound to it. Hence the main classes were the landowning aristocracy, the serfs who were attached to the land, and finally an intermediate class of urban artisans and merchants, with their further subdivisions into guild masters, journeymen, apprentices, and so on. Again there is the possibility of subgradations of property divisions and, thus, of multiple class conflicts. Finally in capitalist society—which is the only society that Engels and Marx knew well—the major form of property is industrial capital. Hence, the major classes and class divisions are between the capitalists—who own the means of production—and the proletariat or workers—who own no property of their own and are forced to sell their labor to stay alive.

Classes are the major actors on the historical stage. It is the classes that fight economic and political struggles, make alliances, and produce historical change. Each class has its own culture, its own outlook. Hence, the ideas and beliefs of each historical era and each sector of society are determined by its lineup of classes. It should be stressed that Engels and Marx do not present us with a mechanical conception of classes flowing from each mode of production. In their concrete historical and political writings—for example, on the peasant wars in Germany or the revolutions in France—they discern quite a few important class divisions. Thus, the midnineteenth-century upper classes included not only the owners of industrial capital, but also the financiers and the landlord class: and these three segments of bourgeois society may often be wrapped in political struggle with each other. There is also an intermediate lower-middle class of small tradespeople, shopkeepers, small manufacturers, and artisans. These, too, are an independent cultural milieu and can be political actors in their own right; Marx and Engels often refer to "petit bourgeois radicals" coming out of this group. But such classes are not fixed forever; as the cycles of capitalist economy produced more and more industrial concentration, Marx and Engels expected the petit bourgeois would lose their small-scale property and sink into the ranks of the proletariat.

All these classes are clearly enough defined by the relationship to some type of property. But there are other classes whose base is more mysterious in the Marx/Engels scheme. They nevertheless can play an important political and cultural role. For instance, there is the *lumpenproletariat:* beggars, thieves, itinerant workers, and entertainers as well as bourgeois outcasts, gamblers, roués, prostitutes, what in general was then called "la bohème." Marx described this group as the shock troops of the counterrevolution in France between 1848 and 1851; earlier Engels had described armies of vagabonds playing a duplicitous role, coming and going on both sides in the German peasant wars at the time of the Reformation. The *lumpenproletariat* class—the structural outcasts of society—derives neither from society's economic base nor from its property owners; nevertheless it is the floating class par excellence, capable of being bought off by either side. It is these structural side forces that make class conflict complicated. Another example would be intellectuals, who usually cater to the whims of their wealthy patrons but who set themselves up as independent and even revolutionary when a truly revolutionary class appears in the economic structure of society.

In the higher classes, too, there are structural groups other than the property-owning ones. Marx mentions especially the army and government officials: what might be called predatory classes living off the superstructure. These classes would later play an important role in neo-Marxist theories of revolution such as those of Barrington Moore, Jr., and Theda Skocpol. Engels found these kinds of political divisions in the upper classes of feudal society as well; he pointed out that the German nobility of the 1500s was sharply split between the large princes, the upper clergy (the Catholic Church was a wealthy and privileged property owner of the time), and the smaller knights. The wars of the Reformation involved not only an uprising of peasants (with an input from armies of beggars) as well as an urban bourgeoisie (for whom Martin Luther was the spokesperson), but also those different sectors of the nobility fighting among themselves over the property arrangements of society.

Engels and Marx did not invent the concept of social classes; it was part of the common terminology of their European ancestors. What they did contribute was to begin a *theory* of classes, to show their causes and consequences. Their analysis is stronger on the side of consequences: they showed how any political struggle could be analyzed into the conflicts and alliances among social classes pursuing different economic interests. They also proposed a general scheme of the causes of social classes, that is, the conditions under which they arise. This part of their theory was merely suggested and not extensively worked out. In general we see that the type of property system of every era creates certain major class divisions. But we see that there are numerous auxiliary classes; the conditions that produce them and that turn their interests in particular directions in class struggles have remained topics to be developed in the tradition of conflict sociology after Engels and Marx.

THE THEORY OF IDEOLOGY

The basic principle of materialism is that human consciousness rests on certain material conditions without which it would not exist. Marx and Engels stated this argument quite early in their careers when attacking (and inverting) Hegelian idealism. But the argument goes beyond a mere abstract claim that the "superstructure" of ideas reflects the material base. It is not simply a matter of the basic economy determining a set of ideas. There is an intervening set of processes that take account of multiple social classes, their conflicts, and even their degrees of relative autonomy. As Marx and Engels state in *The German Ideology*, the ruling ideas of any epoch are the ideas of the ruling class because they control the *means of mental production*.

There are two refined notions here. One is that social classes have a propensity to see the world in a particular way. Ideas reflect their economic interests and also the social conditions that surround these interests. Ideas as ideology serve the double purpose of exalting oneself but also of acting as weapons to cloak one's interests in an ideal form and to gain deference for them. The aristocracy of the feudal era, for example, espoused the ideals of honor and loyalty. This reflected their position as soldiers and it also implicitly upheld their hereditary claims to own land and to receive humble obedience from their serfs. For "honor" meant both bravery in combat and chivalrous politeness to "honorable" opponents of the same class; the idea also implied that "honor" came from family and breeding and that it excluded both mere profit-making pursuits like those of the merchants and artisans as well as dirty productive work like that of the peasants who supported them. Similarly the bourgeoisie created a new set of ideals: freedom, equality, "the eternal rights of man." Behind this abstract universalism was a class message: it spoke revolutionary words against the hereditary aristocracy, proclaiming the dignity of commerce, working for a living, and rising by amassing one's own wealth. It simultaneously elevated the universal rule of money, which knows no pedigree; put down the aristocracy; and tried to keep the workers in their place by holding out the abstract notion of equality without mentioning that the competition of the marketplace was stacked against them.

In political battles, different ideals become the rallying point for antagonistic classes. Marx cut through the contending parties of France before the 1848 revolution—the "Legitimatists," who wanted to restore the old Bourbon monarchy, and the "Orleanists," who supported a rival royal house—to point to the economic interests that clustered in each camp: the landed property holders speaking for "Legitimacy" and the new finance capitalists advocating the "progressive" policy of Orleans. Politics is fought out in terms of a code, which always must be translated; classes rarely sail under their true colors.

The ideologies of the higher classes always reflect their own interests, albeit in idealized form. That is because they have the capacity to control the *material means* by which ideas are produced. These are the means of mental production: the books, printing presses, newspapers, or church pulpits that announce the viewpoint of those who can afford to pay the bills. Intellectuals, too, are specialists in ideas who nevertheless have to make a living by fitting into the economic structure of the time. In medieval feudalism, intellectuals could only live either by becoming priests or monks and drawing income from the landed estates of the church, or by attaching themselves to some noble patron who expected to be entertained. That is why intellectuals, although free in principle to formulate whatever ideas they can conceive, nevertheless tend to create ideologies favoring the class that feeds them: medieval poets who extol the noble virtues, or priests whose theologies declare the hereditary ranks of society to reflect the eternal order given by God.

When an economic era changes, new forms of support for intellectuals open up—the market for books and newspapers that began in capitalist England and Western Europe in the 1700s, for instance, or the school systems with their demand for teachers. When intellectuals have a choice among alternative means of support, their intellectual autonomy is enhanced, and they can formulate criticisms of the old order and even go over to the revolutionary side. But this does not mean that ideas are simply free floating and autonomous: they always reflect the social and material circumstances of intellectuals and become revolutionary precisely at those times—like the late 1700s when French intellectuals were the harbingers and drumbeaters for the coming 1789 revolution—when the material basis of society and of intellectual production are changing.

Engels and Marx never developed the theory of the means

of intellectual production systematically. But the general conception has been quite fruitful in later sociology. Engels and Marx were mainly concerned with the production of political ideologies. The theory of the material and social conditions applies to various forms of intellectual creation. Arnold Hauser and others have used it to explain the changing forms of art and literature in different historical periods. This line of thought also set off the sociology of science, which began in the 1930s when Marxist scientists such as J. D. Bernal, Joseph Needham, and Boris Hessen attempted to show how science arises only within certain historical and economic conditions. That is not to say that the sociology of science has proceeded in a strictly Marxist direction; Robert Merton and others reacted to the Marxist challenge by attempting to show the inner normative social organization of science in its own right.

In recent years we have gotten closer to a conception of science as a series of *nested layers* of institutions: economic and political systems at the outside that under certain conditions (some of which we have seen in the Prologue) allow university systems or research laboratories to exist. These in turn become an intermediate layer of social and material conditions within which scientists and other intellectuals can operate. But inside this realm, scientists carry on their own conflicts: they break up into separate networks attempting to exploit particular kinds of laboratory equipment; they treat ideas as "intellectual capital" to be invested (in the terminology of the French sociologist, Pierre Bourdieu); and in Thomas Kuhn's words, they divide into conservatives defending their "paradigms" or into radicals carrying out intellectual "revolutions." Recently sociologists who have examined what actually goes on in scientific laboratories point out that what is considered to be "knowledge" is shaped by the material setting of the research equipment itself and by the ways that results can be announced through the material medium of print. We understand now a good deal more about the means of mental production and are moving closer to Engels and Marx's aim of showing just how ideas reflect their material social circumstances.

I have considered the theory of ideology in two of its offshoots: the explanation of political ideas held by the dominant classes and the production of specialized ideas by intellectuals. The general theory of ideology has other ramifications as well. It implies that each social class has its distinctive culture and outlook on the world, reflecting the social circumstances in which it lives. This analysis of class cultures, as we will see, took on considerable refinements with Weber's concept of status groups, and it has been developed much further with the empirical research of the twentieth century. In Chapter 3, I will attempt to show how even the Durkheimian tradition adds an important link to the theoretical explanation of why different classes inhabit different intellectual and moral universes. Engels and Marx, with their overriding concern for politics, did not go too far in this direction. But they did contribute some important leads.

In his discussion of the German peasant uprisings at the time of the Reformation, Engels attempted to show why the peasants had to put their revolutionary claims in a religious form. Marx took up Engels's idea in *The Eighteenth Brumaire* to explain why the peasants of France supported the dictator Louis Bonaparte against the Paris revolution. In both cases the general idea is that peasants are immobilized and isolated in their tiny villages and farms. These material conditions kept the peasants from forming any conception of themselves as a class with common interests against other social classes. All they could see was their own local interests plus an unknown but hostile world outside. For this reason peasant consciousness took the form of a mystification: in the one case, it consisted of religious ideas about the impending millennium and the downfall of the Antichrist who ruled the world disguised as the Pope; in the other case, it consisted of a nationalist mythology about the Emperor Napoleon who had come to save France. Both of these ideologies left the peasants at the mercy of political forces they could not realistically comprehend.

From a theoretical viewpoint, the explanation given by Engels and Marx opened the way to an understanding of some crucial mechanisms of class cultures. We can begin to see that all social classes do not form their ideologies in the same way. Higher classes, which are better interorganized and can control the means of intellectual production, have ideologies that are more abstract and self-exalting; subordinated classes have ideologies that are much less serviceable as weapons for their own interests but that nevertheless reflect the material condition of their own lives. We begin to see that there is ideological stratification and ideological domination as well as sheer economic and political domination. We enter the realm where there is a relationship between real violence and what Bourdieu calls "symbolic violence." And we see the mediator between these two realms: the social and material conditions of everyday life that make up the means of mental production.

THE THEORY OF POLITICAL CONFLICT

Politics, economics, and social classes are crucially linked. For the economic system is organized around property, which defines classes, and *property is upheld by the state*. Property is not the thing itself that is owned; the thing is owned by someone only because the state establishes their legal right to it and will act to enforce that claim with the power of the police and if need be the army. Marx and Engels in *The German Ideology* poke fun at bourgeois ideologists who think that property somehow is an inalienable right of the individual, having nothing to do with society. Particular kinds of property emerge only in particular social systems. The man who legally owns a piece of land but who has no capital to cultivate it has nothing, only possession of a fiction. Paper money similarly is worth nothing at all unless one submits oneself to the conditions of the society that make it legal tender.

For this reason, any dominant economic class must be concerned with politics. That does not mean it has to be concerned with the day-to-day running of the state. But it has to make sure that the state continues to protect its property interests, and it wants the intervention of the state's power to help it make even greater fortunes. The feudal aristocracy wanted the state to keep the peasants in line, but it also wanted the state to carry out wars that would give lucrative opportunities for conquest, to award monopolies on the profits of foreign plantations, and to tax goods moving along the roads. The capitalist society is even more entwined with the state because it depends on a monetary system and on a complex network of stocks, loans, interest payments, taxes, monopolies and regulations, lawyers, courts, and lawsuits.

We may conceive of an inner and an outer form of politics. The outer involves the personalities of politicians, their scandals, their dramatic foreign policy crises, their slogans of nationalism, corruption, reform, liberalism, and conservatism. The dominant economic class does not need to take an active part in this, although there is always an opportunity for the wealthy to go into politics personally. But the inner form of politics, too boring for the newspapers and the public generally, is what makes the class system operate: here there are little-known maneuvers between the treasury and the banks, the funding of public debts, the setting of contract law and innumerable other technical regulations. Here the dominant class has a real interest and, according to the Marxian conception, almost always gets its way.

Politics is a struggle to control the state. In Marx and Engels's conception, the dominant propertied class always wins this struggle, except in the historical situation when the basic form of production is shifting. Then the political control of the old ruling class breaks down and is replaced by a new class. Here we have to distinguish between the way Marx's economic system was supposed to work and the sociology that Marx and Engels attached to it. Marx's economic conception was that the internal contradictions of capitalism would bring about the concentration of capitalist property, the growth of a huge unemployed and underpaid proletariat, and eventually an economic crisis so large that the only way out of it would be the abolition of the system of private property. The economic prediction has not yet come true; for various theoretical reasons, it can be argued that it never will. Modern Marxists have generally gone another route to look for the causes of revolution, one which is not dependent on economic crisis per se. It would probably be true that if the capitalist economy worked the way Marx said it did, then politics would be overwhelmingly dominated by the capitalist class until the point at which an abrupt transition of power took place from them to the political leaders of the proletariat. In actuality politics looks much messier than this.

Revolutions, when they have occurred, have always had a mixture of different social classes fighting it out in complex coalitions. Marx and Engels themselves, when they analyzed the revolutions of their day, paid a great deal of attention to the struggles between different portions of the capitalist class (or for the Reformation wars analyzed by Engels, struggles between different portions of the aristocracy). In short Engels and Marx's sociology is much more realistic than their economics. If their economics had worked, their sociology would just be one more flywheel on the machine, grinding out political results of economic processes. But if the economics does not work well, that does not mean the political sociology should be abandoned. Far from it: their political sociology provides the opening wedge of a realistic conflict theory that is applicable to all sorts of situations, not just the particular economic scenarios they envisioned. The sociological flywheel comes loose; we can discard the economic machine entirely if we like. We are still left with a series of principles that show who wins what degree of political power, and why. The bourgeoisie need not always win; it becomes possible to explain the conditions under which we get various liberal reforms, representation of working-class interests, as well as class splits. In short we have a powerful tool for understanding all the messy realities of politics.

One crucial principle is that *power depends on the material conditions of mobilization*. This principle goes back to Engels's formulation of why the German peasants could be dominated by the aristocracy. The peasants far outnumbered their oppressors; during the peasant revolts, they created armies many times larger than those of the nobles sent to fight them. Nevertheless the nobles always won. They did so by splitting the peasants, buying off one local group while attacking another. What the nobles had was superior *means of mobilization*: they were organized precisely as a group specializing in long-distance movement and intercommunication, with their horses, their alliances, their familiarity with military maneuvers. Just as the peasants could achieve only a mystified consciousness of the world outside their little local worlds, they had no material means for organizing themselves in political combat. Marx stated the point even more forcefully in regard to the French peasants of his own century: they were split, he declared, "like potatoes in a sack," merely lumped together externally but never achieving any unity. Their material conditions separated them and kept them from achieving any power.

The property-owning class dominates politically because it has more of the means of political mobilization. Capitalism itself is an interconnected system. Business people are actively engaged in trading among themselves, watching competitors, taking loans, forming cartels. The financial network and the market itself are means of communication that bring the capitalist class into a close network. For this reason the business class, especially in its upper financial circles, is already extremely well organized. The business class has a network at its disposal that it can easily use to enter politics when it wants something done. The working classes, on the other hand, have no such natural means of organization. For them to take part in politics, they have to make special efforts to create political organizations and painstakingly try to connect workers from different places together into a common force. Thus, although the workers far outnumber the business elite, the superior means of political mobilization of the latter tends to put the balance of political power in their hands. This together with the upper-class control of the means of mental production—in modern society the ownership of newspapers, television stations, and the like—means that a fairly small business minority can usually define political issues from their own slant and gain political power far out of proportion to their numbers.

For this reason, the capitalist class has historically preferred some form of republican government. A democracy of voters turns out to be favorable to business interests because the business class is most strongly mobilized to win the struggle for power. One might say that the same material conditions that constitute the business system itself are readily turned to dominating the market for votes. Barrington Moore, Jr., a few years ago used this principle to help explain why and where democracy was created rather than socialist or fascist governments; we will take up this and other ramifications of Marx and Engels's political sociology below.

There is one other important reason why capitalists find it relatively easy to dominate the politics of a democracy, at least in the matters of greatest concern to themselves. This is the importance of finances in any government, especially the national debt. Marx pointed out that the revolutionary government of France in 1848 did not dare put into effect any radical economic policies because its own solvency depended on the strength of the French currency. The banks held the government hostage because any policy that disturbed business confidence automatically brought unemployment, fewer government taxes, and generally exacerbated the problems of the government in paying its bills. A government could of course take over the banks and command what it wants by force, but only at the cost of having the entire business system collapse. The government in relation to a capitalist economy is like the owner of a goose that lays golden eggs only as long as it is treated well. Because a government cannot survive unless it can feed its own army and its civil servants, not to mention keeping the confidence of the general population, it needs to maintain economic prosperity. Any shifts to the left tend to be automatically self-negating because they cause a reaction in the business community that creates an economic crisis. We have seen the same mechanism operating many times in the twentieth century: socialist and liberal governments in Europe in the 1920s, or in Latin America throughout this century, have fallen because of the rampant inflation that followed their taking office. In effect this means that any half-way socialist reform is not likely to work. Only an extremely strong revolutionary government can overcome the loss of business confidence and the resulting period of economic crisis by taking all business and financial affairs into its hands immediately and imposing a completely regulated economy.

The scheme also explains the conditions under which the power of the working class can grow. In the *Communist Manifesto* Marx and Engels pointed out that capitalism itself was overcoming the isolation and fragmentation that characterized the older lower classes. Where the peasants were isolated on their little farms, the very process of business concentration that took place in capitalism was bringing the workers together. As small businesses were bought out, increasingly larger numbers of workers came into huge factories where they became easier to organize. Not only trade unions but working-class political parties were forming; eventually, with the projection of the business trend toward one huge monopoly, the workers would be brought into a corresponding unity that would finally realize their strength of numbers and overwhelm the capitalists.

This is not quite what happened, but Marx and Engels were partially right on the historical trend and even more so on the right track theoretically. Historically, working-class parties were created as capitalism became more concentrated, although this did not go as far as Marx and Engels expected because the means of political mobilization also shifted and the process of monopolization stabilized at an intermediate point. Within the big capitalist corporations that emerged, the organizational structure itself mobilized different groups of employees into different layers. Below the top management, a middle layer of office workers came to acquire their own consciousness based on their peculiar conditions of work; hence, they became an intermediate political force of their own. Outside these giant corporations and interconnected with them there grew up networks of specialists and professionals: small innovative firms, engineers and architects, lawyers, media people, investment consultants, academics, intellectuals. These various professions have often in their own way been even more mobilized and more interconnected into networks than even the business class. The means of political mobilization remain all-important; what has happened empirically, though, is that these means have mobilized a large number of different, self-interested occupational groups. Modern politics instead of simplifying into the showdown of capitalists and workers has, instead, fragmented into the complex maneuvers of many separately mobilized interest groups. Politics has thus turned into the negotiation of complicated coalitions.

In fact it has probably always been so. Engels and Marx wrote brilliantly on coalitions in their analysis of revolutions in their own time. Their theory of politics still applies, as I indicated, even to new circumstances. It shows us not who the actors are going to be at any given time, but, instead, what political weapons they can use and what outcomes will result once we know the lineup of players. Modern theories of social movements, especially the resource-mobilization theory of Charles Tilly and Anthony Oberschall, carry forward this line of analysis.

THE THEORY OF REVOLUTIONS

Marx and Engels had a general conception of the revolution that they expected would bring about the final downfall of capitalism and usher in socialism. But their more valuable theories of revolution are found in their specific historical studies of the smaller revolutions of their own times (also, in Engels' case, in reflections on the revolutionary aspect of the Protestant Reformation). Their basic analysis is that revolutions go through various phases because of *unstable coalitions among a variety of social classes*. The lower classes often do the largest part of the actual destruction of the old regime by their riots and uprisings. But the lower classes tend to act in the interests of a higher social class. In 1789 and 1848 the proletariat and the petit bourgeoisie fought the battles of the upper bourgeoisie for them, just as in the 1520s the German burghers fought the battles of the German princes against the Roman Catholic Church.

Why is it that revolutions have this peculiar quality of false consciousness and action in the interests of someone else? We have already seen some parts of the answer. The differential control of the means of the mental production results in the higher social classes being able to define what the revolution is about and who the enemies are. The workers or peasants do the fighting, but the bourgeois or the nobles tell them what they are fighting for. Also, because there is a complicated set of classes vying for power, coalitions form and interests get submerged within them. Coalitions are necessarily ideological because they need some general slogans around which they can rally. Thus, different social classes who may be at each other's throats at some time, at other moments have to rally together to defend what they believe is their common interest. In 1848, the Legitimatists and Orleanists (landowners and capitalists) had to bury their feud because property of all sorts was being threatened by a revolutionary republic. One general principle, then, is that a coalition is held together by its enemies. Only after the enemies disappear are the partners free to fight among themselves. Similarly, the revolutionary party in 1848 was a coalition of two antagonistic classes: the lower middle class of small shopkeepers, who favored a form of capitalism, and the workers, who were pressing for socialism. These strange bedfellows were held together by *their* enemies, the reactionary upper classes, who threatened the Republic. The battle between these two groups was fought out in opposing slogans, both of which misrepresented the actual interests involved. The conservatives attacked by branding all of their opponents as socialists and enemies of social order, whereas the revolutionaries had to bury their economic differences and concentrate on their common slogan of defending democracy.

Eventually the conservatives were able to mobilize more resources and to split their opponents, lopping off the radical workers' wing of the republicans. But here another principal came into play: *the danger of victory for a coalition.* The lower-middle classes, having dispensed with their allies to form a smaller group for splitting the spoils (what modern political theorists call a "minimum winning coalition"), now found themselves weakened vis-à-vis the conservatives. Power shifted to the right. But even this was unstable because the conservatives found themselves heading a republican government whose very right to exist they had just been denouncing. They were trapped in their own ideology and further immobilized by the outbreak of squabbles between the coalition members (Orleanists and Legitimatists) in their own ranks. The way was opened to yet another political force: Louis Bonaparte and his dictatorship, drawing his shock troops by mobilizing the *lumpenproletariat* and getting his ideological support by playing on the nationalism of the peasants. The only stable stopping place in the war of coalitions was to exhaust and discredit all the class forces.

This model of revolution emerges as a byproduct, a series of comments as Marx analyzed the history unfolding in front of him. It is not a full theory. Subsequent theorists have gone on to examine not only the mobilization of different classes, but also the conditions that break down the state in the first place and open the way for the revolutionary crisis. We will meet these theories below.

THE THEORY OF SEX STRATIFICATION

After Marx's death, Engels formulated a general historical theory of the family.[2] This opened up the issue of equality and inequality among men and women and the social causes of these shifting patterns. Engels put forward the concept of sexual property: that the rights of sexual access are appropriated and guarded in just the same way as are the rights to use economic property. At one time, he argued, there was sexual communism in early tribal societies. Then, as private property was introduced in the economy and classes were created, private sexual property was also enforced, with dominant males making sexual property out of women. Engels's model of a series of evolutionary stages is not too accurate, although he did draw on the leading anthropologists of his time—a period when anthropology was just beginning. Thus, Engels believed there was a stage of matriarchy intervening between primitive communism and the rise of patriarchy. But Engels's attitude about this sort of thing was not dogmatic, and he would have been happy to see his theory modified to fit a better construction of the historical facts.

His theory is nevertheless correct in several important points. Although there almost certainly was no such thing as a universal stage of either primitive sexual communism or of matriarchy, it is true that the kind of sexual property relationships changed from one general type of society to another, though in a more complex fashion. The patriarchal household of the ancient and medieval states was indeed the most male-dominated family system that has ever existed, and women's status generally took a sharp decline with the transition from tribal societies to these class-stratified societies. Engels also pointed to an important phenomenon when he noted that the rise of capitalist society and its private household only gave a formal freedom to women; though they were now free to make their own marriages, they did so on a marriage "market" in which they lacked any economic property of their own. Hence, the typical capitalist form of courtship and marriage consisted of a woman having to trade domestic subordination and sexual favors for a marriage contract with a man who would support her.

Engels also provided an important general explanation of the different systems of sexual stratification by arguing that they are related to the economic system of the surrounding society. Engels's theory was thus capable of considerable refinement to fit a better understanding of the complexities of the historical data. It took a long time before his theory was seriously developed in this direction. Max Weber, who was interested in feminism because his wife was a leader in the German feminist movement, took up Engels's theory, which he criticized for its weaknesses of historical data but praised as a fruitful starting point. Weber developed a comparative theory of the family that also emphasized the variety of economic structures of the household and the form of sexual property within it. Weber characteristically added political factors as a crucial determinant of the kinds of sexual stratification.[3]

Most refined theories of sexual stratification have only opened up within the last 20 years, and efforts to put together the various explanatory factors are still being developed. Engels' basic ideas have an important place in this. One line of argument has taken his conception of the economic basis of the family, to argue that women's household labor is part of the capitalist class structure. Women working as wives and mothers, even though they are not paid for their labor, are a crucial part of the reproduction of the labor force, without which the wage laborers necessary for the capitalist economy would not exist. There is, thus, a hidden economic pressure and a hidden class struggle underneath the more overt class relations of the markplace. Debate still goes on over whether this means that women are a part of the more general working class, or whether homemakers constitute a second, female working class in implicit struggle with both the capitalist system and the male workers who are their husbands.

This is an application of the economic theory to sex stratification within contemporary society. Another application is to use the theory to explain the historical differences among societies with different kinds and degrees of sex stratification. Theorists such as Rae Lesser Blumberg and Karen Sacks find a relationship between the degree of women's social power and freedom, and the extent to which they contribute to economic production and manage to control their own economic property. This more refined version of the Engelsian theory does not require a set sequence of evolutionary stages that all societies pass through. Different kinds of tribal societies, for example, can have great male dominance or various degrees of female power, depending on their specific sex-based economies. In the ancient and medieval ("feudal") state societies, women's status tended to drop because they were squeezed out of the core economic production, although some aristocratic women were able to make gains where the system of marital politics gave them control over property. And in our own society, the relative status of men and women within each family is strongly influenced by their own economic positions. Women who have broken into the more lucrative careers have also tended to break the pattern of the traditional marriage market as well.

Engels's theory is pivotal because it emphasized not only economic determinants of family and sexual relationships, but also recognized the phenomenon of sexual property—the propertylike nature of controls over sexuality itself. This line of analysis has developed somewhat separately from the analysis of economic factors. It has given rise to various theories of the politics of sex. Anthropologists like Claude Lévi-Strauss or Marvin Harris have developed "alliance" theories of the family structures in different tribal societies, analyzing them as ways in which sexual exchanges are used as political strategies to tie groups together militarily and economically. I have applied this type of analysis to the shifting patterns of sexual relationships that have characterized both the patriarchal households of medieval agrarian societies and the "Victorian" period of the early modern marriage market, as well as the sexual transformations that have happened in the twentieth century and are still going on today.

Sex stratification is a topic that many sociologists, as well as other people, ignored for a long time. No male-female stratification was seen because a male-dominated social order was simply taken for granted. Engels was a pioneer in bringing this to light as a question for theoretical explanation. More than half a century after his death, his line of conflict analysis of the family, economy, and sex has begun to develop into a sophisticated general theory.

Max Weber and the Multidimensional Theory of Stratification

Weber's sociology is often seen as antagonistic to the Marxian approach. Actually Weber is more of a continuer of it, a later generation of the historical conflict tradition in the German intellectual world. Weber was born in 1864 and grew up intellectually in the 1880s and 1890s, which is precisely the period in which Engels and his followers were making an impact on German intellectual life. Marx had been generally unknown during his own life, except in the revolutionary underground. But in the 1880s the German socialist party, based on trade unions and following the Marxist theory as their official doctrine, had become a large force in German parliamentary politics. The party itself was participating in elections and becoming gradually less revolutionary, but it was big enough to be able to support its own newspapers and party schools as well as full-time political representatives. It had acquired the material base to support its own intellectuals. Thus it was in Germany that Marxism (maybe really Engelsism) moved above ground and broke into the attention of the academic and intellectual world.

Weber was very much aware of these developments. His father was a member of another political party in the Reichstag at Berlin, a bourgeois party representing the large manufacturers. Prominent politicians, lawyers, and academics met at their home, and Max Weber early became privy to the maneuvers of backstage power politics. Another influence came from his mother, who was devoutly religious in a Protestant denomination. She urged him to take part in a Christian social welfare movement, which was something of a religious response to workers' socialism: instead of the workers gaining reforms for themselves by class warfare, the charitable upper classes proposed to give it to them out of religious duty. Weber, thus, was politically involved from an early age and in contact with two different political forces, each of which was in its own way concerned with the growing power of socialism. Weber himself was no socialist, though he was rather opposed to existing policies of the conservative government. As already mentioned, he married a young woman, Marianne Schnitger (Weber), who became one of the leaders of the feminist movement in Germany. He opposed the persecution of the supporters of socialism, especially in the academic-freedom fights that arose in the universities of the time; Weber even considered joining the socialist party to show his solidarity. But he concluded that it would be dishonest of him to do so because he truly did believe that capitalism was a superior social system for enhancing human freedom and economic productivity. For all his opposition to socialism as a political program, Weber nevertheless learned a great deal of substantive sociology from Marx and Engels. He took up their questions, even if he gave them different and more complicated answers.

Of course there were other intellectual strands in his makeup. Weber was an economist in the German style. That is, he did not use the abstract general theory of the market, either in the marginal utility form recently developed by Carl Menger in Austria, Léon Walras in France, Vilfredo Pareto in Italy, and William Jevons and Alfred Marshall in England; nor the classical form that Marx had used for his economic system. The German school of economics was what might be called "institutional" and "historical." It did not accept any universal laws of economic processes (such as supply and demand, the movement of prices, etc.), but, instead, attempted to show the various historical periods of development of different types of economies. Such theories focused on such possible stages as the household or manor economy, the putting-out system, local markets, the world market, and so forth. Weber in a sense was simply the latest of a series of historical economists who attempted to show what kinds of economic systems had pre-

ceded capitalism and by what processes the rise of capitalism
had come about. Weber also had studied and practiced law; he
knew a great deal of the history of all parts of the world—
indeed far more than Marx and Engels could have known because the discipline of history was only getting underway in
their lifetimes. Although Weber was not personally religious,
he was extremely aware of the religious motivations of people
around him and of religion as a force in past history.

One might sum up Weber's main theme as the problem of
capitalism, the same as Marx's central concern. But where
Marx was primarily concerned with the economic laws of capitalism and with its crises and future breakdown, Weber was
concerned with the background of capitalism, the puzzle of
how it came into existence in the first place. Weber approached
this not by looking for a sequence of stages, but by a world
comparison: Why did modern capitalism emerge in Western
Europe rather than in one of the other great civilizations—
China, India, Rome, the Islamic world? Weber's sociology was
an offshoot of this question. His sociological theories were an
attempt to create the tools with which to analyze the institutional underpinnings of the economy, to show what forces
fostered or hindered it in various societies. One might say that
economics was what Weber wanted to explain, but his explanations took him into the world of sociology, especially into an
appreciation of the role of political and religious factors.

This is not the only possible interpretation of Weber. Some
commentators (such as Talcott Parsons), set him up as a kind
of idealist in opposition to the materialism of Marx. Weber was
seen as the defender of the role of ideas in history. This school
of thought focuses on Weber's earliest important work, *The
Protestant Ethic and the Spirit of Capitalism* (1904), which seems to
turn Marx on his head. Whereas Marx regarded religion as an
ideology reflecting economic classes, Weber seemed to be
showing that capitalism itself was produced not by economic
forces but by the influence of religious ideas: the drive of Puritans to work out their anxiety over their salvation or damna-
tion, which was left in doubt by the theological doctrine of
predestination. At about the same time Weber also wrote an
essay in which he argued that the basic method of the "human

sciences" should be *verstehen* (understanding). One could not explain social processes by abstract laws, but must get inside the subjective viewpoint of the actor, and see the world as he or she sees it, in order to capture their motivation.

These are two pieces of evidence that Weber was really an idealist, or at least tried to give ideas as much influence as possible even in the material world. For Weber never let go of the hard material realities surrounding people. There is another type of "idealistic" theme that can be found in Weber, however. He was often concerned with the rationalization of various institutions: the development of an abstract, means-end calculation. He described modern capitalism as the rationalized economy, bureaucracy as the rationalized organization, the modern state as based on the formal procedures and rules of rational-legal authority. He even argued that what is distinctive about European music since about the time of Bach is that it rationalized the musical scale, turning music into a kind of abstract mathematics. Thus, some commentators, especially recent German ones such as Friedrich Tenbruck, Jurgen Habermas, and Wolfgang Schluchter have claimed that the trend towards rationalization is Weber's master theme of world history. If Weber's *verstehen* method and his emphasis on religious ideas is a version of the idealism of Kant or the "human science" of Wilhelm Dilthey, this world history of rationalization makes Weber sound like a modern heir to Hegel.

The central reality of Weber, though, was that above all he saw the world as *multidimensional*. He gave all factors their due, striving hard to be neither a one-sided idealist nor a materialist. Rationalization, which he certainly saw as a major trend in recent centuries in the West, he nevertheless did not worship in the manner of Parsons and some of Weber's recent German interpreters. Rationalization for Weber was a two-sided sword, simultaneously an increase in formal procedures *and* an undermining of substantive human capability for consciously achieving one's goals.

Weber above all was detached, aware of the distorting possibility of value judgments and biased interests coming from many different directions. His multidimensional perspective made him *fundamentally* a conflict theorist. For conflict is not merely just one more factor among others, it is an expression of the very multidimensionality of things, the plurality of different groups, interests, and perspectives that make up the world. Ultimately the world does *not* hold together as one great social or metaphysical unity. Though there is consensus and solidarity inside some components of society, the whole thing is a mixture of contending parts. This is one important reason, besides the specific things that Weber learned from the Marxians/Engelsians, why Weber had such a fundamental effect in shaping the entire subsequent conflict tradition in sociology. Weber not only saw that there are multiple spheres, but also that there is a struggle for domination going on inside each one. Economics for Weber is a class struggle, though of a more complicated sort than Marx and Engels had seen. Politics is yet another realm of struggle, both among contending political interests and between the politicians and the economic classes. Even the world of ideas is divided among its own interest groups. Religions, for example, have their own internal struggles—based on the social organization of the church itself—that divide professional theologians from the "church politicians" and these in turn from the pious followers. Even where Weber seems to be defending the autonomous influence of ideas, he contributes what may be seen as a sophisticated development of the theory of ideology.

Weber consequently saw history as a messy, multiple-sided process of conflict on many fronts. He was an enemy of simplified notions of evolutionary stages or other neat patterns that theorists tried to impose on the complexities of historical reality. For this reason alone, one has to doubt whether he really thought rationalization was the "master trend" of history. Was Weber, then, an historicist, a believer in the doctrine that there are no general laws, only the endless unfolding of historical particulars, with the principles of each era differing from the next? Often Weber sounded like this, especially early in his career when he was writing methodological pronouncements. This would seem to make sociology impossible, at least as generalizing science. But Weber actually left a way out. He subordinated sociology to the task of showing the elements out of which history is made. For this purpose he created *ideal types*, abstract models of bureaucracy, class, markets, and so forth, that could capture an aspect of the complex historical reality, always keeping in mind that several different ideal types would have to be applied at once to capture the various sides of things.

These ideal types have become the germs of post-Weberian sociology. Each one is a kind of encapsulated theory, much in the same way that the chemical table of elements is a theory of how molecules are put together. Weber denied that there were laws for the overall pattern of history. How that went depended on just which combinations of "molecules" were put together in each case. But these social "molecules" have turned out to be quite structured and lawful on their own level, and they have given rise to theories of classes, organizations, and the like, to give a real content to Weberian conflict theory.

Weber's famous three-dimensional model of stratification is as close as one can find to a key for his complicated system. His American translators, Hans Gerth and C. Wright Mills, introduced this under the terms: class, status, and party. All of these are kinds of interest groups that can fight both among themselves and against each other. They are also connected to each other, and each describes a particular realm about which Weber had a theory.

Class, for Weber, was the same realm Marx and Engels were talking about. One might say then that Weber incorporated Marx and Engels's sociology as one element in his system. In doing so he changed their model. Class conflict for Weber is more complicated than it was in Marx and Engels. They dealt mainly (in their theoretical writings at any rate) with the conflict of capitalist and worker, the owner of the means of production versus the producer of labor. Weber elaborated this to add conflict of finance capitalists (whom Marx described in the 1848 revolution in France) against borrowers of capital, and also the battle of sellers versus consumers. This scheme was pointed up more recently by Norbert Wiley to show that American politics has indeed been full of class conflict; although the capitalist/worker battle has been less apparent, the debtor/creditor battle dominated the farm-based politics of the

1800s, and the racial uprising of the 1960s involved consumers attacking ghetto merchants. For Weber class conflict is a three-ring circus.

Weber's class conflict differs from Marx's in a further and more crucial way. Marx's classes are defined by ownership or nonownership of the means of production. Weber's classes are defined by their position on a market. Recent Marxian theorists, reacting against Weber, have criticized his scheme as putting stratification on the superficial level of economic circulation rather than the basic level of economic production. Nevertheless I would say that this is a strength of Weber rather than a weakness. For Marx's scheme attaches classes to his theory of economics—which is the part of the Marx/Engels system that has proven least realistic as a guide to historical change. Changes in the means of production or in the ownership of them do not follow the path that Marx had set forth, neither since his day nor even in the history that went before. Moreover I think that Marx and Engels tacitly acknowledged this whenever they wrote the actual history of some political event such as the French Revolution of 1848. In those cases they always dealt with many more classes than the owners of production versus the workers. In fact the action always centered on the intermediate classes and on various complicated splits in the upper classes: the financiers and landowners (whom Weber would point out were likely to be a class of debtors) as well as the large and small industrialists.

Weber built his class theory on economic conflicts where they are most real: a struggle to control a place on some market. For Weber, monopoly is not simply something that emerges at a late stage of capitalism. It is a fundamental process found throughout its history. Social classes are based on different ways of trying to gain control over particular markets: money and credit, land, various manufacturing industries, various labor skills. This both gives a more realistic picture of class conflict as it actually happens, and also provides a general theoretical conception of the process of stratification. The dominant classes are those who manage to achieve a tight monopoly on some lucrative market; less dominant classes get only partial monopolies or monopolies in less desirable kinds of markets. Classes who achieve no monopoly at all and are forced to compete on the open market are subject to its leveling forces.

We come now to Weber's second stratification category, *status groups*. These are usually understood as the opposite of economic class stratification. Whereas classes are based on cold economic considerations—the grouping of similar interests by virtue of similar market positions—status groups are supposed to be in the realm of culture. They are not mere statistical categories but real communities, people with a common lifestyle and viewpoint of the world, people who identify with one another as belonging to a group. This makes us think of ethnic groups, races, religious groups, small-town communities, urban neighborhoods: groups that tend to deny social class or to cut across class boundaries. But in fact there is a deeper connection between class and status group. Remember: classes are groups that share a particular degree of monopolization on some market. They do this by becoming organized, by forming a community, acquiring a consciousness through some legal or cultural barriers around themselves—in short by becoming status groups.

Any successful, dominant class must become organized as a status group. In fact historically this has always been the case. Marx and Engels' historical ruling classes were organized legally and culturally to keep control of property within their own ranks. The Medieval landowners did not just hold land and exploit serfs; they did this by becoming the noble Estate, with their requirements of hereditary pedigrees, their chivalrous manners, their knightly style of life, which prevented them from getting their hands dirty with anything other than blood. In India, occupational groups went even further and turned into castes, avoiding each other as ritually polluting—justifying their avoidance by a religious doctrine of past karma and future reincarnation. From the Marxian viewpoint, these classes were simply cloaking themselves in ideologies. Weber's theory agrees with this but with the added proviso: the ideological or cultural side is absolutely necessary for a group to become more than merely a set of persons with the same economic position, a real social community. Moreover the status group reacts back upon the economic situation: it is the way the group becomes powerful enough to monopolize the desirable part of a market, instead of merely competing on equal terms within it. Status-group organization is an economic weapon.

For this reason, status groups are not noneconomic. Their very lifestyle and outlook depend on their economic resources and their position in society. The nobles' castles, along with their horses and costumes, were only possible because of their wealth. In the modern equivalent, the upper class puts on debutante balls and contributes to symphony concerts and art museums as a process of turning economic capital into cultural capital, as Bourdieu calls it. Even their religious propensities are affected by their class position. Weber pointed out in a comparative analysis that the higher social classes always prefer a dignified religion, full of stately ceremonial but not calling for too much personal commitment; the striving middle classes prefer an ascetic, moralistic religion that bolsters their respectability and motivates them to work hard; and the lower classes treat religion as a form of magic, supernatural interventions to bring good fortune and strike down one's enemies. These different cultural outlooks can make higher and lower status groups seem like alien beings to each other. They also help to cloak the economic basis underneath. This is especially true because a dominant group that has become organized as a status group always idealizes itself and claims that it is different not because of its wealth or power, but because of its greater nobility, its honor, its politeness and artistic taste, its technical skills, or whatever the prevailing status ideology happens to be.

Possessing this kind of status ideology in turn makes it easier for the group members to monopolize economic positions. Outsiders can be excluded and competition limited automatically because only persons who seem like "the right kind" are allowed into the preferred positions. The type of status ideology can shift from time to time, but there is always some process of this sort operating. Although the proliferation of educational credentials was not yet very great in Weber's day, he saw that they were creating modern status groups that served to monopolize the more lucrative occupational positions. The growth of the modern "professions" shows how much our work force has become permeated by these kinds of monopolies. Doctors, after all, are really just engaged in a form of specialized labor, but they have cut themselves off from the rest of the working class by building an elaborate occupational culture buttressed by educational degrees and state-licensing requirements to monopolize medical knowledge. In effect they have built a lucrative monopoly on the dispensing of drugs by maneuvering politically to be sure that medical drugs are not sold on the open market. The same type of analysis may be made in many other modern occupational spheres.

One key development Weber evolved from the Marxian theory of classes, then, is that economic struggle is much more multisided than Marx had shown. Classes become subdivided into status groups and gain control of particular sectors of economic markets. A secondary market for status attributes arises, and this tends to blur over the primary economic lines. But the economic struggles go on underneath nevertheless. They are less easy to see, but they remain the skeleton inside the system.

Finally *parties* or power groups: here Weber points to yet another realm of struggle, among political factions. He asserts that politicians and their maneuvers are not simply reducible to the struggles of economic classes or even of status groups because they have interests of their own. This sounds anti-Marxian, a claim that class struggle isn't everything. But in fact Marx and Engels were not so far away in their actual sociology. Recall that in addition to the various classes fighting it out in their revolutionary scenarios, they also pointed to political groups per se: the army and the bureaucrats in 1848 France, the Emperor versus the princes versus the knights in Reformation Germany. These were real interest-group struggles, and although these groups allied with different class factions, they were not reducible to them.

But political factions are not an inexplicable epiphenomenon, a "superstructure" spun free into the realm of indeterminacy. They are organized groups, in a different sphere than classes but nevertheless on the same footing with them. As Weber put it, parties live "in the house of power": in other words they inhabit the state. Now the state is an organization; indeed Weber's analysis of the state gave rise to his theory of bureaucracy and, hence, to the modern sociology of organizations. But an organization is a real material thing—at least if it is to have any permanence, it must acquire property, land, buildings, weapons, claims of sources of income to feed its own members, and so on. Every state has its economy. (Incidentally, Weber said the same thing about every church: as soon as it stops being merely a charismatic sect and starts taking on some permanent leaders, it acquires property and becomes transformed into an economic entity.) Hence, political factions have their own economic interests: the power and wealth of their own organization, the state itself. The same thing can also apply within smaller political organizations such as a political party: its official staff acquires an interest in the prosperity of the organization itself because it is where they make their careers.

It follows that political factions, living in "the house of power," are living in a real house, alongside other organizations of business, finance, and the rest of the class realm. What is distinctive about the state is not the ultimate interests of its members, but its unique weapons. The state is armed and, hence, can dominate all other organizations. Marx and Engels already saw this, in the implication that the force of the state upholds the system of economic property. The state needs to invest in arms and in troops and in police to wield them; the extensive state apparatus of bureaucrats, tax collectors, law courts, and the like, arose to maintain and supply these forces. But this creates a distinctive economic problem for the state: its own fiscal problems. States also have their distinctive enemies: namely, each other. States and their leaders vie over power in the international arena and in its offshoot, national prestige. It is these conflicts above all that increase the power of some states while threatening the power of others. But even militarily successful states risk economic troubles owing to the costs of their armies. The modern conflict analysis of revolutions, as we will see, places considerable emphasis on this kind of economic-and-military strain in the state.

The state also has another crucial weapon: legitimacy. This

is an aspect of the cultural and emotional realm. In Marx and Engels's terms, the state is the great engine for generating ideology; in Weber's terminology, the successful state makes most people within its borders feel they are members of a single status group, the nation. There are various ways in which legitimacy can be generated: Weber enumerated the charisma of forceful leaders, the tradition of hereditary arrangements, and the rational-legal authority of constitutional law. Each of these rests upon a certain material and organizational base. Legitimacy does not just come out of nowhere; it is produced, and the various kinds of organization that produce it might well be called another aspect of means of mental production (or what I have more recently called the "means of emotional production.") Later neo-Marxian analysis has picked this up. For example, the German theorist Jurgen Habermas has claimed that the revolutionary struggle of the modern state occurs not because of economic crisis, but because of a "legitimacy crisis." A more economic analysis was given by the American James O'Connor, who argues that the modern "fiscal crisis of the state"—the galloping situation of government debt, escalating taxes, inflation—is due to the way the state tries to buy legitimacy by providing welfare services at the same time that it is being milked by the monopoly sector of the economy. Both Habermas and O'Connor illustrate the way modern Marxian theories of the state have drifted in a Weberian direction.

The Twentieth Century Intermingles Marxian and Weberian Ideas

Weber deserves to be named as the individual who set off modern conflict sociology. Not that Engels and Marx were not more fundamental, but for them sociology was buried in politics and (especially for Marx) in economics and philosophy. Weber, although an economist and a lawyer by academic training, nevertheless helped found the German Sociological Association and identified his own work as sociological. Furthermore Weber's comprehensive efforts to lay out all the factors that would go into understanding the development of capitalism set the contours of the field. In the generations after

Weber, sociology became much more directly empirical, relying not only on historical comparisons, but also on systematic research efforts to gather new data. The historical and comparative data—which are of course empirical, too, though collected in a different way—have come to be treated in a more explicitly theory-building and theory-testing way than Weber himself treated them. His pioneering efforts and his ideal types provided the nucleus of concepts and theories that were fleshed out by subsequent research and of course transformed as our theoretical viewpoints continued to develop.

Politically, of course, Marxism has maintained a distinctive identity throughout the twentieth century. This has obscured the fact that *intellectually* the conflict tradition, common to both Marx and Weber, has gone on from both of them and that there has been a great deal of crisscrossing between the lines. We even see this in the young generation that followed right after Weber. One of the intellectuals that frequented Weber's salon at Heidelberg was a young Hungarian Marxist, Georg Lukács, whom Weber greatly respected despite their disagreements. Lukács, like his Italian counterpart Antonio Gramsci, bucked the tide of Marxian economism and materialism and developed a Hegelian account of class conflict that emphasized the "false consciousness" of the higher social classes. In Lukács's view, the higher social classes were more alienated from reality and from true human essence than the oppressed lower classes because they purveyed the reified ideology of the permanence of the capitalist order. How much Weber influenced Lukács's ideas is not clear, but it does illustrate the way in which Marxians and Weberians were already part of the same intellectual circle.

Another instance of this intermingling is the development of sociology at Frankfurt. There the so-called "Frankfurt School" of Marxists, led by Max Horkheimer and Theodor Adorno, had a research institute endowed by a wealthy supporter (again the material means of mental production). Adorno's ideas went in the direction of Lukács' philosophy of alienation and reification, whereas Horkheimer brought in Freudian theories to synthesize with Marx. Another member of the school was Herbert Marcuse, who took both of these themes and fashioned a critique of capitalist culture that later served as a rallying cry for the radical wing of the student movement in the 1960s. A more materialist form of Marxism was produced by Karl Wittfogel, who tried to show that China and other forms of "Oriental Despotism" were distinctive because of their own economic base. In Wittfogel's view, they were "hydraulic civilizations," based not on the private landed property of an aristocracy or slave owners, but on irrigation works built by the state. Hence, the state itself was the key economic entity in the Orient and private classes did not strongly develop. Here again we see that the Marx/Engels scheme was not simply a finished set of stages, but an incentive to understand the variety of societies in world history by the variety of economic factors. And it fits with the point just made above that the state itself must be seen as an economic entity in its own right.

ORGANIZATIONS AS POWER STRUGGLES

One of the most influential lines of analysis that came out of Frankfurt was more directly a confrontation and synthesis of the Weberian and Marxian approaches. At the University of Frankfurt—not the Marxian institute for social research—the chair of sociology was held by Karl Mannheim. Mannheim became famous in 1929 with his book *Ideology and Utopia*, a work that turned the Marxist theory of ideology against the Marxists themselves. If conservative ideologies represent the interests of the dominant class, the political claims of the working class are equally ideological and take the form of utopias. Even more important for the development of conflict sociology was a Weberian theme that Mannheim developed in his next book, *Man and Society in an Age of Reconstruction*, written in exile from the Nazis in 1935. Following Weber, Mannheim pointed out that organizations can operate by two different types of rationality. There is *substantial rationality*: the human insight into how certain means lead to certain ends. This is the kind of rationality that we usually exalt, that is supposed to be the hallmark of our unsuperstitious, scientific, professionalized era. But there is a second type of rationality that has become even more prominent: the *functional* (or *formal*) *rationality* of bureaucratic organizations. Here rationality becomes the following of rules and regulations, going by the book, which is supposed to cover comprehensively the most efficient way to function.

The formal type of rationality tends to undercut the substantial type. As we have become more enlightened and scientifically expert, we have embodied our expertise in massive organizations that no longer think in a human way, but merely follow general procedures. The organization develops an inertia of its own and slips out of human control. Mannheim had in mind the military arms races carried on by government bureaucracies from the beginning of the twentieth century—a pattern we still see today, but with the added awesome threat of total annihilation in nuclear war. This was a pattern that Mannheim had already discerned in the buildups that had led to World War I. It was a war no one wanted, but once a minor crisis in the Balkans in 1914 set the machines in motion, there was no way to hold back mobilization and countermobilization until the entire world had escalated into an extremely destructive war. Mannheim asserted that the same process held in the civilian sphere as well. The formal rationality of capitalism in the search of profits nevertheless led to no one looking out for the substantial rationality of the whole economic system. Rationality on one level coincided with irrationality on another level, precipitating an economic depression that could not be controlled. Mannheim argued that Fascism—an antimodernist and antirational ideology—was, thus, not merely a bizarre aberration, but a reaction to the deeper lack of rationality in the world of impersonal modern organizations. Fascism asserted the power of the human leader—exalting a Hitler or a Mussolini—as an antidote to the faceless efficiencies and larger irrationalities of the bureaucrats.

Hans Gerth, a student at Frankfurt, brought Mannheim's message to America. As a professor at the University of Wisconsin, he collaborated with the young C. Wright Mills in a series of books. They attempted to synthesize Freud (an approach the Frankfurt Marxists were using) as well as George Herbert Mead with Weber in their *Character and Social Structure*. In 1946, they brought out the most influential collection of

Weber's writings, the famous Gerth and Mills edition, *From Max Weber: Essays in Sociology*. This brought attention to Weber's stratification theory under the title of "Class, Status, and Party" as well as to his theory of bureaucracy. In general Gerth and Mills stressed Weber as a conflict theorist, counteracting the image given by the earlier translation of *The Protestant Ethic and the Spirit of Capitalism* brought out by Talcott Parsons. Over the next 20 years, a struggle went on over which side would appropriate and define the meaning of Weber for American sociology. Parsons and his collaborators brought out Weber's abstract definitions of capitalism (which stressed its rationality) and then his writings on law and on religion, whereas Gerth and his colleagues countered this idealist image of Weber by bringing out his more fully rounded historical studies.

During the 1950s, the conservative mood dominated American sociology. Talcott Parsons and other functionalists produced abstract categorizations of social institutions, everywhere finding a benign function contributing to maintaining the social order. Conflict sociology was not dead, but it was scarcely noticed. It was, however, making progress on the empirical front, racking up studies of power politics in organizations and charting the realities of stratification. Virtually the only loud voice upholding the insights of the conflict tradition was C. Wright Mills. These were the days of rabid anticommunism in American politics, led by right-wing witch-hunters such as Senator Joe McCarthy, but the mood in a less extreme form was shared by virtually everyone. Liberal academics were afraid to use the word "Marx" in public, and they denounced anyone who had a critical stance lest they themselves arouse the ire of the right-wingers, whom most people felt could easily turn into Nazis. Thus, Mills acquired a reputation for being an extreme leftist. It was not quite accurate. C. Wright Mills was simply an individual of considerable personal courage who wrote clearly and did not mind being a minority because of his sharp criticism of the prevailing trends of his discipline.

Mills's theory was actually an application of that of Mannheim and, hence, of Weber. His most famous book, *The Power Elite* (1956), argued that America was not under the control of individual decision makers—that is, elected officials—but was actually controlled by three massive, bureaucratic organizations. These were the corporate business establishment, the military bureaucracy of the Pentagon, and the bureaucrats of the federal government. One can see the Weberian theme: Marx's capitalists are there, but they are only one part of a larger concatenation of power groups, in which the state (Weber's realm of "party," "the dwellers in the house of power") is importantly represented. Mills also discusses the elite status groups, "high society" and the Hollywood-style celebrities, though he claims that these are more of an offshoot or camouflage for the real power centers. The key point is a variant on Mannheim's: the policy of the United States at the highest level is not really set by any substantively rational, thinking human being and the voters do not exercise control through the mechanisms of democracy. The real forces in control are the huge bureaucracies, following their own logic of self-aggrandizement. Mills argued that the short-run self-interest of the capitalist establishment had become meshed with the interest of the Pentagon bureaucrats in expanding the military arms race. The flow of elite personnel back and forth between top positions in corporate business, the military, and the top federal bureaucracy cemented this structural convergence. All three sectors were drifting out of control and in the same direction. Mills feared it was leading directly towards World War III.

For decades a good deal of what Mills pointed out remained equally true and equally frightening. The personnel of presidents, generals, and cabinet officials changed, but most administrations, both Republican and Democrat, seemed equally unable to disengage themselves from the drift of the war machine. Nevertheless we have learned about some countervailing forces. The machine drifts out of control but that is only one tendency among several. Wars and nuclear confrontations have happened, but we have not yet entirely gone over the brink. One of these countervailing forces was pointed out by a theorist we have noticed earlier. James O'Connor pointed out that the modern state has undergone a fiscal crisis, which is due in part to the economic strains of the same military-industrial complex that Mills talked about. It is true that to some extent the military arms buildup spurs the capitalist economy, but this is more important at some times than at others. It also contributes to burgeoning government costs; hence, periodically we become involved in efforts to adjust to the economic strain by cutting back.

Another shortcoming of Mills's viewpoint is that it considered the United States in isolation, as one capitalist/bureaucratic complex in itself. We have subsequently begun to pay more attention to the larger world system and to discover some of the laws by which it operates. There is a larger geopolitics of military expansion and contraction, involving all states and not fueled merely by one of them. Various aspects of geopolitical theory were put forward by Arthur Stinchcombe, Kenneth Boulding, the world historian William McNeill, and others. In the late 1970s, I put together a synthetic theory that fitted well to the patterns of expansion and contraction of states over the past several millenia. Big, resource-rich states tend to expand at the expense of smaller and poorer states. A second principle is that marchland states, those off "on the edge" of the populated area, tend to expand at the expense of those in middle, which face enemies on several sides. Both of these principles are cumulative over time; the big get bigger, the marchlands eat up the middle states. This would lead to one huge state eventually ruling the world, except that there are two further principles that intervene. One is that states on opposite sides of the world-system (say Russia coming from one direction, the United States coming from the other) eventually meet as two giant empires or alliances facing each other in a showdown for world domination. The other principle is that even without opposition from another super-power, states tend to break apart if they overextend themselves; when the outer borders of their empire are too far from home, the costs of empire start to make a state go bankrupt, and hence become susceptible to a rapid breakup when a crisis point is reached.

In the early 1980s, I applied these principles to the nuclear arms race which Mills had said was inevitable, and came to an unexpected conclusion. Geopolitically, the Soviet Union, which had inherited the position of the old Russian Empire, had lost all its geopolitical advantages by the mid-twentieth century; all predictive factors indicated that it would break apart. The big danger was, would it break up before a showdown war took place with the other great power, the United States, thereby destroying the world in nuclear war? During the 1980s both trends were apparent: increasing economic strains in the USSR, leading to a reform movement that tried to scale down the costs of military over-extension; and on the other hand, an escalating nuclear arms race in an atmosphere of showdown, which threatened to destroy both superpowers and take the rest of the earth down with them. Fortunately it turned out that the strains in the USSR brought about breakdown on that side, before the confrontation of the great power blocks came to its climax. Mills's theory turned out to have its limitations, but it was touch and go for a while.

Let us return for a moment to the development of the conflict sociology of organizations. Mannheim and Mills helped develop this by applying an aspect of Weber's theory of bureaucracy. For another important aspect, we need to go back to Weber's own day. One of Weber's protégés was a young Marxist socialist named Robert Michels. Because of his political beliefs, Michels was denied a position in the German academic world, although Weber crusaded on his behalf. But Michels was already turning cynical. He was thoroughly familiar with the Marxist party of his day, the Social Democrats with their elaborate bureaucracy based on trade unions and their officials. On this organization, Michels trained an eye opened by Weber's notion of political conflicts in their own right. He noted that leaders of an organization are locked in an implicit struggle for power with their own followers: inside every organization there is a kind of miniclass struggle. Just as the small upper class in the economic system is able to dominate the much larger but unmobilized lower classes, the organizational elite is able to get its way, though outnumbered, by its followers because it, too, is much better mobilized. The organization should be seen as a political environment in which internal power struggles are won by those who control the material means of administration. This is a development of the Marx/Engels theory of political mobilization and of the means of mental production. The elite controls the organizational machinery for intercommunicating among themselves and also for defining reality to its members. The members of the elite, too, tend to identify the interests of the organization with their own career interests. Whatever makes the organization safe, secure, and wealthy, benefits its leaders, who thereby derive prominent and cushy jobs. This is another reason for the "organizational drift" that Mannheim discerned. Leaders become attached to the status quo; they compromise with their environment and do whatever they feel is necessary just to keep the organization surviving, no matter how far it takes the organization from the official ideals for which it was set up.

Michels' theory laid the basis for a series of empirical studies of organizations in the 1940s and 1950s. Philip Selznick showed how the same process of organizational "goal displacement" Michels had found in the German workers' party also existed in the liberal bureaucracy of Franklin D. Roosevelt's New Deal, undermining its reform-minded goals in the interest of softening the opposition of local elites. Selznick also showed some further tactics in organizational power struggles: for example, the way dissenters can be co-opted by putting them in positions of formal power where they have no room to maneuver for their own ideals. In effect this is a mechanism whereby the organizational position itself brainwashes the opposition leaders. Other researchers like Alvin Gouldner dealt with the power conflicts of the "change of administration" among top executives; Melville Dalton revealed the techniques of power struggle at the level of middle managers and their efforts to control workers; and Michel Crozier, a French sociologist, pointed out the crucial weapon of control over areas of uncertainty as a key to victory in these power struggles. A host of other studies—some coming not only from sociologists, but also from business schools or public administration—filled in many facets of organizations.

By the 1960s, it was possible to synthesize a full-scale theory of how organizations operate. Amitai Etzioni, for example, used Weber's three dimensions of class, status, and power, to show three alternative techniques of control. Each of these works best in a particular kind of technical environment; each

also gives rise to particular kinds of strategies of struggle between bosses and workers. *Economic controls*, essentially
through the power of the paycheck, are most usable in organizations that have clearly measurable outputs by each worker,
but such controls lead to the displacement of the workers' attention—from the quality of the work itself to a struggle over
just how the output is measured. Sheer *coercion* as a form of
control—brute force and threat—works best when it is easy to
maintain surveillance over the workers; its drawback is that it
is extremely alienating and results in workers who are brutal-
ized and dull if they are not able to escape. Finally for tasks
that require a great deal of initiative and judgment, Etzioni
coined the term *"normative control."* Here the management
needs to manipulate status groups and their ideologies in order
to get the tasks done: thus, the huge sector of professionalized
and credentialized organizations that exist wherever work becomes highly esoteric and technical.

Further developments in the theory of organizations reveal
many of the principles by which they operate in different circumstances. We have fitted in the varieties of technology that
make organizations different from one another, and recently
we have begun to map out the principles of interorganizational
relations as they form an environment, or competitive ecology,
for each other. Organizations survive, grow, or are picked off,
not merely because of their internal processes, but as part of a
kind of local "world system" of the organizations around
them. This is particularly apparent in the case of capitalist business organizations, but it applies to government, religious, and
other kinds of organizations as well. This type of theory is still
being developed. Harrison White theorizes that "markets" do
not consist of competitors but of cliques of organizations that
try to separate themselves into noncompetitive niches. This
type of theory has the potential for overturning the whole conventional economic way of looking at the capitalist system.
Through all this work, a guiding thread is an extension of the
conflict sociology that grew up around the time of Weber. The
struggle for domination does not go on merely among aggregate social classes, but takes place in organizations. This makes

the world of conflict more complex, as there are struggles among organizations, and within them as well. But the complexity is not a chaos. Organizational theory has shown, with considerable insight, how organizations create particular interest groups at the same time that the organizations themselves give these interest groups the weapons that bring about varying degrees of domination. Organization theory, when understood in its broadest context, is a key for understanding the whole workings of society.

CLASSES, CLASS CULTURES, AND INEQUALITY:
THE CONFLICT THEORISTS

Empirical research also got going in the 1940s and 1950s on the stratification of social classes in general. A lot of this research might be called an effort to soften the class model: to show, for example, that there is a continuum among occupations ranked by prestige. This eliminates class boundaries and thereby presumably does away with class conflict, at the same time that it shifts attention away from economic interests and towards the subjective or cultural differences among individuals. Another popular form of stratification research has concentrated on social mobility, which focuses on the extent to which social class membership is not permanent, especially between generations.

Nevertheless social class positions exist, however long people may happen to be in any one of them. During the time they are there, class positions exert a powerful influence on the way people think and behave. Economic inequalities still exist, even if we avert our faces from them to look at prestige or mobility. And as organizational analysis has already shown us, there is a continual struggle for advantage among occupants of different sorts of positions. The key question is: What is the nature of the dividing lines? Given that there are all sorts of organizational factions and that gradations of prestige can become fairly minute, is there nevertheless a basic line of cleavage that strongly affects what people will do?

In the late 1950s and the 1960s, a position emerged that

arrived at some consensus on just such a crucial factor. It did not turn out to be economic property per se. Inside the complex bureaucracies of modern society, the main social dividing line has been between workers and managers. These groups belong to different networks, have different cultures and outlooks, and engage in struggles with each other. But the managers, especially at the middle levels, are not actually property owners at all, but only administrative labor. Conversely, small independent businesses (like plumbers, electricians, and so on) are in many respects more similar to workers than they are to big business owners. The German sociologist Ralf Dahrendorf proposed a revision of Marx to deal with these anomalies. The major class dividing line is between *power groups*, between those who give orders and those who take orders. Sometimes property may be the basis of power: in those cases power classes coincide with economic classes. This was the situation observed by Marx and Engels in the early 1800s that had mislead them into thinking that property was the basis of class conflict. Instead of property, Dahrendorf proposed that power divisions are more fundamental.

Dahrendorf's position generated a self-conscious tradition of conflict theory that is more general than Marxism, although it includes Marxism as one of its intellectual predecessors. Dahrendorf took the Marx/Engels conception of class and generalized it in a Weberian direction, making Weber's conception of power conflict more basic. In my opinion, this is a strategically important move for several reasons. As we have seen, Weber's theory of power conflict connects directly with the theory of organizations because it is in organizations that power is mobilized. Furthermore it enables us to bring what has been learned in organizational analysis into the service of a theory of social classes. Organizations and classes are just different ways of slicing up the same social reality; classes always have their basis as parts of some organizations, and organizations create classes and class conflicts.

There is also a payoff on the level of understanding the subjective and individual side of class, the way in which individuals think and act differently because of their class posi-

tions. If the fundamental reality of classes is the division between giving and taking orders, that points us to the social
psychology of just how those experiences take place: What is it
like to be an order-giver? How does that affect one's consciousness? What kinds of maneuvers must one go through in the
course of an ordinary day in such a position? The same questions of course must also be asked about the experience of
taking orders. Now it happens that Erving Goffman, starting
from an entirely different point of view, showed us a model of
social life as a series of frontstages and backstages, a kind of
theatre of everyday life. The persons who control the frontstage (i.e., official parts of the society) turn out to be the order-
givers, the higher social classes, whereas those who are merely
compliant audiences for these official performances are the
order-takers, the working classes of society. I will leave the
details of this theory for Chapter 3 because Goffman came out
of the Durkheimian theory of social rituals, not from conflict
theory at all. But as my *Conflict Sociology* (1975) attempts to
show in detail, putting together Dahrendorf and Goffman's
models enables us to explain fairly rigorously why different
classes have the kinds of outlooks that so much empirical evidence tells us they do.

One other sign that the power-conflict model is fundamental was provided by a successful theory of the distribution
of wealth. Gerhard Lenski's *Power and Privilege* (1966) was the
first major comparative analysis to ask the question: What
conditions determine whether a society will have a large or
small degree of economic inequality? Lenski examined all
types of societies, ranging from hunting-and-gathering tribes
on through the great agrarian (medieval-style) empires and
the modern industrial societies. He showed that as the
amount of economic surplus increases, the total wealth is increasingly distributed not by economic need or by productive
contribution, but by the organization of power. The most severe inequalities occur where there is a sizable surplus *and*
where power is most concentrated. Historically, the most unequal societies fit this description: they are the agrarian empires, where the economy produces a considerable surplus

but where the military aristocracy, the only politically mobilized group, appropriates virtually all of it. In industrial societies, the distribution of wealth becomes somewhat more equal, precisely to the degree that there has been a *political* revolution that has given more power to the masses of the population. In capitalist countries, it has been mostly the middle and upper-middle classes that have been the beneficiaries of this power shift. In countries where there has been a *political* shift towards socialism, as further research has shown, the degree of inequality is reduced still further. To the extent that inequalities remain in the socialist states, it is not because of economic property but because of concentration of power in the hierarchy of party officials. The Lenski and Dahrendorf models together, thus, throw considerable light not only on inequality in modern capitalist states, but also on the quite apparent class divisions and conflicts that have been going on in Poland, the Soviet Union, and elsewhere.

CLASS MOBILIZATION AND POLITICAL CONFLICT

We have already seen in the discussion of Marx and Engels how fruitful their model has been for a sociology of political conflict. As sociology began doing survey research in the 1940s and thereafter, it inevitably had a rediscovery of many of these insights. Seymour Martin Lipset (in his youth a Marxist, though he later moved sharply to the right) summarized the evidence of the class influence on politics by calling elections "the democratic class struggle." Social classes have been among the most essential dividing lines in explaining how people vote, although the other dimensions that also predict political attitudes are often versions of Weber's status groups. Social class has been shown, moreover, to strongly affect the mobilization of people in modern politics. The conservative parties have not disappeared in modern democracies, even though they represent only a minority of the people, because their higher-class supporters are much more likely to vote, to contribute financially, and to be active in party affairs than are the working-class supporters of the more liberal parties. The material means of mobilization continue to be crucial in the modern struggle for political power. Although the more spectacular conflict theories have dealt with revolutionary uprisings and other social movements, "resource mobilization" is equally applicable to the mundane class conflicts that go on through the medium of voting.

Though the model is generally correct—in the sense that the higher social classes tend to favor the status quo and the maintenance of property, whereas the lower social classes tend to favor reforms and economic redistribution—there have nevertheless been some major refinements in it. Marx and Engels were not just interested in liberal/reforming politics, but in a revolutionary working class. The question that has been addressed is: Within the general left/right continuum of politics, how far will the left go? Under what conditions does it produce reformism, and when radicalism? For that matter, when does one find reactionary movements emerging from the lower classes? Comparative sociologists have made considerable headway on this question.

The first part of this analysis dealt with the early phase of capitalism: the penetration of the capitalist economy into the agricultural societies of Europe as early as the 1700s, as well as subsequently around the world. Both Arthur Stinchcombe and Barrington Moore, Jr., proposed models of agricultural class politics. They both pointed out that the capitalist market itself tends to mobilize social classes. Hence, it made a great deal of difference whether peasants marketed their own crops or whether this was done by some feudal landowner. The French Revolution of 1789 gave peasants their own land. But as a result it made them not a radical force, but a conservative one: as small farmers, unprotected by any monopoly position, they were always kept on the brink of ruin by the ups and downs of the market for farm products. Thus, like small farmers everywhere, they became a typically reactionary force in modern politics, hostile to urban society and to the socialistic or trade-union policies of the workers, which the farmers regarded as just so much featherbedding at the expense of honest citizens.

Paradoxically, Moore pointed out, the establishment of modern democracy proceeded most smoothly in countries such as England where the landlords drove the peasants off the land and into the cities, where they were then transformed from a reactionary force into a liberal one. The worst possible outcome, Moore argued in his *Social Origins of Dictatorship and Democracy* (1966), is when feudal lords keep the peasants on the lands and force them to produce goods for the market by an intensification of traditional discipline. This is the formula for fascism, which developed in Germany and Japan. Finally, there is also the possibility of agricultural workers going radical. This happened, for instance, in China, where the peasants did not own the land, but had to pay rent to absentee landlords. The result was that the peasants were left to absorb the pressures of the market while being squeezed by landlords who demanded rent in good times and bad. Peasants in this case reacted by supporting a movement to overthrow the entire property system.

In Craig Calhoun's book *The Question of Class Struggle* (1982), this type of analysis is extended to urban workers as well. Marx and Engels expected that the coming together of workers in factories would make them "capitalism's gravediggers," revolutionaries mobilizing to bring down the system. But their sociology of political conflict was not quite right on this point. For factory owners themselves are the *most* directly exposed to the market; and it is this market experience that mobilizes them and makes them politically active and aware of their national interests, whereas the workers are somewhat shielded by the organization itself. The workers, thus, fight their class battles within the factory itself, striving for better employment security and for better wages—but not on the national level. They do not direct their attack on the institution of property itself; their basic stance becomes not radical and socialist, but local, trade unionist, and reformist.

The real radicals, Calhoun points out, were those workers who were most directly exposed to the market. These were the small craft workers, self-employed artisans or those in domestic enterprises who were involved in the "putting-out"

system of working up raw materials sent to them by mer-
chant-entrepreneurs. For them, there was no cushion against
economic downturns, which could immediately drive them
out of business. Moreover the crafts workers had no local
enemies they could fight—enemies in the form of factory
owners and bosses. They could not fight for organizational
reforms because they did not work in someone else's organization. Instead, they had to direct their protest against the
whole system. It was these workers who made up the radical
movements Marx and Engels observed in the early 1800s, the
decades of their own youth, and who convinced them that a
still larger radical socialist movement was in the offing.

    This is not to say radical socialist movements cannot reap-
pear at later times. But Calhoun's type of analysis is in keeping
with the general growth of modern sophisticated conflict theory. Organizations are capable of containing and localizing
class conflict, just as they create and shape new conflicts of
their own. For a full-scale revolutionary transformation of the
system to occur, we need to look beyond the localized conflicts
to structural forces that focus conflict on the level of the overall
property system itself. And this brings us again to that dominant superorganization, that upholder of property through its
means of exerting force: the state.

THE GOLDEN AGE OF HISTORICAL SOCIOLOGY

The last 30 years, right up to the time in which we are now living,
has seen many of the finest and most ambitious projects in historical sociology ever attempted. I have already mentioned some of
its high points: the studies of class conflict and the rise of the
modern state by Barrington Moore, Jr., and by Craig Calhoun,
Charles Tilly's studies of revolutionary social movements that
produced his resource mobilization theory, Gerhard Lenski's
comparative model of inequality across all of world history. For
recent years, we can add Tilly's demonstration that the modern
states were created in different forms because of the ways they
gained control of economic resources to build their military organization. Another triumph of historical sociology is Robert

Wuthnow's analysis of how three-sided conflicts between the state, social elites, and cultural entrepreneurs caused the great ideological movements such as the Protestant Reformation, the Enlightenment, and Socialism. Inevitably the realistic treatment of history has led into the paths of conflict sociology. In these works, the themes of Marx and of Weber have come together.

Some comparative/historical work has stayed closer to a Marxian identity. This includes the British sociologist Perry Anderson's *Passages from Antiquity to Feudalism* (1974), which traces the distinctiveness of the West not only to capitalism but also to its foundation upon the downfall of the ancient Roman empire. The most ambitious of these projects is Immanuel Wallerstein's *The Modern World System*, three volumes of which have been published between 1974 and 1989. Wallerstein's work is perhaps the closest to a classic Marxian interpretation in that he regards economic processes and contradictions as the driving engine of history. But he differs from the classic Marxist model in that the economy is located not within any particular state but is organized as a world economic system, with its long-term cycles of expansion and contraction. These long waves of global economic boom and depression, taking over 100 years each, are connected with imperialism towards the periphery in their upswings and with wars among the core powers in their downswings, bringing about the hegemony of a new state. Wallerstein's project is not yet finished. Already it promises to be the grandest and most comprehensive view of the mechanisms that drive human societies since Weber's comparative studies of the world religions— and Weber's project was only a fragment, never finished.

Even though Wallerstein is the most "orthodox Marxian" of the major historical/comparative sociologists of today, I would still maintain that the logic of his world system leans in a Weberian direction. The military hegemony of the core states is a key device by which they are able to dominate the world system economically, and the question remains unsettled as to just which of the core states wins hegemony at each showdown period. I would suggest that there is a further process of the geopolitical relations among states themselves that determines these things. These involve such factors as the sheer geographical positions of states vis-à-vis each other: states on the outer ring of a settled area have a military advantage over states in the middle, as the latter tend to get chewed up in the long run through multisided wars. There are processes of cumulative advantage and disadvantage as conquering states build up their momentum and add further to their size and resources, whereas their rivals fight from successively weaker positions. But there also seems to be an outer limit to a state's ability to conquer territory; a principle of military overextension applies that can be a prime source of the kind of fiscal crisis of the state that we have already discussed above. When such overextension happens, states can collapse much faster than they grew originally, and they are carved up to the benefit of their neighbours.

The principles of geopolitics, I would contend, are more general even than the principles of capitalism. Geopolitics determined the military cycles of ancient and medieval empires, and the same principles operate today, even though a capitalist world economy has been superimposed on them. A state's geopolitical position, furthermore, has a crucial effect on its internal politics, including its experience of revolution. Theda Skocpol, in her now-famous book *States and Social Revolutions* (1979), showed by a comparative analysis of the French, Russian, and Chinese revolutions that revolution needs more than merely the mobilization of social classes making economically radical demands. Revolution always begins with a crisis of the state, a breakdown due to war or fiscal crisis that paralyzes the ruling clases in a battle between the administrators of the state sector and the dominant propertied classes outside that sector. The theory is compelling as far as it goes. What can be added is the point that the strain on the state that starts this off is not accidental. It flows systematically from the position of the state in the larger geopolitical situation. Pre-1789 France, pre-1917 Russia, and pre-1949 China were all in the peculiar position of having great geopolitical strengths in one aspect, but crippling geopolitical weaknesses in another. All were states with great cumulative resource advantages that nevertheless had overexpanded and taken on neighboring powers in too many different directions. In this view, the revolutionary upheaval is a convulsion nested within the larger state system in which the classes that directed the disastrous geopolitical policies had to pay the price. Once these inefficiencies were eliminated, post-revolutionary states, as Skocpol aptly demonstrated, reestablish a militant—and militaristic—national identity and become once again aggressive powers on the world geopolitical scene.

The state-breakdown theory of revolutions developed by Skocpol has been further expanded by Jack Goldstone. Comparing a whole series of state breakdowns in Europe, as well as in the Ottoman Empire and the Ming Dynasty in China, Goldstone has been able to demonstrate with considerable precision just what conditions bring a state to the point of revolution, and what conditions will keep a state intact. Goldstone expands Skocpol's model by showing that the state fiscal crisis, as well as internal conflicts among elites who tear the state apart, are affected by the entire system of taxation, economic development, and population growth. Goldstone is particularly concerned to show that the early modern boom in population upset almost every aspect of states' fiscal health, and thus prepared the way for breakdowns and revolutions. Does this mean revolutions can no longer happen in states that control their population size? Not necessarily; the Skocpol/Goldstone model, taken as a whole, shows that the core of a state's ability to maintain control is its fiscal health, and that can be strained in a number of different ways: from population growth, from an inadequate taxation system, from geopolitical strains, or from any combination of these, provided that the strain reaches high enough levels. The age of revolutions is probably not over. Even behemoths like the USSR have shown themselves vulnerable to collapse through resource strains, and the fiscal problems of states elsewhere in the modern world (including even the United States) suggests that problems loom on the long-term horizon.

The tradition of conflict sociology is very much alive today and continues to make intellectual progress on many fronts. To some extent it is divided within itself. There are ideological debates between Weberians and Marxists and between different viewpoints within each camp. To some extent this is due to the fact that the conflict tradition is the most politically activist of all the brands of sociology. We tend to choose our intellectual stances because of the ammunition they provide for the political programs we would like to advance. But besides these inevitable debates over policy questions, there is a genuine core of insight into the principles of how the world works. Conflict sociology is necessarily conflictual, like everything else. For all that, it adds up to a tradition of sociological realism that has become truly sophisticated. If we ever felt like rising above our own social conflicts and merely contemplating the science of how society operates, the conflict tradition would have to be a central part of that vision.

Appendix: Simmel, Coser, and Functionalist Conflict Theory

The term "conflict theory" is sometimes used for a rather different tradition of analysis begun in Germany by one of Weber's contemporaries, Georg Simmel. In the 1950s and 1960s, it was revived and formally expounded by the German-American Lewis Coser. Nevertheless its tone and its analytical apparatus cuts in quite a different direction than the Marx-Weber lineage of ideas. Coser tried to show that conflict could be incorporated within the perspective of functionalism as another support of social order. If one looks at Simmel's original arguments, the conservative themes are even more marked.

Simmel's one major sociological work, his *Soziologie* (1908), shows a programmatic structure that could have been most fruitful. He pushes for a structural perspective, the social forms that are to be analyzed beyond their specific empirical contents and beyond a merely psychological outlook. And if the emphasis on forms comes from a Kantian philosophical tradition, Simmel is equally German in the emphasis he gives to stratification and conflict. Hierarchy ("superordination and subordination") is a fundamental topic for Simmel. He treats it early in the book and follows it with an analysis of conflict, so often the concomitant of hierarchy. No utopian idealist he.

Nevertheless it is apparent that Simmel's interest in these hard-nosed aspects of society is largely negative and polemical. The very first chapter [translated as "The Problem of Sociology" in Kurt Wolff (ed.), *Essays on Sociology, Philosophy and*

Aesthetics (1965)] starts off by criticizing the existing approach to sociology, which Simmel saw as stemming from the rise of the socialist movement in the nineteenth century. It is this movement (perhaps Simmel had Comte in mind as well as the Marxists) that exalts the class over the individual and, hence, substitutes a new level of analysis. Fair enough, Simmel will enter into that level; but he will do it by proclaiming that sociology must detach itself from the usual contents of social issues and give a formal analysis of the structural forms underlying all sociation. The justification for doing so, he declares (in a passage entitled "How Is Society Possible?"), is by allusion to a neo-Kantian concern for forms.

Simmel's approach to sociology is ambiguous. He does catch a vision of a structural science of sociology, but this works out largely as a cover for his polemical intent: to attack the socialistic world view and defend individualism. For instance, his first substantive chapter begins with a section "On the Significance of Numbers for Social Life." A promising beginning. But where we would expect an abstract analysis, his opening example is labeled "Socialism," and its point is to declare that socialism is impossible as a modern political ideal because equality is possible only in a small group. It is not even a good theoretical point; empirically small groups may be quite authoritarian and hierarchical (think of the patriarchal family) and large-scale societies certainly can approach social equality to some degree. Even if absolute equality is ruled out, economic differences between today's socialist and capitalist societies are substantial.

The example, unfortunately, is all too representative of what Simmel does with his formal approach. Over and over again he makes points of an allegedly universal and theoretical nature, but they represent (more than anything) his own prejudices. Large groups, he declares, are mindless and authoritarian—hardly an original point but a common charge among the conservatives of his day. (And of earlier days as well—elements of this are found in Aristotle's attacks on democracy.) When Simmel discusses the poor, he throws in a section on "The Negative Character of Collective Behavior." He speaks of "The Sociological Error of Socialism and Anarchism" as search-

ing for freedom in directions that always bring about domination because large groups must always be hierarchical. (Must
they always become steadily more hierarchical the larger they
are? Simmel assumes so, but he never proves it, nor even
seems to think any variation is possible.) When he speaks of
coercion, it is in a rather unrealistic fashion; coercion is not the
basis of domination, merely something that is sometimes added onto it. Simmel discusses force only in the philosophical
context of the doctrine that people ought to be coerced for the
good of the social order. Simmel does not entirely agree (he is
after all a nineteenth-century Liberal), but he still believes that
the majority of people may well need to be coerced into behav-
ing (Simmel is an elitist Liberal, no John Stuart Mill).

And so it goes. Time and again Simmel's headings get up
one's hopes, but his content is usually disappointing. The reason is that Simmel is carrying on an underlying polemic almost
from beginning to end. The contrast with Weber, who shared
many of Simmel's political views, is instructive. Weber really
did take his value neutrality seriously; Simmel by comparison
seems shallow. The same holds on the empirical side. Simmel
is not without empirical reference; in fact he fills his pages with
examples of different types of groups. But they are mainly
casual observations, good stories of just the sort that would
entertain a dinner party but that are never checked for their
truthfulness (e.g., Simmel illustrates the place of numbers in
social life by an anecdote of a group of friends who broke a
plate into a dozen pieces and each kept one to represent their
unity). Or else there are historical examples: the customs and
political constitutions of the ancient Greeks and Romans, the
New England township, the structure and practices of the
medieval Papacy (the last quite a favorite source of examples
for Simmel). But they remain merely examples. Unlike Weber,
Simmel never goes into a comparison of cases nor makes even
the most rudimetary effort to see if the preponderance of the
evidence is on his side. Instead, he is content to provide a
colorful illustration for each of his categories.

One point that Simmel is at pains to make is that bourgeois society is the precondition for individualism. He does not
put it quite like that: it would be too overtly polemical and not

"formal" enough, but the message comes through nevertheless. The great danger is the mass society touted by socialists: it destroys individualism. (This sounds like Friedrich Nietzsche, whose vogue in the 1890s and early 1900s coincided with Simmel's activity.) What makes possible individualism is a large-scale society with considerable internal differentiation. Where individuals are simultaneously members of various groups ("the intersection of social circles"), that is where individualism flourishes.

That this is part of a specifically bourgeois, capitalist order is made plain in Simmel's other major book, *The Philosophy of Money* (1900). Incidentally, this work is genuinely philosophy, in much the same way that Marx's early economics was simultaneously philosophy. Simmel reads like almost a direct refutation of Marx (as well as of other economists). Economic value is an objectification produced by separating the individual from the object. Whereas for Marx this is a definition of alienation, for Simmel this is a positive result, analogous to aesthetic values, which he declares are produced by the same objectifying process. Simmel goes on to argue that this objectification and transcendence of subjectivity is due to the exchange process; contrary to Marx, exchange value is absolutely central and use value is not economic value at all. Money is a symbol of objectivity that emerges in a relationship among subjective elements; as such, Simmel pointedly remarks, money is analogous to truth itself. He goes on to attack the Marxian labor theory of value. Not only does Marx's theory ignore mental labor in favor of physical; but, even more, physical labor derives its value from the psychical effort involved in it!

Simmel's evaluation of money is thus very much of the positive side. Money allows for anonymity and emotional detachment among persons; thus, it breaks down the omnipresent group controls of traditional society. Money is the basis of individual freedom. This is not to say that Simmel sees nothing negative about modern capitalist society. He expresses his opinions (of the sort that have become clichés among modern intellectuals) that modern life has become calculating, emotionless, and, hence, characterized by greed, wastefulness, miserliness, cynicism, and boredom. Money generates the "decadent

personality type." Simmel is explicit that these are two sides of
the same coin: the price of modern individualism and freedom
is the deracination of personality. On the whole Simmel is
willing to pay the price. He speaks of how personal culture
lags behind material culture. The latter, we may surmise from
his sociological writings, means the exalted conversation and
aesthetic appreciation of *fin de siècle* salon society, that is, Simmel's own upper-bourgeois milieu. Simmel was known as a
fascinating conversationalist, and the best aspects of his sociology come through in the Goffmanesque portraits of the "play-
ful" world of talk, of secrets (Goffman's backstages), of intimacy, and of sexual affairs. It is here that individualism is in its
element, especially if one is a cosmopolitan insider/outsider
with entrée to many groups but permanently enclosed by
none.

This makes sense if one realizes what kind of career Simmel was pursuing. As a private lecturer (*Privatdozent*) in philosophy, he made his reputation by publishing a large number
of popular articles in newspapers and magazines as well as
both long and short books. He wrote a great deal on art, culture, women, coquetry, and other subjects of the drawing-
room culture of his day. His *Soziologie* (1908) was his eleventh
book, sandwiched in between *Schopenhauer und Nietzsche* (1907)
and *Hauptprobleme der Philosophie* (1910) (*Major Problems of Philosophy*). The truth of the matter is that Simmel was not particularly serious about sociology, and his writings show it. Even
his bourgeois background did not set him in a serious direction. It apparently gave him his political prejudices, but no
insight into the economic side of the world. And this too
makes sense when one realizes that his family connections
were all in the luxury side of business. His father owned a
famous chocolate factory; the father died when Simmel was a
boy, and Simmel acquired as a guardian the head of a music-
publishing house. Georg Simmel inherited a considerable fortune and never had to enter the grubby world of work, except
at his own pleasure. The background to be sure is not too
dissimilar from that of Weber. But Weber's family was in basic
industry, not luxury trades, and Weber grew up in the inner

milieu of Reichstag politics. Both men were privy to secrets; but for Weber these were the backstage secrets of political manuever, whereas Simmel's backstage was merely that of sexual gossip at elegant salon parties.

When Simmel writes about conflict, then, it is in order to disprove the contentions of the Marxian conflict theorists (and perhaps also the military *Realpolitik* theorists). For Simmel, conflict does not produce social change; it is merely another structural relationship endemic to any social form. He sees that it has something to do with domination, but it does nothing to change the system of domination. It is merely another drama of social life to be appreciated, scarcely more than another salon entertainment.

Simmel really only became part of the larger conflict theory tradition in the 1950s, when Lewis Coser reformulated his ideas, and Kurt Wolff and Reinhard Bendix (the latter a Weberian political sociologist) translated his key texts about conflict. Coser was still attempting to adapt the model of conflict to the functionalist theory of social order that was dominant in the United States at the time, but Coser himself was more sympathetic to left-wing movements for social change. Coser purified Simmel by eliminating the anti-socialist polemics and pulling out the principles that have wide-ranging application to all kinds of conflicts. Conflict sharpens the sense of group boundaries. Conflict is most intense when it breaks out between individuals or groups who are already closely related, because then it is most threatening to the group. External conflict draws a group together more cohesively; for this reason, groups often search for external enemies in order to maintain internal order. Ironically, antagonists become bound to one another, much as in an arms race the militarists on both sides owe their influence to each other; in the same way, the militant ideologists in opposing social movements are surreptitiously bound together more closely than are their followers. And conflicts tend to spread, by the process through which each side tries to bring in neutral parties into a coalition.

Coser's formulation of these principles began a modern school of research on the process of conflict itself. Coser's work appeared at about the same time as Dahrendorf's theory of class conflict (which overlaps with some of these principles), and the combination of the two lines of theory made sociologists aware that there was a major tradition that could be called conflict theory.

NOTES

1. Some commentators have noticed a difference between Engels and Marx. For the most part they have made the distinction to the disparagement of Engels, who is regarded as more dogmatically materialist and doctrinaire. Engels's late essay (1873–1874) applying the dialectic to physical science was criticized by philosophical Marxists of the 1920s such as Georg Lukács and Karl Korsch. Recent Marxists (e.g., Norman Levine, *The Tragic Deception: Marx Contra Engels*, Oxford: Clio Press, 1975) have attacked Engels for lacking Marx's humanistic vision, which was derived from the Young Hegelians. As a result Engels was allegedly the forbear of Stalinist oppression that the more humanistic Marx would have disavowed. The attack is completely wrongheaded. It is true that increasingly "soft" Hegelian reinterpretations of Marx have become popular in the last few decades (and the revival of interest in Lukács and Korsch, both of them Hegelian philosophers, is part of this mood), but this is largely because a declining faith in the economic inevitability of capitalist crisis, and a general mood of antagonism to science: a mood that neither Marx nor Engels shared. The Hegelianism is largely an element of mystification, which keeps us from seeing the actual sociological processes that Engel opened up. The real difficulty of Marx's economic system, in fact, is the way that he continually tried to fit it into the frame of Hegelian categories.

Engels opposed paying so much attention to the Young Hegelians (he did not want to add a long section on Feuerbach to *The German Ideology*, regarding him as unrealistic; among all the manuscripts of Marx that Engels did publish posthumously, he did not include the "Economic and Philosophical Manuscripts of 1844"). This has been taken as a weakness on Engels' part, and so has his lack of interest in the more abstract convolutions of Marx's economics. But one could say more justly that Engels had a better sense of what was worthwhile as a realistic analysis of the social world. Moreover it is hardly the case that Engels was the more dogmatic of the two. His essays on the "dialectics of nature" are not notably successful and only point out a kind of metaphorical resemblance between the dialectic and various physical and biological processes. But the effort showed Engels' intellectual breadth and his interest in the laws of nature, which was part of his general push towards making a science of society as well. He used the dialectic on his own turf merely to sensitize one to processes of conflict and change, as one can see in his historical writings. In fact Engels gave considerable weight to the priority of empirical complexities over preconceived theory, and he used the dialectic as a way of *overcoming* any crude materialism. He was willing to give the "superstructure" of politics and ideology the dignity of an independent pole in the dialectic with the economic "base" (Leonard Krieger, "Introduction" to Friedrich Engels, *The German Revolution,* Chicago: University of Chicago Press, 1967: xx).

2. Characteristically, Engels gave credit to Marx, whose ideas he claimed he was merely elaborating. This seems dubious. Engels's theory became the rallying point for radical feminism; under its influence, the German socialist party took a strongly pro-feminist stance, claiming that the only way to achieve sexual equality was to replace capitalism by socialism. Marx, on the other hand, was rather strongly antifeminist. In 1872, he ordered the International Workingman's Association to expel an American chapter, led by Victoria Woodhull, that had feminism (along with Negro rights) among its top priorities. Marx declared that the association must rid itself of those who gave "precedence to the women's question over the question of labor" and who advocated "women's franchise, and . . . all sorts of nonsense" (in Hans Gerth, ed., *The First International: Minutes of the Hague Conference of 1872,* Madison: University of Wisconsin Press, 1958: 177–78, 194–95, 248, 264–67). Privately, as well, Marx was very much a traditional sexist. He ran an authoritarian, Victorian home, regarded his wife as little more than housekeeper and mother of his children, and referred to her in his letters to Engels as merely a harried, "silly" creature (Levine, 1975: 232, 238–39). Marx's daughter, who worshipped him, lists his answers to the questions: "Your favorite virtue in man: Strength. Your favorite virtue in women: Weakness" [quoted in Erich Fromm, ed., *Marx's Concept of Man* (N.Y.: Frederick Ungar, 1961: 257)]. Marx seemed to think that the relation of man to woman was simply a natural relationship [in his "Economic and Philosophical Manuscripts of 1844," *Ibid.,* p. 126]. Engels was on the contrary somewhat of a romantic and a supporter of the new underground ideals of sexual liberation. He supported and lived with a working-class Irish woman, Mary Burns. But Marx and his wife pointedly snubbed Mary Burns when Engels tried to introduce her

to them because she and Engels were not married; their moral disapproval fell totally on Mary Burns, not on her male partner. The one time in their relationship that Engels was genuinely hurt by Marx was when Mary Burns died and Marx refused to extend any condolences. Given these sharp differences in their attitudes, it is not surprising that Engels did not publish *The Origin of the Family, Private Property, and the State* until the year after Marx died.

3. Weber's theory is not well known and has remained buried in his lengthy works, especially his encyclopedic *Economy and Society* as well as in his lectures on *General Economic History*. For an exposition and development of this theory, see Randall Collins, "Weber's Theory of the Family," in my *Weberian Sociological Theory* (Cambridge and New York: Cambridge University Press, 1985).

2: *The Rational /Utilitarian Tradition*

So far as the pursuit of rationality entails study, forethought, and calculation, and such things hurt, as they often do, the pursuit of rationality is itself irrational unless their costs are reckoned in the balance. The costs of rationality may make rationality irrational.
George Homans, 1961

The second tradition we will treat is also a very old one. But its importance in social thought has fluctuated a good deal over the years, and its identity has shifted, along with the name by which it has been known. At first, during the 1700s and 1800s, it was called Utilitarianism, and its advocates were British social philosophers. At that time it was closely connected with economics, a discipline just coming into being. In the late 1800s, Utilitarianism became unfashionable in philosophy, and economics became more professionalized and broke free of its old philosophical connections. All was quiet until the 1950s, when sociologists began to formulate a position known as "exchange theory." In other disciplines too there were stirrings, in political science, in philosophy, and among economists who decided their approach had application outside of their own field. By the 1970s and 1980s there was a widespread movement that was usually known as "rational choice," although some called it "rational action," and one policy-oriented segment of the movement called itself "public choice" theory. I am going to use the term "rational/utilitarian" to refer to this whole tradition. (Sometimes, for convenience, I will abbreviate this to simply "utilitarianism.")

SOME MAIN POINTS OF THE RATIONAL/UTILITARIAN TRADITION

1690	Locke, social contract	
1720	Mandeville, private vices and public virtue	
1740	Hume Hartley association of ideas	
1760–1780	Adam Smith, moral sympathy	laissez-faire economics
1800	Bentham, utilitarian legal reform	
1860	J.S. Mill, utilitarian ethics	
1870–1900	Bradley Moore anti-utilitarian ethics Durkheim criticizes social contract	academic economics general equilibrium
1930	Waller, sex and marriage markets	
1940	game theory	
1950	prisoner's dilemma March and Simon, satisficing	Downs, economic theory of democracy

1960	Homans
	Blau exchange theory
	
	Olson, free rider
		Riker, minimum winning
		    coalition
		
		Schelling, coercive coalitions
		    crime and illegal markets

1970	distributive justice
	    Kahneman and Tversky
	       choice anomalies
	   educational inflation
	   split labor market
		Rawls, theory of justice
		
		Buchanan, public choice

1980	Cook Willer power in exchange networks	state protection rent
1990	Harrison White, market networks Hechter Coleman solidarity theory	

The rational/utilitarian tradition is not strictly speaking a sociological one. It has overlapped some parts of sociology, while it has been bitterly opposed by other parts. It was involved in the formation of the social sciences as specialized disciplines, but has gone in and out of fashion over the centuries. We can picture the rational/utilitarian tradition as a meandering stream across a low marshy plane. Early on it was a spring torrent, creating the river bed itself; then it narrowed and became a mere side channel to some better established rivers; then again—in our own lifetimes—it has begun to flood, submerging the meadows and washing out the banks of the rivers that have been the separate social disciplines for the past century. Advocates of rational choice today visualize their movement as something that will unify all the social sciences into one mighty river flowing to the sea. Its opponents think it is just another period of bad weather, though some of them are working with new energy to put up the dikes. Perhaps both extremes are wrong; but there is no denying that the rational/utilitarian channel is widening again, and that it is reshaping major parts of our intellectual landscape.

Leaving aside the metaphor, we should say that the rational/utilitarian tradition has taken several different forms. One aspect of utilitarianism has a lot in common with conflict theory: a rather hard-nosed way of looking at individuals pursuing their own interests, calculating their advantages; the material world, monetary gains, and physical costs loom large in the picture. People are interested in more than money, of course, but there is a tendency to treat all human interests as analogous to monetary calculations. This version of utilitarianism sounds somewhat like Marxism, which isn't surprising when we consider that both of these intellectual traditions were originally tied to economics. On the other hand, there is an aspect of modern rational choice or exchange theory that is quite unlike conflict theory; it doesn't pay much attention to stratification or inequalities among people, tending instead to describe a world in which people rationally make exchanges among themselves, so that everything works out for the best. This latter type of theory tries to show how norms emerge and how exchanges are carried out under standards of justice and equity so that people get a fair exchange. This part of the tradition, quite unlike the critical and rebellious tone found in Marxism, sounds like the utopian ideals of the early economists, who believed that the "Invisible Hand" of the market makes everything right.

So we are going to find that the rational/utilitarian tradition has not just been invading various topics in social science; it has also been involved in intense disputes within itself. One version has been rather critical of social institutions; it sees politicians as like businesses out to make a profit at the expense of their constituents, and the educational system as similar to a monetary system in runaway inflation. The criticism isn't always from the left, unlike Marxism; some movements, like public choice theory, are considered to be conservative critics, who argue that free-spending politicians need to be kept under control to protect the public; still others try to show what incentives are needed to control crime, or to make families take responsibility for bringing up their children. Whatever the various political positions, what these kind of rational choice theorists have in common is that they bring a viewpoint of unsentimental realism to analyzing policy issues.

Other kinds of modern rational/utilitarian theorists aren't much concerned with issues of policy conflict, but attempt to show that it is technically possible to explain society by the rational motivations of individuals. They become embroiled in conflicts with nonutilitarian lines of theory, especially those that we will consider in the following chapters as the Durkheimian tradition (which emphasizes nonrational or transrational values and emotions), and also with the microinteractionist theories (which see human cognition as interpretive and symbolic rather than as rationally calculating). The utilitarians have created the controversy known as the micro-macro issue: that is, they see society as put together out of the actions of individuals on the micro level, and oppose the image of society as a macro entity or structure that exists over and above individuals. The utilitarians also have been hostile to explanations that invoke such concepts as a culture that determines what people do; the utilitarians instead want to understand how individuals are motivated to do whatever they do, out of their own self-interest.

Here too the utilitarians have turned up controversies in

their own ranks. Starting in the 1950s, a series of paradoxes have been uncovered: the issue of whether individuals can really maximize their interests, or only "satisfice"; the problem of how social cooperation is possible at all, if rational individuals are motivated to become "free riders"; the "prisoner's dilemma," which pits one individual's self-interest against another; evidence that in real life people do not calculate very rationally. Faced with these problems, the modern utilitarian tradition has not collapsed; on the contrary, it has grown richer and more complex in dealing with them.

To set these developments in perspective, let us trace our steps back in time to the beginning of the utilitarian tradition three centuries ago in England.

The Original Rise and Fall of Utilitarian Philosophy

In its first incarnation, the utilitarian tradition was essentially the liberal wing of public philosophy. The term "utilitarian" was not invented until around 1800, but this mode of thinking had been important among British intellectuals since the Glorious Revolution of 1688–1689, which limited the power of the king and put England on the path to parliamentary democracy. Many of the basic ideas of utilitarian philosophy were laid down by John Locke.[1] Locke was the ideologue of the Glorious Revolution. He had had to go into exile for his opposition to the old king, and when he returned from Holland with the constitutional monarch William of Orange, Locke brought with him the manuscripts of his books, which laid down the philosophy of the new social order.

For Locke, the starting point is always the reasonable individual. The individual has certain basic rights, which cannot be taken away by the government, for the government itself is only the creation of a social contract among individuals. Among those basic rights is the ability to hold private property created by one's own labor. The purpose of the state is a minimal one, to protect individual rights and their property. One can see how from Locke's emphasis on individual labor and property could develop the position that economics is the basic science of human beings. Everything else, including government and religion, plays a quite secondary part in the scene.

Locke had lived through a period of intense political conflict over the power of the state to impose Catholic or Protestant religion, and he was particularly concerned to establish social peace by putting the religious issue aside. Toleration of personal belief is the most important thing; belief is individual, and it cannot be imposed on other persons from without. Locke thus opposed any philosophy that held that ideas are innate, or that they come from anywhere other than individual experience. The individual's mind originally is like a blank sheet of paper, and what is written upon it comes from one's experience. Locke is an empiricist out of political conviction. Each person builds up his ideas as the result of his own sensations; each one experiences the material world, and by associating various sensations together builds up a picture of what exists. Locke depicts the individual as living in a mundane, practical, and material world, because this is the way to avoid giving any privileged position to traditions imposed by social pressures. Religious ideas, the theologies that had caused so much violence between Protestant and Catholic, have no real authority; Locke believed that the only religion the individual can rationally accept is a few basic ideas about a world creator and human morality that can be build up by reasoning from experience. We would say that Locke rejected the force of cultural tradition in shaping what an individual believes.

As we shall see later on, the utilitarian tradition has continually had difficulties on this point. The rational individual only builds up his or her own ideas from experience, and he or she certainly ought to reject ideas that don't come from one's own experience. Why is it, then, that ideas and traditions have so often been imposed on people? Why did they have the religious wars in the first place? In the same vein, why was it necessary for individuals to fight a revolution to throw off the despotic power of the king, if the government was created by the people in the first place? In other words, how can utilitarians explain what they regard as false ideas and disadvantageous behavior? The utilitarians are ambiguous between explaining what they believe the rational individual *ought* to do, and explaining the way people have actually behaved. Is it a theory about the ideal, or the actual? The history of the rational/utilitarian tradition has been animated by sorting out these problems.

Locke's empiricism was followed up by British thinkers for over a century. Some of his early followers were concerned, however, that Locke's dismissal of innate ideas went too far. If every individual is following his or her own physical sensations, how is it that people ever feel a sense of morality, a sense of obligation to do what is right for other people? To avoid this image of the selfish individual, Shaftesbury and Hutcheson argued that the individual must possess an innate moral sense, just as one has an inborn sense of beauty that enables one to distinguish between what is beautiful and what is ugly. Other empiricists felt that to admit an innate moral sense was to open the door for a return of religious dogmatism; they wanted to protect the mind from superstition and external control by showing how all beliefs are built up from experience. David Hume advocated the principle that all our beliefs are built up by the association of ideas based on the order in which our sensations have occurred to us, and this holds for every kind of idea, about the physical and social world alike. The only reason we believe the sun will come up tomorrow is because we have seen it come up many times before; but there is no guarantee the sun will come up, only our habitual belief. For Hume, habit and custom rule the mind; and since everything comes through the mind of the individual, the habitual association of ideas is the "cement of the universe."

One can see that Hume was moving to overcome the ambiguity in Locke's philosophy, between describing what the rational individual ought to do, and what he or she actually does. Hume comes down on the side of the actual; if individuals act in certain ways, it is because of their habitual experience, not because it is ultimately rational for them to believe as they do. Hume opens the way to explaining why people may put up with social institutions, even if the institutions do not benefit them or fit their rational interests; for if institutions have been customary for a long time, the individual just takes them as a matter of customary experience. Hume never satisfactorily answered the question of why unfavorable institutions might have emerged in the first place, nor how it is possible to break through the caked-up layer of custom into social change. Again these are problems that modern utilitarians have had to grapple with as well. Hume, in trying to explain why things are as they are, rather than criticizing and reforming them to fit the rights of the individual as Locke had done, has become a conservative. But Hume is not a reactionary; it is just that he lives after Locke's revolution has already succeeded, and Hume sees no reason for further change. On only one point he is a radical: he sees no rational basis for religion, and would be happy to do without it.

Hume's principle of the association of ideas soon gave rise to what we now regard as the classic utilitarian position. David Hartley, in 1749, argued that all of our ideas are selected because of their association with pleasures or pains, and this holds for our aesthetic and moral ideas too. In other words, there are no innate ideas of beauty or morality; these too are learned by experience. Ten years later, a young friend of Hume named Adam Smith wrote his first book, the *Theory of Moral Sentiments*. Smith tried to show that what we call good is what brings us pleasure, and what we call bad is what has brought us pain. How then can there be any morality that goes beyond the selfish experiences of the isolated individual? It is because each of us has the capacity for imagining oneself in the place of other persons; we sympathize with their pains and pleasures, and so we are able to conceive of what is good or bad for them. Like most utilitarians, Smith saw no serious conflict between individuals; one person's selfish concern for his own pleasures and pains does not generally come into conflict with anyone else's selfishness. To be sure, Smith was accurate in noticing that sympathy does sometimes exist among persons; but he did not ask whether the range of sympathy does not vary, so that sometimes individuals extend their sympathy to a narrow group, at other times extending it much further to include an entire class, nation, or everyone in the world. These are sociological questions that were not asked until much later, beginning with Durkheim, and outside the utilitarian tradition.

There is another reason why Smith was not very concerned about possible conflicts among individual interests. Smith is most famous for his system of economics, which he published in

1776, and in this he argued that individuals following their self-interest end up benefiting everyone. This economic thread was present in the utilitarian tradition from the beginning (for instance, Locke defending the right to private property), and Hume too was a famous economist in his day. The utilitarians opposed government interference and championed the freedom of the market. This was not just a matter of individual rights, they argued; everyone would be better off as a result, because the total economic wealth would increase. The theme had already been expressed by a London doctor, Bernard de Mandeville, in 1723, under the slogan "private vices are public benefits." Mandeville shocked his contemporaries by arguing that vain and fickle consumers of luxuries stimulate production and full employment; even thieves are useful because they provide business for locksmiths. Everything comes out for the best as long as the free flow of trade is unimpeded.

Adam Smith systematized the doctrine of *laissez faire* into a set of economic principles. The pleasures and pains of the individual become economic goods and costs; the rational individual attempts to maximize returns relative to costs (in other words, seeks a profit for his or her investment of goods and labor). Both individuals and society are best off if this profit-seeking is carried out on an open market. For in a competitive market, the laws of supply and demand ensure that goods will be offered at the best quality and for the lowest prices; anyone who tries to sell goods that are inferior or priced too high will be outbid by someone else. Economic competition increases production, so a society with an open market grows steadily richer. There is no need to interfere with individuals who are pursuing their own private profits, for the market is a huge "Invisible Hand" that disposes everything for the best.

Smith was not so extreme that he believed no one should ever interfere with the behavior of individuals. He well recognized that merchants might try to cheat, or that sellers of goods or of labor entered into collusion to create monopolies and keep up prices above what they would get on a competitive market. Smith favored a minimal regulation, to prohibit monopolies and enforce fair dealing on the open market; the government was to be a kind of neutral referee, and certainly should not be using political power to license its own monopolies. Here again we see that Smith, like other utilitarians, had in mind a kind of ideal individualism that would constitute the best society; at the same time, he believed that the laws of rational individual behavior—in his case, the laws of the market—explained how things actually happened. But he implicitly admitted that these laws only operated if society allowed them to operate; it was necessary to clear a space for them, and to cut back certain irrational patterns of social institutions that inhibited the working of the market.

Smith's laissez-faire economics appeared at the same time the industrial revolution was taking off in England. His theory seemed to explain and to give a guide for the economic transformation. Utilitarian thinking became enormously popular. At this time the term "Utilitarianism" began to be explicitly used, as the label for a movement of social reform. Jeremy Bentham, a lawyer, led a crusade for legal reform, especially of the criminal law. His aim was to do away with the harsh punishments that were normal in English law (as well as in most other states) up to this time. Hanging as a punishment for penniless people's stealing bread; mutilation, such as cutting off the ears of felons; imprisonment for non-payment of debts: these sorts of punishments, Bentham held, were irrational. As long as a man was in debtor's prison, for instance, he could do no work that would enable him to pay off his debts or create any benefits for the rest of society. There should be no punishment for actions that cause no one harm, such as tabooed sexual behavior; and for crimes like theft which do harm a victim, the punishment should be no greater than necessary to deter the action and should not inflict gratuitous pain.

Bentham attempted to replace such practices with a code of law based on a calculus of rewards and punishments. The overall aim is to promote good and eliminate the bad; one did this by finding the right mix of incentives and sanctions that would produce the best overall results. This calculation was applied to individuals, and then summarized for the entire society. The criterion was "the greatest good for the greatest number." Utilitarianism is based on considering the rational actions of individuals, and this is founded on individual self-interest. But it is important to note that utilitarianism does not begin and end with the selfish individual; it goes on to balance the interests of all the individuals in the group. This is not necessarily a contradiction. In the background of Bentham's thinking was the well-established tradition that individuals are capable of sympathy, of putting oneself in the place of other persons and calculating their pleasures and pains as well as one's own. In addition, Bentham's Utilitarianism drew upon the popularity of Smith's economics, with its demonstration that the selfish interests of individuals could be reconciled for the common benefit. Bentham in effect was looking for an equivalent of the market's "Invisible Hand"; and he believed this could be created in the form of a rational legal code.

From 1800 to the 1860s Utilitarianism was the cutting edge of Liberal reform in England. Its advocates fought for widening the political franchise and reducing the traditional privileges of the aristocracy and the state-supported Anglican Church. John Stuart Mill, who was both an economist and a Utilitarian philosopher, laid out the principle of unrestricted freedom of speech and advocated the rights of women. Nevertheless, toward the end of the century Utilitarianism had faded away. There were several reasons. In part, it died of success. Many of the political and legal reforms for which it fought had been won; and the new social issues that had emerged, especially with the rise of the labor movement, cut against the tradition of laissez faire economics and social harmony. The old reform movement split into what came to be called "Liberals" with a large "L"—the defenders of individualism and the open market—and "liberals" with a small "l"—those who favored collective action and government regulation.

Another reason for Utilitarianism's demise was that its offspring, the discipline of economics, had grown up and had moved out of the home. As I have discussed in the Prologue of this book, it was in the 1870s that economics became firmly established as an academic discipline; simultaneously it began to change into a technical discussion carried out in mathematics. Marginal utility, a technical concept that lent itself to formalization in the differential calculus, replaced the labor theory of value used by economists up through Mill. Economics was becoming divorced from the concepts of common sense that had made utilitarianism accessible to the general public; one of the main props for utilitarianism's popularity disappeared. Around the same time, sociology split from economics and also became an academic discipline. Some of the first sociologists, such as Herbert Spencer in England and William Graham Sumner in the United States, favored old-fashioned laissez-faire Liberalism. But more characteristic of the sociologists were small-"l" liberals or even moderate socialists. Sociologists like Émile Durkheim wanted collective reform against the social conflicts and anomic individualism which they saw as the main traits of industrial capitalism. Durkheim laid down his principles of sociology in a new direction: critiquing the utilitarian claim that the individual is prior to society, and trying to show that moral ties among people are more basic than exchanges in the market. We leave this aside for now, since it is the subject of Chapter 3 in this book.

What remained of Utilitarianism was a doctrine in the philosophy of ethics: the identification of good with pleasure and of bad with pain. This doctrine was criticized and repudiated by such philosophers as F. H. Bradley and G. E. Moore. They argued that pleasure is not what we mean by calling something good; the good is an end in itself, and it would be good whether anyone desired it or not. How else can we say that some persons have bad desires? Or that something is painful but good? The Utilitarians would have said that something painful is good only if it is part of an overall package in which the pleasures outweigh the pains; but don't people regard it as supremely good if someone sacrifices oneself for someone else, or for an ideal such as telling the truth, no matter what it costs? Religion or art are not good because they bring pleasure; they are good in their own right, and if someone says they are good only because they bring pleasure, one can be sure that person does not really value religion or art.

This criticism of utilitarian ethics was devastating. Philosophers of ethics turned away from trying to calculate individual pleasures and pains, and instead focused on explicating how ethical concepts are used and how meaning is expressed in ethical language. From the point of view of the philosophers, utilitarianism was just a bad example of the mistake of trying to derive an "ought" from an "is." By the 1930s, the Logical Positivists were arguing that ethical terms aren't meaningful at all, since they cannot be verified by empirical evidence. To say that something is good or bad is only a disguised imperative, a way of saying "Do this!" or "Don't do that!" Such statements are not logical, but emotional; they have no more truth-value than saying "Ugh!"

We have come a long way from reformers like Locke or Bentham, who felt it was necessary to give morality a firm grounding in the interests of individuals, so that there would be a criterion by which to criticize and rectify social injustices. An old-fashioned Utilitarian would not have accepted the argument that religion is good in itself; for Hume and Mill religion was not a good if it oppressed the individual and had no basis in empirical reality But thinkers were now convinced that there is no way to calculate values, since values exist in a realm apart from facts, and there is no common denominator by which different values can be compared. Values are merely premises from which one begins. At the intellectual level, the twentieth century had become relativistic about values; for one's own values, one could only believe and act. Of course political battles still went on: for and against socialism and communism; struggles with fascism, antisemitism, and racism; struggles for civil liberties, and intermittently for women's rights. But utilitarianism was no longer a part of these debates; other social philosophies had taken its place, and they were more inclined to argue for the rights of groups rather than the pleasures of individuals, or else to proclaim that certain principles are good in themselves.

Utilitarianism by this time was dead. What we have to discover now is how it came to life again.

Bringing the Individual Back In

Skip ahead now to the 1950s. A version of what looks like utilitarian theory begins to crystalize in sociology, but its roots and concerns are quite different from the old utilitarian philosophers and their economic offshoots. In fact, sociology never had much to do with utilitarianism, at least since the very early period when it wasn't clearly differentiated as a separate discipline.

Spencer and Sumner argued to some extent on the basis of social contracts and markets, but the leading sociological theorists— Durkheim, Weber, Mead, Parsons—had argued in very different directions, often by starting from what they maintained was left out by the utilitarians.

In the 1950s, though, George Homans launched an attack on the way sociological theory had developed. His target was the structural-functionalism of Talcott Parsons, who claimed to synthesize the essential insights of Durkheim and Weber. In Parsons's theory, individuals generally do what is required by their roles in the larger social system. The standards by which individuals behave are given by the culture, and their motivations are created by a process of socialization; some individuals may deviate, but then they are considered abnormal and are kept in line by the surrounding society. Homans protested that this social system is a myth, a theoretical construct made up out of Parsons's mind. Individuals are the living, breathing realities of the social world, and whatever happens must be caused by the motivations of individual men and women.

Homans argued that sociology did not need to depend upon concepts formulated for abstract social systems that no one had ever really seen, for it had already accumulated a solid basis of research studies on the ways humans interact. Researchers had gone inside the factory and had discovered that workers are organized into informal groups; it was these groups, rather than the orders of the boss, that determined how hard they worked. Other researchers had hung around with street gangs in big-city slums; anthropologists had lived in tribal villages and had observed who interacted with whom and who evaded each other's contact. By reviewing and synthesizing these studies, Homans formulated a series of principles of how people actually behave.

His most important principle, known as Homans's Law, states that the more individuals interact with each other, the more they come to like one another, the more similar they become to one another, and the more they tend to conform to a common standard. In other words, if a bunch of people are thrown together so that they have to interact—by working on the same job in the same place, by living in the same neighborhood or village—they start becoming a cohesive group; they develop a group culture that didn't exist before, and they enforce their standards upon each other. The factory work group makes individuals slow down their work rate so that it fits a common pace; the street gang makes its members fight to protect their turf. Homans's Law explains how group pressures emerge from interaction. His principle has a crucial proviso, however: this process of group-formation occurs *only* if the members of the group start off as equals. The boss who comes down to the factory floor and gives orders is not a member of the group; in fact, the group puts up with the boss only to the minimum necessary and avoids interacting with him or her. So interaction across authority lines does not set Homans's Law in motion; only interaction that occurs within the same level of authority does so.

How can one explain in deeper theoretical terms why this happens? Homans argued that the group processes emerge because of something that individuals must be doing to each other. The reason that individuals come to like one another, and thus to have influence over each other, must be because they are giving each other something that they find rewarding. This is the basic reward of social approval. The group is formed as long as individuals exchange these rewards. The group leader, the most popular person in the group, is also the person who interacts most with the others in the group; he or she is the person giving out the most rewards to other persons, and receiving the prestige of leadership as an extra reward in return. This argument also explains why this process does *not* take place between unequals in authority. When one person has the power to give orders, it is distinctly *unrewarding* to have to interact with him or her, so other people tend to avoid interacting with someone of this sort. Both types of evidence fit the same principle: people pattern their interactions according to where they get the greatest rewards.

It is easy to notice that Homans was not only shifting sociological theory back towards the individual, but also that he was placing the emphasis on processes whereby individuals made exchanges with one another. For this reason, this line of thinking became known as "exchange theory." If one kept going in this direction, one would head back towards an economic way of analyzing things, as exchanges occuring in a market. It took a while for this implication to emerge, however, because Homans placed greater stress on the point about individual motivation than the point about market exchanges. Homans launched what was later called the "micro-macro debate," arguing that systems never do anything, only human actors do. He created a furor by arguing that the basic principles of sociology are really applications of psychology. On the other side of the debate were not only Parsonian functionalists, defending the higher-order existence of a social system, but also many other sociologists who felt that psychological principles do not tell us enough. Even if we agree that all social action must be motivated by the rewards that individuals get, don't we still have to answer the question as to why the rewards are distributed among people in a certain way in the first place? Both in a dictatorial hierarchy and in a small eqalitarian group people are motivated by rewards; but why are there differences in these social patterns? And so on for all the other forms of social organization.

In the next stage of exchange theory, sociologists became less interested in reducing sociology to psychology, and more concerned with the social patterning of exchanges. Here the lead was taken by Peter Blau. Blau began to show that exchanges are found in many different places in social relationships. Take, for instance, what happens in a conversation when people are first introduced to each other. Typically, one starts out by making oneself important, bragging about your job, who you know, the places you've been. Blau analyzes this as an effort to raise one's value on the market for conversations or friendships; you are attempting to make yourself an attractive person to talk with. Later on, one begins to play oneself down, to make self-deprecating remarks, showing that you are just an ordinary person, easy to get along with. This is the phase of adjusting the conversational bargaining: if you pitch yourself at too high a level, the other person may not be able to match the price, so you have to come down to a lower level to make an equal bargain.

This kind of social interaction is a market for equal exchanges. What happens if the exchanges are not equal? The result will be either that the two persons find they cannot deal with each other, and will walk away from the relationship; or if they stick with it, then the relationship will be dominated by one person over the other. Blau analyzes love affairs as often fitting this second type. Suppose one person is more in love than the other one. Who will have the upper hand in the affair? It will be the person who is *less* in love, because he or she is more likely to make moves towards leaving the relationship, and the one who is more deeply in love will give in in order to keep the relationship going. This is called the "principle of least interest." Actually this insight was not original with Blau; it had been formulated by novelists like Stendahl a century before, and other sociologists examining dating and marriage had also formulated it. Blau, however, used it as part of the evidence for a widely applying model of explanation of social behavior, an explicit exchange theory.

Sociological exchange theorists now began to study the phenomenon of power quite extensively. Laboratory experiments were set up in which individuals were allowed to make exchanges with some persons but not with others (this is typically done now by having them linked together by computer hookups through which they can make offers to exchange various kinds of reward points). We have thereby accumulated considerable knowledge about how proper is negotiated in social exchanges: exactly how much power someone can extract in relation to what each has to offer the other, and how this is affected by the extent to which there are alternative exchanges one can make with other persons elsewhere in the network. These formulations have developed into several ongoing research programs, most notably David Willer's Elementary Theory and Karen Cook's exchange network theory.

We should note that sociological exchange theory, although bearing a resemblance to utilitarian theory, has gone off in a direction of its own. Utilitarian theory was not very concerned with questions of inequality and power, but instead concentrated on arguing how the greatest good could be produced for the greatest number. Sociology, on the other hand, has found that the most interesting question is precisely how power and inequality comes about. That is not to say that the exchange theory of power is a full and complete theory of all the ways in which power occurs. The most typical exchange analysis of power is that one individual has something to offer that the other side really needs; and if one cannot reciprocate by giving something of equal value, one can only keep up the relationship by giving up power to the most resource-laden individual. In one of Blau's famous analyses, the way in which someone becomes the informal leader of a work group is by being the expert who gives advice to newcomers; hence the leader gets power in return for giving his expertise.

Oddly enough, exchange theory has so far emphasized a rather benign techocratic model of power. Sociological exchange theorists, unlike economists, don't like to mention money; they prefer to give the impression that the boss in a factory has power over the workers because he or she has more expertise than they do; whereas it would be more straightforward to say that the boss has power because he or she controls the money to pay them. In addition, exchange theory has put virtually all its attention onto the rewarding aspects of exchanges; little investigation has been done concerning coercive sources of power, such as an army's conquering power or a revolutionary movement's coming to power in an armed uprising. That is not to say that these kinds of coercive situations cannot be analyzed by using a model of rational individuals bargaining over their own interest. The economist Thomas Schelling has analyzed coercive situations as a coordination game, in which it is dangerous for anyone to be left out of the dominant coalition; so one individual will only resist coercion if a large alternative coalition can be formed at just the same time. This leads to a theory of so-called "bandwagon effects" or "tipping phenomena" as periods of coercive stability are punctuated by sudden breakdowns and jumps of loyalty to the other side. Another application of economic theory to coercive power, which we will discuss below, is the theory of "protection rent."

What we see here is a lesson that is repeated many times over in the history of the rational/utilitarian tradition: our explanations need to focus not only on the calculations of the individual, but also on the kind of structural situation in which individuals bargain with one another. Markets are one kind of exchange situation; so are the more restricted networks studied by laboratory sociology experiments, in which only a few possible exchange links are possible; yet another type of social bargaining structure exists when power is coercively imposed. One might say that a big part of the task of building rational action theory is to lay out the various structural situations, as well as the kind of bargaining that is found in each.

Sociological exchange theory has given rise to branches that have gone off in quite different directions. We have noticed how one emphasis has tended to go in the direction of analyzing power as it arises from positive exchanges. Another direction, which we will explore a little further in the following paragraphs, has continued to look for places where markets are found in social phenomena. Yet another direction of research has focused on what is now called the theory of equity or social justice. This arises from a point which both Homans and Blau raised in regard to social exchanges. Exchanges operate according to an underlying principle: if I give something to you, you should give me something of equal value in return. Homans makes this principle of reciprocity part of his basic explanatory system; people become angry if reciprocity is violated, so that they feel unjustly treated if someone does not pay back something of equal value. This has given rise to a whole sub-area of research on how people feel about social justice, how they calculate the justice of particular exchanges, and how they react to violations.

It is noteworthy, though, that this line of argument pushes the boundary of exchange theory, up to a meta-level that is not the exchange itself, but the basic rules that govern it. But how is the underlying principle established? Does it itself arise as a result of exchange? Blau attempted to argue that principles of fair exchange emerge the longer an exchange has been going on, but he admits that there had to be some initial reciprocity to get things going in the first place. Ironically, the exchange theory, which began with Homans's criticism of Parsons's normative approach to social order, comes back to the same kind of normative principle in order to allow the exchange system to operate.

Sociology Discovers Sexual and Marriage Markets

Probably the main part of exchange theory that has led to the increasing spread of a rational or economic approach to social phenomena has been the tendency to find many kinds of social markets. Economists have moved into sociological topics rather late in the game; sociologists have been discovering marketlike systems in society for quite some time. As we shall see, sociologists have given a somewhat different emphasis to these social markets than economists do.

One of the earliest of these discoveries was by the sociologist Willard Waller, back in the 1930s. While doing research on high schools, Waller analyzed the process that he called the "rating and dating complex." He found male and female teenagers devoting a great deal of attention on who was going out with whom—an elaborate process of invitations to parties, dances, and dates. Popular girls had many invitations, popular boys could be sure of acceptances from whomever they asked; less popular kids worried about whether they would get the partner they wanted or any partner at all. Waller pointed out that the structure is a kind of market, in which the kids were stratified by their resources (physical attractiveness, personality, money for clothes and tickets, social background) which they can use for attracting partners. But everyone, at every level, whether highly popular or not, had strategic choices to make: some had too many choices and had to eliminate some, others had too few choices and struggled to find a partner that would be acceptable. This dating market, Waller pointed out, was a preliminary version of a marriage market, which eventually resulted in long-term or permanent exchanges. The bargaining system was a process by which each boy or girl found out how much he or she counted for in comparison to other partners. This is why the whole situation could be one of the most emotionally stressful times in a person's life.

Later sociologists took up the idea of the marriage market and used it to explain why it is that typically people tend to marry someone of the same social class (and often the same ethnic group, educational level, and so on) as themselves. This occurs even in modern, individualistic society, in which one's parents have nothing to do with choosing a partner for their children or arranging their marriages. Nevertheless the distribution of social resources, including one's class background and ethnic or racial prestige, results in class endogamy. Here we see the "Invisible Hand" of the market operating to reproduce a stratified society.

Another version of exchange theory was anticipated by sociologists of marriage and family. Even before Blau formulated his principle of power resulting from exchange of unequal resources, sociological specialists were finding evidence that the balance of power between husbands and wives was influenced by such things as how much money they had relative to each other. A woman had less power vis-à-vis her husband if she were a housewife than if she had a job and an income of her own; just how much power she had depended on how her income matched up against her husband's. In addition, a woman generally had less power when she had more children, because this lowered still further her chances of autonomous resources from outside the home. Although this theory of household power was developed before the women's movement began in the 1970s, the theory has relevance to what has happened since. For if a woman's power depends upon her outside career in comparison to her husband's career, then it makes sense that the mobilization of the feminist movement should go along with a greater demand by women for careers on their own; simultaneously, the value of getting married has declined, so that the rate of marriage has dropped, people tend to delay getting marriage until later in their lives, and they are likely to have fewer children when they do marry.

Some sociologists who identify with the feminist movement have attacked exchange theory on the grounds that it is antithetical to women. It is argued that exchange is a dehumanizing way to talk about human beings; that women should not be treated like economic property; and indeed that the entire mentality of cold rational calculation is a male attitude, which isn't applicable to a woman's perspective. To this, an exchange theorist would reply that the theory merely provides a standpoint from which to analyze what happens in the relations between men and women; it does not choose up sides, but only shows what will happen if resources are stacked up in particular ways. Exchange theory does not predict that marriages are always dominated by men, or even that the process of finding partners in love and sex is inevitably initiated by men. What the theory says is that power comes from unequal resources in exchange, and that each side shapes its own way of bargaining depending on what kind of resources it has. Exchange theory predicts quite clearly that whoever has most of the economic resources will be able to dominate the marriage market, and will have most power in the home. When men have had these resources they have dominated. Correspondingly, those women who have acquired greater economic resources now have a higher level of power if they marry.

Changes in women's career patterns have also affected the very way sexual negotiations are carried out. Waller's picture of the "rating and dating complex" from the 1930s and 1940s may seem rather outdated from the period of the 1980s and 1990s; the practice of boys asking out girls to the movies (which the boys pay for) was based on a situation in which males had most of the opportunities for making money. If more egalitarian romantic negotiations go on today, it is because young people of both sexes now tend to expect the same kinds of careers, and initiative is taken more equally on both sides. The pattern of bargaining resources has even produced a change in attitudes about sex. In the earlier part of the twentieth century, sexual behavior was regarded basically as a male province; men would talk about sex among themselves, bragged about their sexual conquests, and frequented prostitutes (or among the wealthy, had mistresses) on the side. Respectable women were those who did not openly talk about sex, and who upheld the principle (at least in public) that sex should wait until a couple were married. In fact, the male/female differences in sexual behavior were not quite as extreme as the respectable ideology; research on sexual activity shows that a certain proportion of women did in fact have sex before marriage, although less often than men did, and with a much smaller number of partners. In terms of exchange theory, women were guarding sexuality as a resource that they used for negotiating marriages; since men had most of the other resources, especially higher occupations and most of the wealth, women made sexual modesty into a compensating resource to attempt to control men.

From this perspective, the reason that sexual manners began to loosen up in the 1960s and thereafter was that women were acquiring more economic and occupational resources of their own. Talking about sex in public became no longer taboo; having sex before marriage became much more common, even openly accepted; and men's and women's sexual behavior has converged towards a similar pattern. The pattern is not yet the same, but exchange theory makes a clear prediction on this point: when men's and women's occupational power and wealth becomes equal, one can expect that their sexual behavior will be similar too. The fact that women and men on the statistical average are not yet economically equal fits with the currenty realities that male and female sexual behavior are still somewhat different too. Breaking down the evidence into subgroups, we see that women who are in occupations that give them resources equal to men's also tend to have sexual behavior patterns more like men's; whereas women who remain in positions of low economic power, especially women in traditional housewife roles, tend to be most traditional also in their sexual behavior.

Some critics have condemned the exchange theory as a male viewpoint; nevertheless the theory is rather successful in explaining why there should be such a thing as male and female viewpoints that exist at particular times in history. It is worth stressing that the exchange theory does not posit that groups of people have cultures that exist throughout history and independent of social circumstances. On the contrary, the theory shows how cultures emerge out of the kinds of exchange situations that exist at a particular time; as those exchange structures change, the theory predicts that the cultures change accordingly. Exchange theory believes in neither biological nor cultural absolutes. Let us look at the recent period of history, in which men generally had most of the economic resources in the marriage market. Does this mean that men will then be especially calculating? Arlie Hochschild argues that on the contrary, men who hold the economic resources don't have to look for a wife who has money; instead, a man can just follow his emotions, fall in love because of personality or physical attractiveness. The evidence, as Hochschild points out, is that in fact men tend to be the more emotional ones in love affairs, in the sense that men fall in love earlier than women do, and they stay in love after their female partners have fallen out of love with them. For a woman, on the other hand, a marriage was a much more consequential thing than for a man, if her entire economic future and her special class position depended upon it, as it did not for a man.

Women are "experts in love," Hochschild says, in the sense that they talk about their love affairs and potential partners much more than men do. But this talking about love is not passively floating on the tides of sentiment; it consists rather in rational efforts to keep emotions under control, to decide which man will or will not be a good match from a woman's point of view. Hochschild thus argues that women's reputation for being more emotional than men is only a crude way of expressing the truth. Women talk about their emotions more than men, and express emotions more; but this is because women have had social incentives to try to shape their emotions, to be rational managers of their emotions. Men, on the other hand, are simply carried along by their emotions, especially in matters of love, pride, or anger. As long as men are socially dominant, they have much less incentive to reflectively control their emotions. Having emotions is neither rational nor irrational in itself; what is rational is the way people live with the emotions they have. These male and female cultures of emotion, then, are shaped by the particular line-up of resources, especially in the sexual bargaining and marriage markets of a particular time in history. The exchange theory would predict, once again, that if these underlying market resources change in the future, then what counts as male and female cultures will change as well.

THREE APPLICATIONS OF SOCIOLOGICAL MARKETS: EDUCATIONAL INFLATION, SPLIT LABOR MARKETS, ILLEGAL GOODS

We should stop here to notice that the way in which sociologists have developed their market theories differs quite a bit from economic models of the market. Economists have developed a mathematical apparatus focusing on prices of goods in relation to each other, and the amounts of each good that will be produced; on another level, called macroeconomics, the theory attempts to explain the business cycle and long-term growth of the economic system. Sociological market theories, on the other hand, have usually not been concerned with prices and production, equilibria, or economic growth at all. When Blau analyzes the power that comes to a work-group leader for giving advice, he is not analyzing the price of advice in general throughout the society; there is in fact no such price, and each price that is worked out in terms of power and deference in a work group is a specific, local bargain. In general, economic theory is not concerned with questions of power; its whole emphasis is on large-scale movements of supply and demand throughout the market, which wipe out local differentiations and make the phenomena of power impossible. In this sense, economists' and sociologists' models are at opposite ends of the continuum from one another. Similarly, a Waller-style analysis of finding a matching partner in a sexual or marriage market does something that economists do not do at all: it explains *who* will exchange with *whom*, not the aggregate results that flow from the sum total of all the exchanges. In fact it is rather hard to imagine what would be the social equivalent of the general equilibrium price of marriages, or of the total level of marriage productivity.[2]

Another way to put the difference is this: economics is concerned with certain quantitative summaries of the things that are produced in order to be exchanged, whereas sociological market models are concerned with the pattern of the social structure that constitutes the exchanges themselves. In addition, whereas economic theory tends towards an idealized picture of an egalitarian exchange system, sociology focuses on the inequalities that are created or sustained by exchanges.

Let us briefly sketch three examples of social market systems that sociologists have dealt with.

In today's society, education has become the center of the stratification system. What social class position one ends up in is heavily influenced by how much education one has. But here we find a paradox: access to schooling has expanded throughout the twentieth century, but our society is not becoming more equal. In the early 1900s, a high school education was completed by only a small percentage of the population; now the vast majority of people finish high school, and about half of the population attends college. Graduate school, professional training, advanced degrees in business administration, and so on have become as common as high school once was. But the gap between the rich and the poor is no narrower (in fact it has widened since the 1970s), and the chances of rising higher in the social scale than one's parents has hardly shifted at all: social mobility rates are at about the same moderate levels as they have been for a long time.

How can we explain the paradox that education has expanded into a huge system, while at the same time the degree of stratification has at best remained the same? A sociological explanation is that education is like a huge market. People invest their time and efforts in getting schooling for themselves and their children. As a result of this investment students expect that there will be a payoff of a good job. However, what is "bought" in the schools is not jobs themselves, but the chances to get jobs; as some sociologists say, one acquires cultural capital; or in other terminology, education gives credentials.

The value of educational culture or credentials is like money. The more money there is in circulation, the less you can buy with the same amount of money, because increases in the money supply makes prices rise. A high school diploma was quite valuable in the 1920s, because only a small percentage of the population had it; one could "purchase" a good managerial job with it at that time. By the 1960s, so many people had high school degrees that one could only acquire a working class or lower clerical job with them; their value had eroded, due to the inflation of the educational currency. The same thing has happened to college degrees in more recent years; when almost half the young people going into the labor force have a college degree, then it is no longer worth much on the job market. Students who want to get ahead are forced to go back to school for longer periods, to get advanced degrees and professional specializations. One can predict that the process will continue to repeat itself at the more advanced level too. If in the future everybody had a Ph.D., law degree, M.B.A., or the like, then these advanced degrees would be worth no more than a job in a fast food restaurant, and the competition would move on to still higher degrees.

Here we have a market theory that explains why stratification continues to exist, even when social institutions expand which, according to widespread cultural ideals or ideologies, are supposed to reduce inequality. Again we should note that the way sociologists use a market model is different from most conventional economists. For economists, the market is an ideal system of competition that results in the best possible world for everyone. This of course was part of the original utilitarian program, which led to the early development of economics. Sociologists, however, have picked up a rather different implication of market analysis: a modification of the theory that enables them to explain how inequality and stratification is created and reproduced.

A key point is that, as classical market economics implies, if there is perfect competition, there should be no inequality. No one can make a profit in the long run (an economist would say, at equilibrium) because if someone charges a higher price for what they are selling, someone else will see that there are profits to be made, so they will come into that market as competitors; and this competition in turn will drive the prices down. This applies to labor markets just as well as product markets. If some occupations get a higher wage than others, then people will leave the low-wage occupations and move to the higher-paying ones. Eventually, as people keep chasing around from one high-paying occupation to another, things should move towards a point at which every occupation pays the same as any other.

This sounds so different from our normal reality that we have to make an effort to get rid of our usual prejudices. Isn't it normal that doctors should make more than garbage collectors? But if there were no barriers keeping people from moving from one occupation to another—and that is a key point in the theory—then more people would come into the medical field, and by overcrowding it would drive the incomes of doctors down to an average level. In fact if huge numbers of people became doctors, far more than the demand for their services, then doctors on the average would make less money than other people. This does not happen in our society, because there are strong barriers to becoming a doctor. The medical profession is organized in a way that makes it difficult for most people to get into the field, and these barriers (which include the inflation of credentials in medical education) keep getting higher as more peple try to enter the field. If we imagine a world without such barriers among occupations, then it would have competitive labor markets everywhere, and anyone who earned a higher income than others would soon be swamped by competitors who brought the income level back down to normal.[3] In such a society, the only jobs that would have higher wages than the average would not be the ones that are especially attractive because of their working conditions and prestige; those occupations in fact would have a surplus of suppliers, and hence their wages would be depressed. It would be the least attractive occupations that would have to pay more to attract anyone to do the job. In this world of completely open and competitive occupational markets, garbage collectors would be among the highest paid people.

All this sounds paradoxical because it is so far from the way our world is actually constructed. But we can directly make use of this kind of market theory, if we see the crucial point: it is barriers that keep people in different occupations from competing for the same jobs; barriers are responsible for inequality. If a truly open labor market spells equality, then a closed market, divided by occupational barriers, is the source of inequality.

One of the most influential theories developed along these lines is the theory of the split labor market. A split labor market exists where some jobs have poor working conditions, long hours, little job security, and on top of all this, are poorly paid. At the same time, other sorts of jobs have good and safe conditions of work, good hours and provisions for overtime pay, job security protected by tenure or union provisions, and these jobs are typically highly paid. Why are all the disadvantages lumped together in one sector, and all the advantages in another? The first type of job is wide open to competitive pressures; the very fact that there are no unions or professional associations in this sector means that entry into this area is easy, and extra labor easily comes in and competes with those in this sector, making it possible for employers to pay low wages and allow onerous working conditions. In this sector are jobs like working in small restaurants, operating little all-night convenience stores, driving taxis, acting as housekeepers and hotel maids. In the other sector, such as working in big manufacturing corporations, the jobs tend to be unionized or bureaucratized and protected by rules. This sector is sometimes referred to as the monopoly sector of the economy (strictly speaking one should say the oligopoly sector, where a few big firms control most of the business); here the employers have a relatively protected position, and can afford to have workers who also have a protected position through their unions and professional associations. So on the one hand there are little, small competitive businesses, operating on a low profit margin and hiring employees who are also paid at the minimal level; on the other hand are big, well-financed organized with protected market positions whose workers also are highly protected and relatively well paid.

Why are any workers willing to work in the low-paid, competitive sector of the split labor market? Edna Bonacich points out that the dividing line between the two sectors is often an ethnic line. In the contemporary United States, the low-paying, competitive sector tends to be the place where workers are black, Hispanic, or increasingly in recent years, migrants from the Middle East or from Southeast Asia. The high-paying, protected labor markets are predominantly staffed by whites of European descent. One can say this is a matter of ethnic discrimination, but the question is, how does this discrimination get started? Bonacich's theory is that ethnic populations only acquire their social identities when migration takes place. Some migrants come from homelands where the economic level is lower than the society into which they are migrating. This means that if someone comes from a poor country, they will be willing to accept relatively lower wages than someone who is used to a higher standard of living. Operating an all-night convenience store for low wages would be considered a real decline in one's standard of living if one has grown up in a wealthy industrial country, but it may be an increase in one's living standard if one has migrated from a poor Third World country. Hence it makes sense that historically these patterns have shifted as to which ethnic groups have occupied the low-wage sector of the split labor market; at the beginning of the twentieth century, it was recent immigrants from Italy or Eastern Europe who came from areas where the standard of living was relatively so much lower than in the United States, and hence were willing to work in the dirtiest, poorest paying jobs.

Bonacich's theory of the split labor market is simultaneously a theory of ethnic antagonism. Workers who are willing to accept low wages and working conditions are regarded as a threat by workers who demand a higher standard of living, and perhaps have fought union battles in order to gain control of their labor markets. Ethnic discrimination, Bonacich is saying, is not simply a matter of skin color or speaking with a different accent; it is basically an economic conflict over wage levels in the labor market. The split labor market starts out with differences among groups in their economic demands; it also perpetuates ethnic differences, because antagonism between the two labor markets reinforces ethnic identifications on both sides of the dividing line. One might say that ethnic groups that are discriminated against are those that initially were willing to accept low-paying and undesirable work; having gotten into that work sector, they meet with antagonism that keeps them from getting out of that sector.

A theory like the split labor market does not sound very much like the optimistic tone of the classic utilitarian thinkers. It sounds more like conflict theory, and split labor market theorists in fact tend to identify themselves with that theoretical tradition. But it is also in keeping with the tendency of rational, market-oriented analyses in sociology in recent decades to turn the optimism of the utilitarian tradition on its head. Instead of extolling the virtues of the open market, it concentrates on showing how social inequities are created and sustained by barriers that separate off sectors from full market competition.

The third example of this kind of undesirable social conditions arising from a distorted market is in the area of crime. This is the theory of markets for illegal goods and services. Consider where organized crime has arisen. When alcohol was illegal in the United States during the period of Prohibition, criminal organizations arose to take over the distribution. Where gambling is illegal, similar kinds of criminal syndicates have arisen. We find the same thing again in recent years: with the war against drugs, the distribution of cocaine and other drugs have become increasingly controlled by large-scale gangs, operating with a high level of violence. In all these cases, the level of enforcement of a prohibitive law has gone along with a rising level large-scale criminal activity and violence.

How can this be explained? Social scientists using economic

concepts have pointed out that the price of an illegal commodity is determined, like everything else, by supply and demand. Stringent law enforcement tends to constrict the supply, but demand for these illegal commodities seems to be relatively inelastic.[4] With a lowered supply, the price of the illegal commodity goes up. Drugs or alcohol, which might otherwise be relatively cheap if left to the open competitive market, rise in price. This has several further consequences. One is that the sellers of illegal goods make more profit, as long as they do not get caught. This in turn brings more potential sellers into the market; even if some of them are caught and thrown in prison, that only opens some room for others to take their place. Illegal business becomes big business. Notice that there is a hidden symbiosis here between law enforcement and the profitability level of illegal business. If there were no law enforcement, then the market would be wide open; many competitors would come in, and that would drive down prices and profits to a low level. So law enforcement, although it is a danger to the individual bootlegger or drug dealer, is also the structural force that tends to restrict competition and thus ensures high profits.

The fact that the criminal organizations that deal in illegal goods also tend to be quite violent can be explained by the same model. The 1920s was the heyday of murders taking place among the gangs of bootleggers, among which the Mafia gradually rose to the top. The killings consisted mainly in rival gangs struggling over control of a territory; in other words, they were fighting to establish a monopoly. The same thing exists in today's world, with the violence among rival gangs trying to control the drug business. In the realm of ordinary legal business, it is scarcely possible for one business to use force to try to exclude competitors from the market; one fast-food chain does not go around and dynamite another fast-food chain, for example. That is because legal businesses are protected and controlled by the state; they can appeal to the police and the courts for protection. But an illegal business, by its very nature, cannot have property rights protected by the government. Criminal gangs thus emerge as a kind of illegal government. Of course illegal gangs also engage in outright robbery too: it is very common in the drug business for armed robbers to find out where a drug deal is going on or a drug stash exists, and to rob it. The uncontrolled condition of an illegal business is a free-for-all.

Big gangs, which might start out as free-lance robbers, eventually introduce some regularity into an illegal business; by controlling a territory, they make it possible for suppliers and dealers to operate in a fairly routine way. Of course they pay a cost for this; the gang either takes over the business or takes part of the proceeds for protection. (The same thing happened in the past in other illegal businesses such as gambling, where the Mafia came in and demanded protection money.) Organized crime provides what economically oriented theorists have called "protection rent"—a concept that we will examine further below, when we come to the rational theory of the state. Gang violence is thus not merely an emotional or irrational phenomenon; it follows directly from the rational interests involved in establishing and protecting a market for illegal goods.

Another consequence of this restricted market is on the side of the consumer of illegal goods. As prices are driven up, the consumer has to pay more. Since these goods are of the kind that tend to be addictive, consumers do not cut down their consumption so much as they attempt to find ways to raise extra money. This produces what is called "secondary deviance": drug addicts engaging in additional crime, such as robberies and burglaries, in order to raise the money to pay for their drugs. The association of drugs with violent crime, which has arisen in the first place because of the expensiveness of illegal goods, now recycles back and reinforces the desire of the straight society to repress drugs. This is a self-reinforcing circle; efforts to eliminate the problem only contribute to making it worse.

In all three of these cases—educational inflation, split labor markets, and illegal goods—the rational interests of individuals have led to social inequalities and undesired consequences. All this suggests that there is something paradoxical about the market model of society. The fact the people do not see the consequences of their actions suggests a weakness in the theory. People crusade against drugs, just as they once crusaded against alcohol, without seeing how their actions contribute to the problem they want to solve. They blame ethnic minorities for undercutting working conditions and wages, and dismiss them as dirty and lacking in civilized standards, without seeing how the split labor market, which the dominant majority benefits from, is responsible for these very distinctions. As individuals, we all push for as much educational opportunity as possible, without noting the consequences that more and more education will be needed for the same jobs. In all these cases, rational actions on the individual level are leading to irrational consequences on the collective level.

It is not surprising, then, that the theoretical attention of the rationalist tradition has shifted in recent years towards the study of paradoxes.

The Paradoxes and Limits of Rationality

All this study of rationality in society came up against a deep theoretical prolem. Both in the model of individuals calculating their self-interest and in analyzing how they make social exchanges, paradoxes and limits on rationality began to proliferate. The study of paradoxes has become a leading part of the rational choice tradition. The effect of this was not to discourage enthusiasm for this mode of analysis. On the contrary, it has stimulated interest, giving theorists a real puzzle to sink their teeth into. One might say it has led to the development of pure theory of the fundamentals of rational action.

The paradoxes that have emerged are of two kinds. On the level of the individual, there are limits on the ability to process information and make rational decisions. On another level, there is the question of how rational individuals can form groups: indeed, how collective action is possible at all.

The first set of paradoxes are sometimes referred to as *bounded rationality*, and the result is called the neo-rationalist position. Here the issue is the limits on the capacity of the individual to be rational. The problem first emerged in the area of research in formal organizations, or what might also be called administrative or management science. Herbert Simon, studying the behavior of managers in organizations, pointed out that a key problem is dealing with all the information that comes in, and selecting which information to act upon. The rational manager tries to maximize rewards and minimize costs; the difference between the two is what constitutes profit for the organization. Well and good; but what is it that he or she should be maximizing and minimizing? Presumably the organization—say it is a factory in the manufacturing sector—should be maximizing production. But if there are too many accidents and too many workers get hurt, that will slow things down and increase costs, so safety needs to be maximized also. Moreover, should one produce goods just as fast as possible, even if it means wasting materials? Presumably cost control needs to be part of the rational aim. The list is easily extended. Keeping down the cost of wages is important, but so is keeping up workers' morale. Quality, quantity, getting things done on time, dealing with breakdowns, planning for the future—all these are part of the package that a rational manager needs to maximize.

In his studies of what managers actually do, Simon came to the conclusion that a manager cannot do everything at once, and does not even try to do so. In the classic formulation Simon wrote together with James March, the rational manager *does not maximize,* but *satisfices.* The meaning of this last term is the following. A manager has a set of things to be concerned about: production, quantity, quality, speed, safety, etc. For each area, he or she sets a satisfactory level; if events go on within that level, then he or she does not have to pay much attention to that area, but lets it follow existing routine. Instead, he or she concentrates his/her attention on one area at a time, the one in which the biggest changes appear to be needed. Usually this is the area in which there are the biggest problems, where things have fallen below the satisfactory level. The rational manager, then, does not try to maximize everything at once; he or she satisfices (accepts a merely satisfactory level) in every area that can be treated routinely for the time being, and concentrates on troubleshooting the areas that are least satisfactory.

This principle, that it is impossible to maximize, but rational to satisfice, is called the principle of bounded rationality. Rationality cannot be universal; individuals have limits on what they can do. It is not rational to try to act like the ideal economic actor, considering every possible alternative on the market before making a choice. The costs of processing all this information about alternatives soon outweigh the rewards; it is better to make a choice relatively early, and get on with adjustments afterwards if things do not work out at a satisfactory level. This is what is called the neo-rationalist position.

March and Simon formulated their principle of satisficing in the late 1950s. Since then, a number of other problems of limits on rational choice have been uncovered. Consider Blau's basic principle of exchange theory: the actor chooses the highest payoff or profit, which is calculated by multiplying the rewards (minus their costs), times the probability of attaining each reward. But how does one do this in real life? For one thing, how do you measure the probability that you will get one reward (say having fun at the beach if you take the day off from work) as compared to another reward (forgoing the beach and getting a good day's work done)? The problem is that real human beings, as opposed to idealized mathematical distributions in an economist's equations, do not usually have clear or reliable information about probabilities of various things happening.

A related problem is that most things people make decisions about are not measured in money, and hence are not strictly comparable. How do you value your day at the beach, as compared to, say, your peace of mind in getting your work done? This is the problem of a common denominator by which to compare diverse things; even if some of those things are in money (your day's pay), how do you set that against non-monetary things (fun at the beach)? The situation is even worse if one strictly follows Blau's model: what is the common denominator that enables one to multiply *Reward* times *Probability of Attaining It?* Rewards and probabilities are not the same kind of things; when you multiply one by another, in what units is the result measured? And are the units of reward-times-probability in one area (having fun at the beach) the same kinds of units as rewards-times-probability in another area (getting your work done)? The upshot of this analysis is to cast doubt on whether it is possible for human beings in social life, no matter how rational, to actually make these calculations at all.

These may be the underlying reasons why researchers, when they have come to study how people actually make calculations and decisions, have found that people don't follow classic rules of rationality at all. This research is called the study of choice "anomalies" or "heuristics." Some of the most famous findings here are summarized by the psychologists Tversky and Kahneman. For instance, when someone is asked to choose between different situations in which there is a balance of rewards and risks of various costs, the person is more likely to take a risky option if the question is presented to them as a matter of gaining something rather than focusing on the possibility of losing. They find a public policy much more acceptable when they are told it will bring 90 percent employment than if they are told it will bring 10 percent unemployment. There are many such heuristic patterns of choice. People tend to regard costs as higher if one has to subtract them from something one already has than if one substracts them for something one could have had in the future. When hypothetical choices are presented to individuals, they are more likely to regard a cost as unacceptable if it is a risk for someone that they know personally, than if it is presented as a risk for just anyone.

In general, people do not pay much attention to statistical information that is given to them; they prefer to act upon information that fits their past stereotype of what is going to happen. Stockbrokers and gamblers, who are occupationally concerned with probabilities, nevertheless use cultural stereotypes rather than pure calculations. Even memory is affected by these heuristic strategies; people remember the cases that fit their stereotype, and forget the cases that disconfirm it. In short, people do not search for a full range of information and perform rigorous calculations upon it. This is not surprising from the point of view of the model of satisficing rather than maximizing. People will choose a medical alternative much more often if it is presented in terms of the number of lives lost than of lives saved. We seek to avoid losses more than we tend to seek gains. No wonder, then, people in real life accept routines as long as they are not too bad, and spend their time on troubleshooting rather than trying to maximize their gains.

The other set of paradoxes in rational behavior is not at the level of how the individual thinks, but at the level of how individuals are able to coordinate their actions into a group. These may be called problems of social coordination, and they cast doubt on whether it is rationally possible for individuals to form a society at all. The most famous of these problems is called the "free rider" problem. Mancur Olson formulated the issue in 1965. Consider that there are some things that are "public goods": things which are provided for everybody, and it is not possible to consume them as an individual without other people being able to consume them too. Having clean air, or trash picked up off the streets, or control of crime, are examples of public goods. Olson's free rider paradox is as follows: the rational individual will not contribute to the costs of providing public goods, but will go ahead and enjoy them nevertheless. For the goods are public; they will exist whether I myself contribute to them or not. It is as if there were a free bus service, maintained by voluntary contributions from the community. (An example which really does exist is public television or radio stations supported by contributers.) I can ride the bus for free, so why bother to make voluntary contributions to it? Of course someone has to make contributions; but it is in my rational self-interest to have other people make the contributions while I do not.

How then does it come about that anyone makes contributions to public goods at all? Olson concludes that it cannot be done by appealing to individual self-interest. Instead, public goods must be provided by an arbitrary or even coercive decision; public transportation or clean air, if we are to have them at all, must be created by passing laws to collect taxes or to prohibit individuals from polluting. If it were a matter of private interests alone, it would never get done.

Notice, by the way, that the free rider analysis cannot be answered simply by saying that people have the interest of the group in mind, i.e., that they have a sense of solidarity with the whole. For that answer begs the question: what we want to know is how selfish individuals thinking only of their own interest would actually come to put the interest of the group ahead of their immediate selfish interest. If we say that in fact people are altruistic (to be realistic, we should say that some people are altruistic, not everyone), then we are stepping outside the frame of theory based on the rational, self-interested individual. And the theoretical problem is to see whether group interests can be

158 FOUR SOCIOLOGICAL TRADITIONS

constructed from individual interests, without positing some other, non-self-interested factors such as altruism or solidarity.

Another version of the free rider problem is called the "prisoner's dilemma." This arises in game theory, a method created during World War II for analyzing strategic decisions. In game theory, each actor has two choices to make, and each one knows that the other person also can make the same two choices. What each one gains or loses depends upon how the choices match up. In the prisoner's dilemma, imagine two criminal suspects who are in jail on suspicion of committing a robbery. The police give each suspect the same choice: if you confess and the other guy does not, you will be given a light sentence and the other will receive a severe punishment. If you don't confess and the other guy does, the situation is the reverse: he gets off and you get the slammer. Of course, if neither one confesses, then the crime can't be proven, and both will get off free. To put pressure on them to confess, the police cover the fourth alternative: if you both confess, then your confession doesn't count for as much, and you will both be given a moderate sentence, in between the lightest and the heaviest.

Obviously, the best outcome would be if both prisoners have faith in each other and refuse to confess. Then they will both go free. This is the best possible world; it comes about if the two individuals have social solidarity among themselves. But supposing they do not trust one another? Given the incentives that each one has, and that each one knows the other has too, it is more in one's self-interest to confess, to rat on the other guy and get off with a slap on the wrist. Morever, there is pressure to rat on the other guy quickly, before he rats on you; because if he confesses first, then my confession isn't worth anything. The strategic interests of the two individuals are antithetical to each other, and that keeps them from forming a social solidarity that would be best for them altogether.

The prisoner's dilemma is analogous to a social world in which public goods would be quite valuable to have, but in which individuals would lose something from contributing to the public good as long as other people do not. There has to be an assurance that the other side will live up to the bargain; but there is no way of knowing that, and in fact one can figure out that other people will act just like oneself. Whether one assumes that the other person is ultimately selfish, or merely distrusting, the outcome is the same. Rational selfish individuals dealing with other rational selfish individuals will never sacrifice anything to the public good, since it would be a waste. That is what makes the situation a dilemma.

PROPOSED RATIONAL SOLUTIONS FOR CREATING SOCIAL SOLIDARITY

In recent years there have been increasingly sophisticated efforts to overcome these problems. After all, social coordination sometimes does exist; it must be possible. But is it possible to account for it starting from the point of view of rational individuals? One way that has been proposed to overcome the problem of social coordination has been by means of iterated games. That is to say, one invokes game theory, while positing that individuals play not just a single, isolated game, but a series of games with the same partners. This leads to long-run patterns that may differ from what happens in a single game. The iterated game approach however has not arrived at any clear consensus as to whether this is a general solution to the rational creation of social coordination. For one thing, does it actually model real life situations? In the case of the prisoner's dilemma, what makes it a dilemma is precisely that the prisoners are given only one chance; they are prevented from learning from the first time and trying again.

In addition, there is a second kind of question: what determines the payoffs offered in a particular game? Indeed, why are the rules of the game laid down as they are, and what rules would determine that people should play a series of games? It is easy to simply set this up in the laboratory in whatever way the experimenter wishes. But why do people in the real world create particular kinds of games? Perhaps there is a higher level on which people have to play a game to decide what sorts of games they are going to play.

This tendency to distinguish first-order games from second-order games is a pervasive direction in current theorizing. We are becoming accustomed to distinguishing first-orders and second-orders of all sorts of things; in a few paragraphs we will encounter first- and second-order free riding, for instance. And there may even be third-order or fourth-order effects, which raises the possibility of falling into an infinite regression of meta-levels. This too is a problem with which current theoretical sophistication is grappling. It is a particularly difficult problem because these kinds of solutions (iterated games and meta-levels) are designed to solve the problem of individuals creating group coordination, not the other set of paradoxes relating to bounded rationality of individuals. Are individuals, operating under cognitive limitations rather than full mathematical rationality, capable of calculating series of games extending far into the future, or taking account of various meta-games? It remains to be seen whether bounded rationality may not make all these games and meta-levels collapse like a house of cards that is stacked too high.

In the late 1980s, several sociologists formulated a different approach to the rational creation of social solidarity. Michael Hechter and James Coleman, working independently, both produced theories that solve this problem in a somewhat similar manner. Both start with the point that in many cases individuals need either other; there are things that people can produce only by cooperating—such as public safety, defense against crime, economic production which increases with a division of labor, and so forth. The trouble is, can they overcome their distrust of one another? On some occasions there is a demand for norms or solidarity. But when are people able to overcome the free rider problem and produce a collective good to meet this demand?

For Hechter, the key condition is that all the members of the group should be able to monitor and sanction each other to prevent free riding. A political party, for instance, will be able to act together as a group only if the members can see whether everyone else is actually voting the party line, joining in rallies, and struggling against their common enemy. Solidarity thus depends upon communications. Small groups more easily can generate solidarity, since the behavior of all members is immediately visible to one another. When groups become larger, solidarity is more difficult, and usually depends upon some group members becoming specialists in checking on the behavior of the members. But this raises a second danger: the possibility that these specialists will abuse their power for their own ends. It is the old question: who guards the guardians?

Solidarity takes more than surveillance. It also requires that individual group members have some resources that they can use to control one another. They must have some way of rewarding one another for their cooperation, or punishing them for failing to cooperate. Hechter argues that positive rewards generally create much more solidarity than negative punishments. The threat of punishment tends to create distrust, and is an incentive to hide one's behavior from surveillance. Thus groups that rely on positive rewards will generally have more solidarity. This isn't easy to maintain, though, since a group that produces material goods out of which to reward its members (a collective farm, for instance, in which everyone gets more to eat if they all work hard) raises the possibility that individuals might be able to get the same rewards for less work elsewhere (for instance by leaving the farm and going to work someplace else where the wages are higher). In general, Hechter shows that solidarity will be highest when the rewards are something intrinsic, such as social approval or protection against an enemy, than if they are extrinsic rewards such as material payments. That is because intrinsic rewards are much more likely to be tied especially to that particular group, whereas extrinsic rewards are more likely to lead into market bargaining, which motivates individuals to go off on their own in search of the best deal.

Coleman gives additional emphasis to the point that positive sanctions (rewards for compliance) are more effective than negative sanctions (punishments for noncompliance). For if there is a lot of negative sanctioning, the costs of sanctioning people will build up. It will be necessary to put extra efforts into seeking out deviance that some individuals are hiding from the group. Sometimes noncompliant individuals may resist control or even fight back, so the norm-enforcers will need to carry extra sanctioning powers with them, perhaps even weapons. All this results in building up a formal organization within the cooperating community, an organization that specializes in exercising controls. This organization demands resources and takes on interests of its own. Now there is a problem of second-order free riding, which has emerged out of efforts to control first-order free riding.

It is better if the whole problem of specialized, formal controls can be avoided or minimized. Coleman points out this is easiest to do if the community consists in a densely interacting network, which is closed to outsiders. In that case, controls can be informal rather than formal. Informal controls are both less costly and more likely to involve positive sanctions than are formal controls. People will more naturally conform to a small, dense group, since they get feelings of belonging as rewards for their conformity, whereas if the controls are exercised in a more impersonal manner, mostly involving punishments, the whole thing is held together less by positive feelings of benefit than by fear of being caught.

This rational choice theory of solidarity has not yet been extensively examined or tested. We do not know yet if it is capable of predicting empirically the variations in where solidarity occurs: the places where solidarity is most intense, as well as the cases where solidarity is only lukewarm, where it breaks down, and where it is never created in the first place. One problem with proving the theory is that a number of the specified conditions may also have a different meaning in the eyes of a different theoretical approach. The Hechter-Coleman theory predicts that solidarity will be highest when there are small groups, densely interacting and closed to outsiders, in which individuals closely monitor each other and exchange positive rewards such as personal esteem. The trouble is that these variables are also found in the ritual theory of solidarity that comes out of the Durkheimian tradition. In the ritual theory (as we shall see in Chapter 3), a high density of interaction, group focus of attention, and the sharing of emotions are the key ingredients for producing feelings of solidarity.

Can we find a way to test which theory is right by separating out distinct measures of the factors which each theory says is operating? Or will it turn out that both kinds of theory have converged on the same basic processes? If the latter is true, then we will have the ironic result that the utilitarian and Durkheimian traditions, which have argued back and forth as rivals over the years—Durkheim versus Spencer, Homans versus

Parsons—would have in the end come back onto common grounds. Whether this will happen or not remains for the future to see.

Economics Invades Sociology, and Vice Versa

An odd result of all this attention to the paradoxes of rationality and the efforts to overcome them is that the market model no longer seems so important. Thinkers who advocate a rational action approach spend more time on showing how nonmarket relationships work than on imitating economists. The rational actor, too, seems to be receding from the center of the stage; it is more like a hollow silhouette which outlines a topic we are concerned about, but we pay more attention now to the ways in which it is overshadowed by limits on its rationality and boxed in by the constraints of social structures. To be sure, social scientists who belong to this school of thought still regard individuals as self-interested. But the up-to-date rational actor doesn't do things that are very maximizing for his or her interests, and he or she is only intermittently capable of being really selfish. It is something like the problem of lying: no doubt unprincipled persons lie whenever they can, but they may end up telling the truth most of the time just because it is too much trouble to keep up lying consistently.

Thus although we talk about the economic invasion of the social sciences in recent years, and the spread of rational choice theory, these terms don't precisely convey what is going on in today's intellectual world. It is not simply that economic theory is now being used all over the place; in order to use economic theory, it has been necessary to modify it. And to speak more generally about rational choice theory as being one of the intellectual popular movements is not to say that we are now showing everything to be based on rational calculation by individuals. On the contrary, what we are finding out is how complicated and subtle our models of rationality have to become if they are to fit the problems of explaining social interactions and organizations. It would be more accurate if we were to talk about the "rationality puzzles" or the "rationality controversies"; for it is questions and approaches, more than solutions, that constitute the intellectual appeal of this approach.

It is true that economists in recent years have been dealing with subjects like the family, crime, education, and politics, areas that have traditionally been outside strictly economic concerns with prices and production. From the other side, many sociologists and political scientists have adopted various items from the economists' way of thinking. But a great deal of modification has gone on in this social and economic discussion, so that it is no longer very traditional economics. The theoretical core of modern economics is the highly sophisticated mathematical model known as general equilibrium theory. This is the attempt to prove, in a rigorous way, that there exists (at least in principle) a general equilibrium of prices for all goods and services, a situation that clears the market (everything is sold; no one is unemployed), and that this equilibrium is stable and unique (there is only one way in which it can occur).

This is an extremely abstract ideal of the market; many theorists of economics believe that general equilibrium does not really exist, even hypothetically; and in any case it doesn't help to solve practical problems such as predicting the amount of inflation or the price of medical care next year. Theoretical economists nevertheless keep working on the general equilibrium problem because it gives such a beautiful ideal of how the market system, in its ideal incarnation, would work, and because it is a challenging mathematical puzzle that calls out a great deal of ingenuity in creating the various proposed solutions, or in poking holes in them. This in fact is characteristic of the way the intellectual world operates; attractive puzzles have a fascination for smart people, and the puzzles take on a life of their own, whether or not they are connected with other problems that people might want to solve. The upshot is that when economists come into a field like sociology, the tools that they bring with them are by no means the whole mathematical kit of general equilibrium (or even partial equilibrium) analysis; often they bring in a few much simpler ideas, which provide some insights, but which are no more advanced than the rival ideas used by practicing sociologists. In other words, economists outside their home field are traveling light; although they bring some fresh ideas, these ideas are not superior in sophistication to sociologists' theories, but only different.

Interestingly enough, at the same time economists have started to invade sociology, some sociologists have been doing a little conceptual invading in the other direction. As the connection between economics and sociology has attracted more attention, sociologists have questioned how markets really operate and whether the approach focusing on the general tendencies of competitive conditions is the most fruitful way to understand how people make economic exchanges. Most people buy or sell over and over again at the same stores, employers, or other economic units; they don't comparison shop or change jobs very often or very extensively, and hence they don't try out even a fraction of the competitive opportunities that are theoretically available. Some sociologists have suggested that the best way to examine such situations is by tracing their connections as social networks, since they resemble local ties rather than wide-ranging markets.

One of the most far-reaching ideas along this line comes from Harrison White, who suggests that what we call a market is usually a network of producers who monitor what each other are doing. For instance, clothing manufacturers watch each other closely, in order to see what sorts of styles are selling well this season. Producers not only imitate each other, they also try to distinguish themselves so that what each one sells is relatively unique. If a producer is successful in finding a distinct niche in the market, it does not have to compete with all the other producers, and the sales prices are not driven down by competition as they would be if everyone were selling the same thing. So a market is not simply a matching of supply with demand; it is more a matter of the suppliers (producers) trying to figure out how to sell goods that are similar to what has already been popular, without being so similar that the goods are in direct competition.

White's version of the market is more dynamic and innovative than the traditional economist's market, and in this respect it better matches the modern world. Another point of realism for White's social-network based market is that it explains why the leading edge of the market is usually in the tendency towards more luxurious and expensive goods—the style-conscious consumer society of today. And it helps explain a fact that has always been a sore point for traditional economic theory: why there is so much inequality of wealth in the capitalist system. For in traditional theory, competition should drive profits down to the lowest possible level; whereas in the network model, successful producers are those who find, at least for a while, niches in which their products are unique and so sheltered from competition. And when the competition catches up with their niche, the greatest wealth goes to those who have most quickly moved on to yet another product. Inequality and innovation are connected. For this reason, we should expect that our high-tech, innovative, consumer-oriented capitalism of today is not going to become any more egalitarian. It is this kind of insight that sociologists offer for understanding some economic issues, perhaps better than economists have done.

Harrison White shows us how a market may be organized so that competition is minimized, and exchange channeled into relatively narrow circuits. In this respect, his model resembles the split labor market theory we have examined above, and both types of theory help explain how market processes can result in inequality. Another modification of market economics is the so-called "market versus hierarchy" question. Oliver Williamson (who is an economist, but whose influence has been greatest outside his home discipline) pointed out that it is rational sometimes to leave the open market. From the point of view of pure market theory, buyers and sellers of labor (i.e., employers and employees) should always be free to enter and leave their particular exchanges if a better opportunity comes along; that is how employers would be able to purchase the cheapest labor force, and conversely workers would move to follow the highest wages. But in fact most labor markets do not bargain on a day-to-day basis, but enter into long-term employment contracts. Instead of constantly bargaining on the open market, workers and their employers enter into a relatively permanent hierarchy. Someone goes to work in an organization; they bargain about pay when they are hired, but once they are in, they follow orders rather than bargain over how much it will cost to comply in every single instance.

It is rational to move from the market to a hierarchy, Williamson theorizes, when there are high *transaction costs* associated with bargaining. If one had to spend a great deal of time and effort finding workers who are willing and able to do a job, then it is more rational to hire them for the long run. Transaction costs are highest where there is a great deal of potential for distrust, so that much effort must be put into checking on possible cheating by the other side. In addition, it is rational to leave the market when the services one wants to buy are relatively unique and only a few people can supply them, or when a good deal of training and cooperation in an job is necessary for workers to be productive. Where these conditions are lacking—such as hiring casual laborers to dig up a construction site—then the jobs stay on the day-to-day market. Where these conditions are present, jobs go off the market and into an organizational hierarchy.

James Coleman, in his big synthetic book, *The Foundations of Social Theory*, points out that not all rational patterns of exchange are markets. If the rational choice theory is correct, then every social institution is going to be shaped by the rational interests of the actors who put it together. This applies to the family, to the collective behavior of crowds, to government, and to any other kind of organization, as well as to the economic marketplace. Rational choice theory is much wider than economic theory; the latter is a branch of the former. This is in effect returning to the position of the earlier utilitarians; though the economy was obviously one of their favorite institutions, it was just one application of the utilitarian approach.

In fact, Coleman argues, the dominant fact about our modern society is not the market, but the existence of huge organizations. Government agencies, the military, schools and universities, big businesses: all these are large-scale bureaucracies. Individuals work in these organizations, but the organization itself is much more powerful than the individual. The only way that individuals can take on an organization is by forming another organization; consumers' groups, social movements, members of any constituency based on gender or ethnicity or anything else, are only effective when they too become organizations. We live in a world of organizations. Much of the modern economy consists of organizations buying and selling or loaning or borrowing money to and from each other, just as modern politics consists in organizations trying to influence one another or suing each other in the law courts.

Coleman shows how it is rational for individual persons to form organizations. (The argument here is not so very different from Williamson's formation of hierarchies out of markets.) In forming organizations, individuals give over some of their individual rights of action to the organization. They become part of the corporation's action, following its patterns and instructions, rather than their own immediate goals. But now a new form of rationality appears. The organizations become what Coleman calls "corporate actors." The corporation itself becomes a rational decision-maker, pursuing its own interests, trying to maximize gains and minimize costs. There is nothing mysterious about this; the corporate actor is guided by the top executive officers or the board of directors, but they are no longer acting merely as individuals pursuing their private interests; typically, the group of top executives or leaders push each other towards doing what they conceive is in the interests of the organization. This corporate identity is encouraged by modern Western law, which recognizes the corporation as a legal individual, a kind of fictional person that nevertheless has the rights of holding property and making transactions with other individuals in society.

The question now arises: are these big rational actors, the corporate actors, beneficial for our society? An early utilitarian might have naturally said yes, if he or she could come to accept that a corporation rising above the human individual is also an individual and would act in rational ways. But Coleman is living in a time when we have explored a good many paradoxes of rational behavior, so he asks whether these kinds of paradoxes do not show up at the level of corporate actors, and indeed whether there might even be some new problems associated with this kind of corporate individual. As we shall see, what Coleman says is in keeping with the tendency of modern utilitarians to see rather serious problems with the large-scale organizations of today's world.

First we need to take a look at the most powerful of these big organizations, the modern state.

The Rational Theory of the State

The most benevolent theory about the state from a rational choice point of view is that put forward by the philosopher John Rawls. Rawls wants to argue that it is rational to have a liberal policy that will help the disadvantaged; if there has been racial or gender discrimination in the past, or if social class advantages and disadvantages are passed along from parents, then the state ought to do something to compensate for these disadvantages. There should be affirmative action programs in education and hiring, or similar policies that put members of disadvantaged groups first in line, ahead of persons from groups that historically have been the privileged ones. This is not a new idea from the point of view of political ideologies, but it poses a puzzle for a thinker in the utilitarian tradition. The utilitarians have always argued from the starting point of the individual; for individuals to have equal chances, they have argued that the competitive marketplace should simply be open to everyone. The role of the government is not to favor members of any group, thereby interfering in the open competition, but to act as a neutral referee. The utilitarian position has been to trust in the open marketplace and the noninterventionist state.

Rawls, however, argues that it is rational for individuals to favor government intervention in favor of the disadvantaged and that this position is rational for everyone to hold, whether personally disadvantaged or not. His reasoning goes like this. Imagine that you are going to set up a state and will choose what sort of constitution it will have. You are doing this from behind a "veil of ignorance": that is to say, you have no idea of what position you will have in this future society, whether you will be rich or poor, black or white, male or female. From this neutral position, it is rational for you to choose the constitution that gives extra advantages to the disadvantaged, in order to compensate them and make them equal to everyone else. For you might be one of the disadvantaged persons, and in order to guard against this, it is rational to adopt this constitution.

Rawls's theory has attracted a good deal of controversy, but no general agreement that his argument is correct. One major flaw is that it ignores the neo-rationalist models of how human reasoning actually works. If the human being operates under bounded rationality, and satisfices rather than maximizes, one cannot expect that people will reason globally and hypothetically about which constitution they would prefer out of all the possible ones. The satisficing model says that people accept whatever arrangements happen to exist as long as these meet some minimal level of acceptability, and concentrate only on one thing at a time; they don't construct big philosophical models from scratch, but make modifications in what currently exists by dealing with the most pressing problem. One could say that this is what has actually happened in the years since the Civil Rights movement of the 1960s; it was only when race, gender, and other inequalities became big enough disruptions that these problems moved into the center of attention, and people were motivated to find a way to patch things up. If we don't do a very good job of creating solutions that solve these problems without generating further problems and controversies, that is not too surprising from the point of view of neo-rationalist theory; we never go back to zero and make fundamental changes, but only make local adjustments in response to emergencies, and hope that things will recede to a normal level of satisfactoriness. Rawls's approach describes an ideal rationality, which does not fit the way people actually operate.

That is not to say that many people might not be sympathetic, at some time in history, to the upshot of Rawls's program: i.e., to favor affirmative action for minorities or other sorts of compensation for disadvantages. But it is unlikely that they are doing it because they have gone through the kind of reasoning that Rawls lays out. Some people favor a compensatory program because it directly fits their self-interest as members of a disadvantaged group. For members of the privileged majority who go along with this, it is likely that they are swayed by a social movement that preaches altruism, not self-interest. Successful social movements preach for justice, taken as an emotionally compelling ideal in itself, rather than appealing to each individual's rational self-interested calculations. The fact that some people favor liberal-altruistic policies, while other people oppose them, indicates that Rawls's explanation in terms of universal human rationality will not tell us why people chose their positions on this issue. More likely, we have to look for an explanation of why people favor some social movements and oppose others.

On the whole, Rawls is rather an exception in his benevolent theory of the state. Most rational choice theories of politics do not paint a very pretty picture. One theory is that the state arose to provide "protection rent": i.e., that the key to the state is its control of armed force. People pay taxes (or historically, some form of tribute) to the government, as a kind of rent for living on safe premises; the state is a sort of landlord, not so much over the land itself, as over the peacefulness of the territory in which one lives. Paying the state is paying for protection against domestic crime and foreign invasion. But the state may extract quite a lot for this protection, since the state is a monopolist (or certainly tries to be, by keeping rival armed force out of its territory). Monopolies are not constrained by price competition from rivals; a citizen of a state cannot usually choose what state they want to buy their protection from. (This theory, we should notice, is like Weber's conflict theory of the state, which also proposes that the state is the monopoly of armed force over a territory, except that Weber adds the additional, non-economic point that the use of force claims to be legitimate.)

In this vein, recent historical sociologists have developed the analysis of how states have actually arisen and expanded. For instance Charles Tilly and others have shown that the medieval state was essentially the army, plus whatever taxation system could be developed to extract goods from the economy to support the army. I will not go into the complexities of these theories here; generally speaking, they are developed by theorists who are coming more from the conflict theory tradition than from the rational/utilitarian tradition. The reason I mention this research here is to indicate that there is a lot of evidence that is generally congruent with the rational/utilitarian argument that the state provides "protection rent." Furthermore, this historical sociology is useful in showing why the monopolistic state does not always squeeze the last drop of protection rent out of its population. The protection rent theory of the state makes the self-interest of the state rather a menace to the economic interests of ordinary citizens. But if the state is in the military business, so to speak, it can also go bankrupt if it runs its business in a profligate, spendthrift manner. Modern geopolitical theory shows for instance that states lose wars when they overextend their resources in fighting too many enemies, in too many directions, or too far away from home, and a state that loses a war is not in a very good position to demand protection rent. Similarly, the costs of wars and government expenditures in general can create a fiscal crisis in the state budget, and most of the great revolutions have come about (as we have seen from conflict theory) when the state is unable to pay its own personnel. So states that have lived by protection rent have also died, so to speak, by being inefficient landlords of the peace.

This is a comforting conclusion in a sense. Even if the state is a military monopolist, there are limits on how much it can extract from society. When states violate these limits, they lose their power. So we see that state crises give an opportunity for reform. This is one of the main ways historically in which democracies have arisen, and in which the rights of citizens against the encroachment of the state have been institutionalized. All this is in keeping with the neo-rationalist model of how people behave: satisficing, not maximizing; putting up with normalcy as long as it can be sustained, even if there is hypothetically a better way of doing things; turning attention to problems only when they get out of hand. The crisis-and-breakdown model of state democratization fits quite well with the picture of the neo-rational individual who takes drastic action only when emergencies arise.

The realistic picture of politics that is emerging is that people only intermittently make any large structural changes in the state; from time to time, in emergencies, these changes may move in the direction of democratization. But most of the time, politics is carried on in a routine, in which the self-interest of politicians and citizens alike leads to results that favor the interests of only a part of the population. The so-called economic theory of democracy argues that politicians are like businesses: they invest their promises of political action in order to attract voters so that they can become elected. The winning politicians are those who make promises that attract more people than the promises of rival politicians. This theory would seem to imply that the majority of the people will benefit from the government. One offshoot of this theory, however, proposes that the majority will tend to be as small as possible while still winning elections. This is the theory of the "minimum winning coalition." For instance, suppose a political party wins an election by a landslide. Now it has most of the vote, say 80 percent. But that means that the politicians and their supporters must share the spoils of victory among a relatively large group of people. If the winning coalition were smaller, say 51 percent, it could still win but would have fewer people it needs to share with. The theory of minimum winning coalition, then, says that all is not harmonious after a party wins a great victory and demolishes the opponents. Instead, after the victory the winners start to split, to fight among themselves, until a smaller winning coalition is formed. The rational self-interest of politicians thus keeps down the level of social harmony, even if a greater harmony of interests were possible.

The New Utilitarian Policy Science

James Buchanan, formulating a position called "public choice theory," has gone even further in drawing out some negative consequences of the utilitarian view of politics. Buchanan points out that politicians have an interest in becoming elected, so they will spend the government's budget on things that the voters will like, whether this is social security, medicine, education, defense jobs, or building construction in one's community. At the same time, citizens don't find it in their self-interest to pay taxes. The rational, self-interested politician resolves this conflict by government spending, but paying for it not by higher taxes but by borrowing—in other words by a budget deficit. This is rational for everyone concerned, but only in the short run. In the future, the debts must be repaid with accumulated interest, and the longer the deficit exists, the larger it grows. For the rational politician thinking of the present time, that may not make very much difference; he or she is elected by making voters happy today, whereas it will be somebody else in the future who will have to pay for the deficit. In short, the self-interest of the current generation is favored against the self-interest of the future generation.

Buchanan argues that the rational interests of politicians and voters cannot resolve this problem. The only way to bring the interests of future generations into current calculations is by changing the rules of the game. Buchanan thus favors a constitutional amendment that mandates a balanced budget and prohibits deficit spending. Now there are various controversies about the side-effects of such a policy (such as what it does to the short-term flexibility of government in emergencies). Leaving this aside, we may notice that Buchanan takes the utilitarian position up to a limit, and then steps onto another level. Traditionally, the utilitarians have regarded the government as a neutral referee, upholding the rules of the game of the economic marketplace. But now we have a theory of how government itself is a kind of competitive marketplace, a competition of politicians for votes. So the neutral referee, according to Buchanan, needs to be kicked up a notch; we need a meta-level above politics, in the form of a constitutional amendment, which will control the rules of the political game.

Here we see that Buchanan, from his distinctive angle, has hit again upon the problem that has existed throughout the utilitarian tradition. It is the problem of who guards the guardians, or how to construct the referee. This is the problem we have discussed above, of how self-interested individuals produce social solidarity or norms that provide for their collective interest. In terms of Buchanan's constitutional amendment, what will actually mobilize people so that they would vote for such an amendment? Wouldn't the rational voter be motivated to free ride, i.e., to keep up the status quo of deficit spending as long as he or she gets something paid by the government and doesn't have to pay taxes for it? Buchanan wants voters to step out of their skins as utilitarian rationalists on the individual level, to rise to a meta-level where they are concerned about the rationality of the collective level. But when do persons conceive of themselves as having interests on the individual level, and when do they switch to thinking of themselves as members of the collective, sharing interests with all? Is there a rational calculation that individuals can make to compare their interests as individuals with their interests as members of the collective? Again we come up against the same problem facing Rawls's theory of justice, even though we would call Rawls a liberal and Buchanan a conservative. To motivate people to make an idealistic decision beyond their immediate self-interest, one would seem to have to transcend the utilitarian frame of reference and appeal to an altruistic, emotion-laden social movement.

In James Coleman's theory, the problems found most generally throughout today's society are problems of this kind: the problem of individual responsibility in relation to collective institutions. The problem occurs on two levels, but the underlying issue is the same. On one level, there are issues regarding the lack of responsibility by individuals to others in their group: parents who are too busy with their own careers or their own happiness to keep a stable family or care for their children. On another level, there is the problem of corporate organizations: businesses that in their search for profit ignore what they are doing to the environment or to the public; government agencies that are concerned to protect their budgets and their jobs, irrespective of what the society needs or can afford. Analytically, these are specific instances of the same problem: a self-interested actor who imposes externalities upon others (i.e., consequences that others in the surroundings have to bear) without having to take into account the interests of others. In one case we are dealing on a smaller scale, with natural individuals such as parents and children in a family; in the other case we operate on a larger level, in which corporate actors themselves are the rational individuals.

Coleman's strategy for dealing with such problems is broadly similar for both cases. He does not propose a route, like Rawls or Buchanan, that would consist in somehow creating a new collective interest or set of rules, over and above individual interests. He does not argue that people and corporations ought to become more altruistic. Instead he wants to find ways to appeal to utilitarian interests to motivate social actors to do things that are more beneficial to others. Coleman seems to feel that it is more realistic to accept self-interested motivations and work with them than to look for an idealistic movement interpreted in the guise of a higher self-interest.

In the case of the family, Coleman argues as follows. At historical periods in the past, it was in the interest of parents to invest a lot of their energy and attention in making sure their children were brought up to become disciplined, productive members of society. Parents depended upon their children to care for them in their old age; lifetime comfort as well as social status depended upon having children who could manage the farm or the family business, or at any rate were successful enough in their own careers so that their aged parents could move in with them. But in our own society, the greater individualism of careers, plus the provision of old age pensions and insurance, has meant that parents have much less to gain from their children. There are few real incentives for parents to make sure their children stay out of trouble with the law, or that they do their schoolwork; for some parents, there is not even a minimal incentive to be home with one's children rather than leaving them alone. The result is that families don't do a very good job of socializing children, and this imposes externalities upon the rest of society: the costs of gangs and crime, the general inefficiency of education. Coleman showed, in a famous research study, that the involvement of parents in their children's education has a much stronger effect on how well the kids do in school than anything the school itself does. All these are external costs that someone else has to bear: crime, poor education, an alienated youth population are things that the community in general has to pay for, whereas the mother and father have their own immediate interests that make it rational for them to ignore their kids.

Coleman thinks it is unrealistic to expect that we will return to the old-fashioned family. It does no good to preach that we need to return to traditional values, if values do not determine what people do. The only realistic way to solve the problem is to appeal to interests in a new way. Thus Coleman suggests that we need new incentive schemes to make it worthwhile for people to put the effort into bringing up children. He argues, for instance, that it is rational for the government to calculate how much it is costing the taxpayer to combat gangs and crime and to pay for the welfare upkeep of school dropouts, as well as the income forgone by the drop in economic productivity. This is the amount that could be saved by investing in bringing up children. This amount in turn would become a fund to be used as incentives, offered to people who are willing to spend extra amounts of time in quality child-rearing. Coleman points out that sociologists could calculate which children, because of their family circumstances, were most likely to end up as a gang member or a school failure, and hence the amount of incentive would be scaled higher for the level of danger. Coleman speculates that these financial incentives could be offered to anyone who would contract to take on the care of these children—their own parents, or some other family or organization willing to make the effort—and they would be paid according to how well the children are doing in staying out of trouble, performing well in school, and so forth.

Coleman offers similar kinds of proposals at the level of corporate actors. If big companies, for instance, are not socially responsible, they could be restructured so that incentives bear directly upon the persons who control the damaging activities. Coleman suggests, for instance, that legal immunity could be lifted so that members of corporate boards become personally responsible for lawsuits against the behavior of their company. Another possibility would be to bring persons who are subject to externalities inside the company: the board could be made to include neighbors of the corporation who feel its environmental effects, consumers, and even respresentatives of children who are denied adequate family care because their parents' lives are taken over by corporate careers. Now, all of these proposals on Coleman's part are rather general and hypothetical at this time; a great deal of investigation would have to be done to work out how they could be implemented in detail—what side effects they would have, auxiliary problems that would arise, how the incentives would actually be brought to bear. It remains to be seen whether particular incentive schemes would actually bring about the benefits sought and be worth their cost.

The importance of Coleman's approach may be not so much in the specific proposals as in the general way of thinking about social issues. His stance attempts to be a realistic one. All right, he says, let us admit that people have selfish interests, that they don't calculate consequences very widely, and that in many cases they have no strong reason to pay attention to the effects of their actions on others. If we want to make policy changes that will really make a difference, we need to calculate how these will affect the incentives, the costs and benefits, for the individuals who are actually involved. This is a shift from the traditional utilitarian position, which believed that the free market was the best possible mechanism for optimizing the greatest good for the greatest number. At the same time, Coleman's approach does not simply reiterate the old left-liberal tradition that direct government intervention can solve problems by simply handing over goods from one group to another. The market does not establish a utopia, nor does avoiding the market and substituting a welfare state. What we need to be aware of is that individuals continue to be self-interested, no matter what circumstances we put them in, so we need to structure their self-interest in such a way that the results will be beneficial in the direction we intend.

Of all the current social theories, the rational/utilitarian tradition, in its modern incarnation, is most finely tuned to a way of making social policies work. The conflict tradition, with its tradition of conflicting movements and revolutionary upheavals, has a tendency to focus on the evils that exist, and the conditions that will bring about an uprising against them. Where conflict theory is weak is in explaining what will happen after the revolution, or after a successful movement has won some power. Its attitude tends to be: put the oppressed peoples in charge and everything will be great. At this point conflict theory stops being realistic. In their own ways, the other lines of social theory also tend to be vague about social theory. The Durkheimian tradition, with its emphasis on the conditions that produce solidarity and its ideals, doesn't see people as very capable of generating specific social results; its victories are symbolic and emotional rather than practical. The micro-interaction theories, with their emphasis on the shifting cognitive interpretations of social reality, are also not very good at specific social policies. They assume either that somehow a social belief will be created that people find satisfactory, or that people live in their own little worlds of cognitive reality-construction, like separate bubbles in a stream. The modern rational/utilitarians, for all their faults, nevertheless are on the forefront in attempting to apply sociological insights to propose policies that have a realistic chance of succeeding.

This is not to say that the theoretical basis of rational/
utilitarian theory is necessarily adequate yet to this task. We have
seen a consistent problem in the utilitarian tradition, on the level
of how to motivate people for collective action. Can the appeal to
interests alone motivate people to adopt great reforms, whether
this appeal is embodied in the legal codes advocated by Bentham,
in Adam Smith's freedom of the market, or in schemes for new
rules of the social game such as those proposed by Rawls, Buchanan, or Coleman? There is an element of pulling oneself up by
one's own bootstraps in these proposals, as long as one starts
from the isolated individual concerned for his or her own interests. As an alternative, we may still need to draw on the conflict
theory, which suggests that people fight for their interests rather
blindly, solving one problem but creating new ones. The other
alternative is the Durkheimian tradition of social solidarity, which
explains precisely the emotional links among people that rational/
utilitarian theory leaves out. To this alternative we now turn.

NOTES

1. Strictly speaking, we could trace some basic utilitarian ideas back
another half century to Thomas Hobbes. But Hobbes was in some ways
a more complicated thinker than Locke. Hobbes's argument that rational individuals should give up their sovereignty to a ruler, in order
avoid a war of all against all, is more similar to the "free rider" paradoxes of the 1960s than it is the benign social harmony outlined by the
utilitarians who followed Locke. So we begin with the latter.

2. From an economic viewpoint, the marriage itself is not something
that is produced; it is an exchange, through which something that has
been produced is being exchanged for something else.

3. It is sometimes argued that high-paying occupations require especially high talent, so that relatively few people could enter them. This
objection misses the point: it is not necessary that everyone in the world
could become a doctor, but rather than the number of people who have
the talent to do so is considerably larger than the number of doctors who
are enough to meet the demand for medical services. If, in fact, the
potential supply of doctors greatly exceeds the demand, then it would be
possible, in the absence of barriers to entry, for competitive pressures to

reduce the incomes of doctors. Similarly, if doctors did not monopolize the power to dispense antibiotic and other drugs by means of government licensing laws, price competition for such drugs would also bring lower prices, as well as less demand for the services of doctors.

4. These are commodities that tend to be addictive, or at least people are willing to continue to consume them even if the cost rises to quite high levels. It is for this reason that such commodities, when they are legal, are usually subject to high "sin taxes," such as the taxes that exist on tobacco and alcohol today. One might also add that all of these illegal commodities—alcohol during the 1920s, gambling at all times, drugs since the 1960s—have been associated in the subcultures of their users with excitement, an escape from routine, and a sense of rebellion against the dominance of ordinary society. Thus rigid law enforcement does not necessarily decrease demand; it actually increases the sense of excitement and rebellion, and hence the attractiveness of illegal commodities.

3: *The Durkheimian Tradition*

Sociology must not be a simple illustration of ready-made and deceptive truisms; it must fashion discoveries which cannot fail to upset accepted notions.
Emile Durkheim, 1909

We come now to the core tradition of sociology. I am labeling it after the name of Émile Durkheim, its most famous representative. It is sociology's most original and unusual set of ideas. The conflict tradition, too, has its novel impact. It begins in the revolutionary underground; it tears away the veil of ideologies. The world revealed is dramatic, conflictual, capable of erupting. Nevertheless the truth of this world is rather cold and bleak. The hidden realities turn out to be economics, resource mobilization, and the struggles of political organization. Not your everyday world of common belief, to be sure, but even more harshly mundane.

What we come to now, though, is a tradition of genuine excitement. Here, too, there is a surface and an underlying reality beneath. But this time the surface is symbol and ritual, the depths are nonrational and subconscious. This intellectual tradition focuses on themes of emotional forces, morality, the sacred, the religious—and declares that these are the essence of everything social. The Durkheimians take us into the jungle; only the jungle is ourselves, and we never escape from it. The tom-toms are beating, the vines entangling around us, emotional tides are sweeping us along—and this is no more than the magic show we call life.

SOME MAIN POINTS OF THE DURKHEIMIAN TRADITION

	Macro Wing		Micro Wing
1740–1770	Montesquieu		
1770–1800	revolutionary *philosophes*		
1800–1830	Saint-Simon		reactionary defenders of religion: De Bonald, De Maistre
1830–1860	Comte's Positivism		
	utilitarian influence: John Stuart Mill		
1860–1890	Herbert Spencer		crowd psychologists
			classicists and anthropologists: Frazer Fustel de Coulanges
1890–1920		Durkheim	anthropology of rituals: Mauss
1920–1960			Cambridge scholars of classical religions
	functionalists: Merton Parsons	Lévi-Strauss's structuralism	British social anthropology: Radcliffe-Brown Lloyd Warner
1960–1990		Bourdieu's cultural capital theory	Goffman's interaction rituals
			ritual and stratification: Bernstein Mary Douglas Collins
			Durkheimian sociology of science: Hagstrom Bloor
			sociology of emotions Scheff

If Durkheim's view of social life was exotic, one reason is because he made no distinction between sociology and anthropology. Institutionally the separation between the two areas was less sharp in the French university system than elsewhere. Durkheim and his followers used the term "ethnology" for the empirical description of tribal societies, whereas "sociology" meant the theoretical analysis of any society, tribal or modern. Durkheim saw the building of a sociological science as very much a collective enterprise, and his collaborative efforts centered on his journal, the *Année Sociologique*, which tried to synthesize the relevant research of each year. The main contents of the *Année* were reviews of anthropological studies plus articles of synthesis written by Durkheim, Marcel Mauss, Henri Hubert, Celestin Bougle, and others, singly or collaboratively. Durkheim was particularly interested in inducting the laws of all societies by the study of tribal and non-Western societies: partly because he thought they were simpler and more likely to reveal the "elementary forms" of social life, but also because they showed more plainly the nonrational sentiments and the symbolism that he believed were involved in every society. The strength of Durkheim and his followers was that they saw modern society through the lens of tribal society.

Sociology as the Science of Social Order

Not that Durkheim wished to be exotic or mysterious—far from it. He was the most scientific of all the great sociologists, and his anthropology played a crucial role in his science. The key to the scientific method is to compare, to look for the conditions under which something happens by contrasting them with the conditions under which it does *not* happen. This is the essence of the experimental method in laboratory science, and Durkheim was its strongest advocate in sociology. Put more precisely: the scientific method is the search for a set of mutually consistent causal generalizations that are based on the systematic comparison of conditions associated with a varying range of outcomes. Durkheim's study *Suicide* is much beloved by American methodologists because it set off the use of this method. Durkheim put suicide into the form of a variable by examining different rates of occurrence; he systematically tested alternative explanations that he wished to rule out by showing that they did not hold up comparatively; and he validated his own explanations by showing that certain factors (the condition of being single, or married but childless, or a Protestant) do increase the propensity for suicide.

But Durkheim was not merely interested in various factors that might be correlated with suicide or with not committing suicide. The state of being married, of having children, of belonging to a religion with a great deal of ritualism and community control of the individual (such as Catholicism or, even more so, Judaism) are all simply different indicators of the more general point Durkheim was trying to prove: that social structures of high intensity prevent the individual from killing him/herself. Durkheim was interested in the theoretical generalization, not in the empirical indicators per se. It is the generalization across various indicators that makes up a science; the synthesis of different parts of the theory is just as crucial as the method of systematic comparisons. Durkheim wanted to reveal the abstract skeleton beneath all aspects of society. His task, as Talcott Parsons would later put it, was an *analytical* one, not merely empirical interpretation. Durkheim actually regarded a certain level of suicide as perfectly normal, the comcomitant of a social structure that did not tightly constrain the individual. In the same way Durkheim shocked his contemporaries—who did not have his scientific detachment—by arguing that crime too is normal and even a necessary part of maintaining society.

Durkheim chose suicide to study because it is at the opposite extreme from *social solidarity:* the case where the social bonds are so weak that the individual finds life meaningless and forcibly removes him/herself from it. Durkheim wished to demonstrate the power of social ties; because these are usually taken for granted when things are going normally, one must compare normal conditions with those in which they break down. Hence, it is hardly to the point to criticize Durkheim (as some commentators have done) for failing to explain all the psychological and individual factors that move someone to commit suicide in each particular case. Durkheim was not interested in suicide at all, but in showing how the conditions for normal social integration work. Suicide merely served as a convenient comparison, a negative screen to set off this positive foreground. As Durkheim stressed elsewhere, the forces that hold society together are invisible. One learns about them when they are broken, like walking into a plate-glass window.

Durkheim used this method over and over again. He was interested in anthropology because it enabled him to show varying structural conditions by their contrast with modern social forms. He argued that the basic contents of sociology should be historical: only by taking a long sweep of time and space could one derive enough comparative leverage to see the conditions determining such large-scale structures as the overall form of society itself. Unfortunately Durkheim himself did relatively little comparison of real historical societies; because of his belief in a linear evolution, he felt he could substitute tribal societies as examples of earlier forms of our own society. But this is an empirical shortcoming of Durkheim's work, not an error in his conception of the scientific method.

Durkheim represents the central sociological tradition not only because he formulated its key method, but also because he made sociology a distinctive science with its own lawful generalizations. Auguste Comte coined the term "sociology" and envisioned the possibility of this science; Durkheim carried onward some of Comte's ideas, and achieved the first success in getting sociology organized as an intellectual discipline. The Durkheimians *are* literally the "sociological" tradition because they are the ones who called themselves by that name.

Comte had argued that sociology is the "Queen of the Sciences," by which he meant that the science of society came last, after all the other physical and biological sciences were established. Society, because it is closest to us, is the hardest for us to study objectively. Hence, science began with astronomy, dealing with objects that are farthest away, next came down to earth with physics, and then gradually crept closer to us through chemistry and biology. Comte did not mean that the laws of sociology subsumed those of the disciplines that came before and "below" in the hierarchy; in fact Durkheim was to argue that this was not possible because each discipline deals with an emergent level of organization that has structural laws in its own right. Comte wished, instead, to stress that sociology was the most important science because its application would correct all social evils and create a perfect society. Though Durkheim was not as utopian as this, he, too, believed that sociology was like medical science and that it should develop laws to distinguish between the normal and the pathological states of the social organism. This aspect of Durkheim's theory, however, is antithetical to conflict theory. Instead of trying realistically to understand the contending interests that make up any real society, Durkheim condemns some of them (the side he wasn't on) as merely pathological.

What Durkheim was able to achieve of lasting value was to cut through to a basic question of sociology: What holds society together? Parsons later referred to this as the problem of social order. As usual for Durkheim, it is not merely a philosophical question, but one to be decided empirically by the method of systematic comparison. We do not simply ask why there is order rather than chaos, but examine different kinds and degrees of social order and look for their causes and correlates. It is a search for the basic mechanism or, if one prefers a different image, for the glue that holds things together. The abstract question can be unpacked into a host of subsidiary questions dealing with all the different kinds of social patterns that can possibly exist. But it also unifies sociology around a quest for a general theory rather than merely a set of investigations of social problems or historical particulars. Whatever specific mechanisms we find should all relate back to a more fundamental mechanism of which these specific mechanisms are variants. Durkheim not only argued that sociology should search for such a mechanism, but he believed he had found it.

DURKHEIM'S LAW OF SOCIAL GRAVITY

Durkheim's key explanatory factor is social morphology, the structural relationships among people. The essential laws of sociology show how variations in the patterns of social interaction determine variations in people's behavior and beliefs. All this is quite concrete. Society determines the individual, not as some vague abstraction, but precisely as the individual is in some structural situation in relation to other individuals. There is nothing mysterious about this: by structure, Durkheim means the actual, physical pattern of who is in the presence of whom, for how long, and with how much space between them. Differences in this social density have profound effects on people's ideas and moral sentiments, hence, on their capacity for rational thought, bargaining, suicide, and anything else one cares to examine.

Durkheim referred to his sociology as the physics or physiology of society. The basic determining factors are the structural relationships among individuals, not the individuals themselves. Historical change happens mechanically, independent of individual wills, by a kind of "law of gravitation of the social world." Individuals develop progressively more specialized roles: not because they simply invent them, but because of the growth of population and its migration into cities plus developments in the technology of transportation and communication. These two changes in the social structure bring about a "progressive concentration of societies". They diminish the spaces between groups and bring more people into interaction with each other. Notice that Durkheim does not say anything at this point about the quality of the interaction; bringing larger numbers of people into more frequent contact with each other has powerful effects on everyone exposed to this situation. These variations in *social density* are the key determinant in every aspect of Durkheim's theory.

We can see this happen on both a large and a small scale. The structure of the entire society is determined by how large a population there is, how spread out it is across the territory, and what means of communication exist that bring about intermittent contacts. Where all these factors make the social density low, groups exist as isolated segments with relatively unspecialized roles among themselves. One can imagine a set of small tribes or isolated farm communities here and there, each relatively self-sufficient; each group has to produce virtually everything it needs, hence, its members are relativly unspecialized, performing many kinds of tasks for themselves. Where there is a high social density, the structure changes towards a complex division of labor. This social density can occur, recall, either by crowding large numbers of people into cities or by bringing people who are physically dispersed into contact by more transportation and communication (or both factors simultaneously). When this happens, social roles become more specialized; individuals produce only small components of what they need and exchange them with others. The entire society becomes more interdependent at the same time that individuals are becoming more different from each other.

Durkheim's conception of this is not necessarily benign; he believes that it is competition that motivates individuals to seek specialized niches when social density increases. Although Durkheim's tone does not sound at all like Marx and Engels discussing capitalism, nevertheless they are talking about the same thing. Durkheim is merely viewing the process from a much greater height of abstraction and with a good deal more detachment regarding its human consequences. The division of labor was one of Adam Smith's major concepts in formulating economics, and the competitive drive to specialization is also present in Marx (who, however, interpreted it as a form of alienation with the individual losing the capacity to be a jack-of-all-trades). Durkheim, however, is claiming a point that is even more general than that of Marx; he is implying that even if capitalism, the private property system, were overthrown, the socialism that replaced it would continue to have its own form of a complex division of labor, driven by the same structural factors of social density and the same competitive efforts to find specialized niches. These might take the form of specialized positions in socialist bureaucracies, political parties, and the like, but would nevertheless continue to exist. (Max Weber, incidentally, made much the same point in forseeing a socialist revolution in Russia.) The historical facts of the twentieth century would seem to bear out Durkheim.

The general argument, then, is that the physical aspects of structure determine the social aspects of structure. They also determine the mental and moral part of society as well. Thus, comparing societies with low versus high social density (small tribal societies or isolated rural groups vs. complex urbanized societies), Durkheim points out that in the former people's ideas are more concrete and particular, whereas in the latter they are more abstract and general. Isolated groups tend to focus on the concrete details of things; in their religions, the gods and spirits are usually visualized as particular people, animals, or the like. History is described in the form of myths because people have little capacity for abstracting general causes. In a complex urbanized society, on the other hand, the personification of social and natural processes gives way to abstract concepts; people talk about inflation, the balance of payments, or the prospects for medical breakthroughs and even their conception of religion recedes into an abstract conception of a Supreme Being that is beyond mere human personality, or sometimes even into pure morality.

Durkheim of course is sketching a large generalization. It is not necessarily true that everyone in a modern society thinks equally in terms of abstract ideas. These rationalistic and abstract conceptions are most likely to be used by members of the specialized professions and managers of the complex bureaucracies, whereas the lower classes are more likely to think in terms of particular personalities (albeit the cult of movie stars and other entertainment figures rather than ancient myths) and to hold to an anthropomorphic, magical conception of religion. But these variants fit into Durkheim's theory if we bear in mind that not everyone in society is equally exposed to the effects of what Durkheim called its social density. It is those people who are in the most specialized positions and those involved in the long-distance contacts coordinating the different parts who have the most abstract ideas (the professionals and managers), whereas it is the lower classes who are most localized in smaller enclaves, making up what Herbert Gans referred to as little peasant villages inside the framework of a modern city. Although Durkheim does not mention social classes, his theory is nicely applicable to understanding their differences. It even offers a theoretical explanation of the phenomenon Marx and Engels noted in regard to the stratification of the means of mental production: why the peasants of rural France and Germany were able to think of politics only in terms of religious beliefs or the crude modern mythology of nationalism and its war heroes. For it is precisely these isolated rural groups that produce a concrete, nonabstract consciousness as the result of their very structure.

Durkheim's principle that the physical density of society determines behavior and ideas holds at the level of smaller groups as well as for the whole society. His major explanation of suicide, for example, is that groups that have a higher social density have less likelihood that their members will kill themselves. This is because the social structure itself creates a kind of cocoon around the individual, making him or her less individualistic, more a member of the group. With higher social density, the meaning of life is attached to participation in the group, not to one's own wishes. The local social structure, in other words, has a moral and emotional effect. It is where this structure is loosened that the individual becomes more capable of committing suicide.

How is this moral cocoon formed? Durkheim eventually traced the mechanism to what may be called social rituals. These are most apparent in religion, but once one sees the basic structure, it can be picked out everywhere, including in the interactions of everyday life. A ritual is a moment of extremely high social density. Usually the more people that are brought together, the more intense the ritual. But it also heightens the contact; by going through common gestures, chants, and the like, people focus their attention on the same thing. They are not only assembled, but they become overwhelmingly conscious of the group around them. As a result, certain ideas come to represent the group itself by becoming its symbols. The tabooed objects of the primitive tribe, the altar of a religion, the flag of a modern political ritual—for that matter, the football team of a college crowd—takes on a sacred significance, transcending the ordinary and enforcing respect.

Durkheim referred to this aspect of interaction as moral density, an added element beyond mere physical density. It is not only the sheer numbers of people in contact that makes a difference, but the extent to which they have "a common life." Suicides are prevented, not by living in an impersonal dormitory amidst many other human bodies, but by living in a family or some other *ritualized* group that goes through periodic formalities to focus the attention of the individual on the group itself. Earlier in his career, Durkheim argued strongly that ideas do not determine social structure, but the other way around. Later, he began to give ideas somewhat more autonomy. We can see this in the way that a ritual is not merely the sheer copresence of people in a place—though that is a necessary condition—but a further, mental element, of focusing attention on the same thing. Families with certain religious beliefs are less likely to have suicides because the belief itself is a kind of mental current flowing through people and reminding them of the group.

Nevertheless ideas are only partially autonomous in this system. It is true that society cannot exist without ideas. But these ideas are efficacious precisely because they are social, because they remind individuals of where their memberships and loyalties lie. Durkheim referred to them as "collective representations." They are best thought of as charged particles, circulating among people and lodging for a while in their individual minds, but particles that originated in group rituals. Not that human consciousness doesn't exist; but it is those moments when people focus their consciousness on the group— which is to say, on the situations of high social density that make up a ritual—that their consciousness becomes a powerful instrument for directing their social lives. People do not have to be constantly in the presence of other people for society to have its influence. Ideas carry over the effect of society when people are between contacts, or when their contacts are low key rather than highly ritualized. Symbols are necessary for society, but they also grow out of it. It is worth reminding ourselves that there is nothing mysterious about this. Ideas are produced and charged with social significance at certain times and places where social rituals take place; then individuals carry these ideas around with them, exchange them with others in conversation, and use them to guide their own thinking and make their own decisions until these ideas are brought back again to other situations that charge up their ideas with further social significance. We can visualize individuals moving around the physical environment and picking up special moral "charges" whenever they get into certain kinds of group situations in which they strongly focus on each other. Just how long and how frequently people are in these kinds of situations has a crucial effect in shaping each individual.

Durkheim's model, thus, gives us a two-level world. We think inside our social ideas, and these ideas form the contents of our consciousness. We do not see the symbolic significance of our social ideas because we take them for granted. They are a kind of glass through which we see the universe and which we don't even notice until it is broken by some social disruption. Even when that happens, we tend to react by punishing the disrupting person, instead of paying attention to the fact that there is a glass wall around ourselves. Thus, Durkheim depicts society as having a conscious, superficial level and an unconscious structure within which the real determinants operate. We think ourselves rational, masters of our own destinies; in fact our rationality itself is given to us by the social structure we inhabit, a structure that forms us to think in one particular way rather than another.

The "unconscious" level in Durkheim's theory is not mysterious or obscure. It is the morphology of social structure, the "social physics" of the physical density of the group that is spread out across the landscape; its pattern in time is people coming together and drifting apart in little rituals of highly focused attention. We are in this social structure and are determined by it, but we do not notice it because we are too busy going ahead with the details of our lives. Durkheim was a severe critic of utilitarian conceptions of psychology or economics that declare people simply move about making rational choices for rewards and punishments, investments and payoffs. Not that people may not try to do this at times, but that is only the surface of society. As we shall see, Durkheim proved that society could not possibly be held together in that way; rationality always has a nonrational foundation from which it emerges.

Durkheim also differs from Marx and Engels on this point. In general, the conflict theorists also regard society as having two levels. One level is the real structure of social conflict and domination, be it economic, political, or organizational; the other level is the ideology that masks the depths of our consciousness and is itself produced by the material means of mental production. But the conflict theorists attempt to tear off the veil, to reveal the realities beneath. Their aim tends to be a more perfect society of the future in which ideologies will no longer exist. Durkheim however implies that this is not possible. If moral beliefs are necessary to society, then to expose their basis does no good, they will always return in some form. If some are delegitimated by the revelation, others will nevertheless arise according to the inevitable laws of social structures and ritual interactions. Even Durkheimian sociology remains part of the same social world, though it gives a reflexive vantage point on it.

Two Wings: The Macro Tradition

Durkheim's sociology applies both to the large-scale macrostructure of society and to the small-scale microinteractions or rituals. This makes the Durkheimian tradition particularly central in sociology. Neither of the other major traditions has this breadth. The microinteractionist tradition, which we will examine in chapter 4, has little of use to say about the macrostructure and sometimes even denies that it exists. The conflict tradition on the other hand is primarily a macroanalysis with its home base in large-scale historical processes. It is true that there are microelements in it: Marx had his theory of alienation, and Weber wrote on the method of *verstehen*, defining sociology by the subjective understanding of social meanings. Actually these have had little impact on microsociology. Marx's vision of alienation really has nothing to do with face-to-face interaction, but it is a philosophical conception of the way the individual relates to the entire macrostructure of capitalism. And Weber's *verstehen*, although seeming to point towards the microworld, it was never used by him in that way. Instead, he used it to justify looking at the world through the eyes of the Protestant ethic or other religious outlooks: a subjective viewpoint, all right, but not a micro one because it has nothing to do with how people react to particular situations. Weber's *verstehen* only meant in practice that one should try to understand people's religious or other philosophies. The theory of situations and their structures, as well as the way these determine people's ideas and beliefs, is worked out in Durkheim but not in Weber.

There are two wings to the Durkheimian tradition, corresponding to a macroemphasis or a microemphasis. Most of Durkheim's forerunners were macrosociologists like Montesquieu, Comte, and Spencer. It is Durkheim himself who added a microapplication by discovering the theory of rituals (with help from Fustel de Coulanges and some anthropologists). The Durkheimians thus ended up with two wings, one coming through Durkheim's macrolevel theory of the division of labor and the social structure generally and proceeding forward to Talcott Parsons and the functionalists. The other wing proceeds from Durkheim's followers in social anthropology, including his nephew Marcel Mauss, and finds a modern application on the microlevel through such sociologists as Erving Goffman and Basil Bernstein. As I have mentioned, it is this part of the Durkheimian lineage that ends up providing a microunderpinning for a theory of class cultures. There is also an aspect of the Durkheimian tradition that tries to weave the microlevel and the macrolevel back together, especially through the theory of exchange and alliance developed by Mauss and Claude Lévi-Strauss, through Pierre Bourdieu's theory of cultural capital and my own theory of interaction ritual chains. We examine first the macrolineage.

MONTESQUIEU, COMTE, AND SPENCER ON SOCIAL MORPHOLOGY

Durkheim defined his own predecessors when he wrote in his doctoral thesis of 1892 about the contribution of Montesquieu to the founding of sociology. Durkheim saw Montesquieu's *L'esprit des lois* (*The Spirit of Laws*, 1748) as the beginning of the science of society. This work follows the fundamental scientific method of searching for general laws instead of writing about history as a record of famous men. Individual instances are infinite and nothing can be said about them except by reducing them to types and then making comparisons to understand their causes. Montesquieu is also worthy of praise because he was the first to understand society is more than the state. Montesquieu is usually considered to be a political philosopher who enunciated the doctrine (which impressed Thomas Jefferson and the founders of the United States) that the best state should have a separation of powers to prevent the abuse of authority. But Durkheim argues that Montesquieu's point is far more general than this.

Montesquieu classified societies into two main types: the old Greek and Roman republic versus the contemporary European monarchy. At its best the latter had a separation of powers among the nobility who controlled the law courts and the municipalities (from which class Montesquieu himself came), the central authority of the crown, and the spiritual power of the church. Durkheim argued that this separation into specialized institutions was not just part of the political structure of the monarchies of early modern Europe, but was the general tendency of all societies with an advanced division of labor. Durkheim thus read back into Montesquieu the basic framework of his of own *The Division of Labor in Society*, which he was about to publish a year later (1893). Montesquieu's ancient republics are what Durkheim called the "mechanical solidarity" type: societies that are small and dispersed over large areas. Within each group, the individual is subordinated to the community. The basic sentiment of this type of society is what Montesquieu called the striving for "virtue," obeying all the old sacred rites and sacrificing oneself for one's family and one's city. Montesquieu's monarchies represent the more modern end of the continuum in which societies have become large, densely settled, and internally specialized and coordinated. The characteristic sentiment of these societies is what Montesquieu called "honor," which is equivalent to Durkheim's spirit of "individualism," the striving to exalt the self.[1]

Durkheim believed that Montesquieu was on the right track in seeing population size as a prime cause of these differences in social structure and prevailing cultural ideals. (Montesquieu had a more famous explanation of the differences among societies in terms of their climate, but Durkheim, who refuted this type of explanation easily in his analysis of suicides, regarded this explanation as an insignificant part of the argument.) For this reason, Montesquieu merits the title of originator of the lineage of

Durkheimian sociology—at least he did in Durkheim's eyes, and we have no reason to contradict him.

The "official" founder of sociology is Auguste Comte. He formulated the idea of society as a system in its own right, analogous to a biological organism but definitely not reducible to the laws of biology. Comte also had a dynamic element that Montesquieu lacked. Whereas Montesquieu merely compared different types of societies "horizontally," so to speak, Comte put them into evolutionary stages of development. Comte also was the first to take an explicitly scientific attitude towards society and to induct its laws. But Durkheim criticized Comte for believing that he had already completed the science of sociology and that its laws were summed up in the so-called "law of three stages"—Comte's belief that societies pass from the military to the legal to the industrial stage, with concomitant changes in beliefs from religion to metaphysics to science, and in moral attachments from the family to the state and finally to all of humanity. It was obvious to Durkheim that Comte was primarily enunciating a utopian doctrine; Comte had pointed the way to sociological science, but the work of building it still remained to be done.

Herbert Spencer was widely regarded as Comte's successor, who freed sociology from Comte's religous quirks and gave sociology some serious content. Durkheim agreed; in fact his model of societies evolving from isolated segments to a complex division of labor is essentially that of Spencer. But Spencer had only gathered facts to illustrate a philosophical principle. He had already enunciated at the beginning of his system the generalization that everything evolves from a state of chaotic, similar particles to a condition of differentiated interdependence. Spencer applied this to the evolution of both the universe and biological organisms before going on to show that it applied to human societies as well. Durkheim wanted, instead, that the principles be established as the result of empirical comparisons and that these should show the causal conditions that brought about one outcome or another.

Durkheim also had a deeper criticism. Spencer thought society was like an organism in that it followed organismlike laws of differentiation of functions, but this was only an analogy. So far so good, as Durkheim also held that it was no more than an analogy. But Durkheim believed that society was a psychic unity (he first called this the "collective conscience," later the "collective representations"): the currents of ideas and emotions that are generated when people interact and that constrain individuals from outside. On this point, though, Spencer was a methodological individualist. He held that society had no central consciousness (unlike an organism) and that such consciousness existed only in individuals; individuals in fact followed their own rational self-interest, forming society by entering into contracts to exchange with one another. In this respect Spencer was a typical British Liberal, in the nineteenth-century sense of the term. He regarded the society of individual liberty and the open capitalist market as the best form of society; he also preferred that societies move from lower forms of coercive regulation towards a contractual system of laissez-faire.

Durkheim regarded Spencer's system, in this respect, as biased by his politics and also scientifically naive. Not only does the structure have laws of its own, which hold independently of whatever individuals may choose. Even more fundamentally, individual choice could not possibly hold society together. A combination of rational individuals leads only to a war of all against all. Spencer held a more benign view; he regarded modern society as emerging from a competition on the market guided by freely made contracts. But Durkheim asked how people could have a contractual society unless they trusted one another to *uphold* their contracts because the advantage would always go to the side that cheats. The contractual society of the utilitarians is a myth, and can exist only on the basis of a precontractual solidarity. Durkheim attempted to show how these nonindividualistic, moral feelings are produced by different forms of the social structure itself.

The comparative/historical analysis in *The Division of Labor in Society* was one prong of Durkheim's attack. Another was his study of suicide, which he based on comparisons of the statistical rates in different groups. This material was useful for showing how the intensity of group structure affected the individual. It also, in Durkheim's mind at least, demonstrated the existence of structures over and above the individual, by the very fact that statistical rates remain constant for long periods of time over an entire group. The birth rate is about the same from year to year, even though it is different people who contribute to it each time; and the same holds for suicides and many other examples. Durkheim is thus the founder of statistical sociology, although it did not really get steadily under way until the American survey research institutes of the 1940s.[2]

After Durkheim's death in 1917, his sociology tended to split in two directions. The microdirection was taken up by British and French anthropologists and eventually brought to the United States a generation later. Durkheim's macrosociology was more immediately picked up. His *Suicide* was touted as a methodological guidepost for statistical sociology in the 1950s. The most prominent advocates of Durkheimian sociology, however, were the functionalist theorists, Robert Merton and Talcott Parsons.

MERTON, PARSONS AND FUNCTIONALISM

Robert Merton formalized the functional method: to look at any social institution in the light of what contribution it makes to upholding the social order. Durkheim had made sociology a two-level inquiry, showing how the surface of our beliefs and actions is determined by a structural basis below. Merton interpreted the structural basis as a tendency of the society to maintain itself. There are *manifest functions*, which are results that people consciously try to attain, and *latent functions*, which are produced by the action of the social system itself. For example, the corrupt "machine politics" of American cities resisted all efforts of reformers to clean it up, because it served certain implicit functions for ordinary people who benefit from the machine more than they do from the official bureaucracy espoused by the reformers. The same type of analysis can be applied to any institution: if it exists, it must be serving some function, which is the business of the sociologist to ferret out.

This type of analysis at one time had considerable appeal, especially around the 1950s. It motivates sociologists to look beneath the surface. Sometimes, as in Merton's analysis of the political "machine", it points up the fact than an official view of what is a "social problem" is really only one group's view-point, whereas other people involved actually benefit from the situation. But the functionalist terminology keeps the insight from going any further. Instead of seeing that the big-city "machine" involved a fight between different interest groups and social classes, it diverted attention from the structure of conflict into a more abstract judgment that the institution served some "latent function." To be sure, in this sense one can always find a function for anything. But to talk about func-tions and the maintainance of social order is misleading if one stops there. It is not the whole society whose functions are being met by each particular arrangement, but each group has its own version of social order that it is are trying to uphold. In this sense Merton's functionalism has operated to obscure the clarity offered by the conflict viewpoint on society. Kingsley Davis and Wilbert Moore, for instance, argued in a famous functionalist theory (1945) that stratification and inequality sim-ply are mechanisms to ensure optimal social efficiency by put-ting the most qualified people in the most important positions.

Merton and his followers, however, have sometimes had to admit that not everything works out for the best for every-one. For this they coined the term "dysfunctions" to go along with "functions." Unfortunately this terminology does not get us very far. It merely puts a value judgment on it, admitting that things can be bad instead of good, but it misses Durk-heim's central point that sociology ought to show the condi-tions under which structures produce one thing rather than another. To go around and label things as functional does not answer the question of why certain structures happen to exist to serve that function rather than something else. Defenders of functionalism used to argue that this question could be answered without leaving their framework by analyzing the bases of "functional alternatives." Unfortunatly this has mostly been an empty promise because little of this comparative work has been done. As we have already seen, the main practi-tioners of the comparative art have been conflict sociologists. The functional method at its best is too vague to do more than goad one towards looking for explanations. In actual practice its proponents have tended to give the most benign interpretations of social institutions whenever possible. Their sociology of science claims to reveal an ideal, self-correcting instrument for the attainment of truth; their sociology of the professions takes their altruistic claims at face value instead of seeing them as ideologies for the interest of these monopolistic groups. For these reasons, it is not surprising that functionalism has fallen into disfavor since the political mood became less conservative after the 1950s.

Talcott Parsons produced a more macro theory than Merton's "middle-range" functionalism. For Parsons the key entity was always the social system as a whole, and he developed an extremely complex analysis of categorizing its various functional sectors and subsectors. His work was full of charts, dividing boxes into cells and then drawing arrows between them to show various functional interchanges. Though the basic conception of society is Durkheimian, Parson's method is more like that of people whom Durkheim himself criticized. For Parsons did not give the causes of anything, but merely carried out the preliminary work of mapping out the conceptual scheme. In effect he gave only a description of society at a very abstract level rather than an explanation of it, just like Durkheim's German contemporary Albert Schaeffle, who presented great volumes of information about societies all neatly categorized according to what part of the "body" it was analogous in the great "social organism." Parsons was a good deal more abstract than Schaeffle and other nineteenth-century sociologists, and he spoke about "goal attainment," "pattern maintainance," and other functions with rather more picturesque metaphors such as society's nerves, brain, and so forth. In this respect Parsons was more like the formal sociologists who followed Simmel, as well as other American theorists of the 1930s such as Robert MacIver, who also gave lengthy sets of terminology for classifying every aspect of society.

To the extent that Parsons's system has some content rather than serving as a gigantic grid for categorizing things, it is at the extremely macrolevel. Parsons's societies are not static, and the most dynamic aspect of his system is its long-term historical vision. Parsons argued, following Durkheim, that societies could not be held together rationally. He interpreted this to mean that the whole society has a set of values that are inculcated into individuals. (Various structures have the function of carrying out this value socialization: initially the family, later also the church, and then the educational system.) The basis of historical change, as far as Parsons is concerned, is changes in basic values. Exactly how this happened is a bit of a mystery, a kind of pulling oneself up by one's own bootstraps or even something very much like divine intervention.

Concretely, Parsons used Max Weber's comparative religions to argue that world history is driven by a succession of different religious world views. Initially there were tribal societies with their particularistic symbol systems, that merely reinforced the traditional routine. Then came the great breakthrough into the "world religions," which separated the gods from the world and put spiritual power in some transcendental realm, called Heaven, Nirvana, or some equivalent. This transcendental realm provided a leverage point to focus human striving and enable people to transform their own world into something different. Parsons interpreted Weber to mean that Christianity generated much more social leverage than Buddhism, Hinduism, Confucianism, Taoism, or Islam, all of which ended up reinforcing the static social order rather than changing it. Hence, Christianity alone, and especially its most activist form, Protestantism, generated the value system that ended up creating the modern world.

In a sense, Parsons' explanation of historical change is a gigantic version of Weber's "Protestant Ethic and the Spirit of Capitalism" attached to a Durkheimian macrotheory of society. This aspect of Parsons is probably his most enduring contribution. This is not to say it will necessarily turn out to be right, but it has attracted a good deal of attention in the last few years, especially in Germany, where theorists such as Wolfgang Schluchter and Jurgen Habermas have tried to analyze history as a long-term evolution of human rationality. It should be borne in mind, though, that this interpretation picks out the most idealistic side of Weber and ignores the conflict model, just as Parsons picked out from Durkheim the most functionalist and moralistic side. Durkheim above all regarded himself as a scientist formulating the laws by which the material structures of human interaction produce certain ideas and emotions, which in turn circulate through the system. He would not have been sympathetic to Parsons's effort to show that history follows from certain religious ideas that mysterously appear on the human stage at certain points. For Durkheim religion was explained by the ritual interactions that produced its ideals, not vice versa. Durkheim's theory is much more compatible with a materialistic theory that proceeds through social conflict and physical changes in the pattern of social interaction, than it is to a set of idea-driven stages as set forth by Parsons.

It is true that in general Durkheim himself, like Parsons and Merton, tried to ignore or downgrade conflict and domination in society. They all shared a benign view of the world, one in which conflict is secondary and coercion is interpreted either as serving the good of the whole society or as a temporary and pathological condition. Parsons wrote some illuminating pages on Nazi Germany, for example, but he regarded it as the aberration of a passing stage, a country that tried to modernize too rapidly from a traditional base and, hence, provoked mass psychological reactions to the strain of change. For Parsons all societies eventually evolved toward democracy because this is the most advanced "functionally differentiated" stage. Unfortunately this smacks of wishful thinking. In general Parsons and his collaborators tended to regard any social dissatisfaction or upheaval as a temporary strain of social change. The protests about "conformity" and "consumerism" in the 1950s, Winston White argued, were simply misunderstandings that American society was becoming more functionally differentiated. This raised the level of social efficiency in every sphere; the family and specialized social groups were each able to carry out their own function better—for instance, socialization and inculcating values ("conformity") or producing more goods and more time to consume them ("consumerism"). A little later Parsons explained away the student revolts of the 1960s as simply the temporary response to the further upgrading of specialized educational training; our more differentiated society was demanding longer years in school, and this created a temporary strain as people had to adjust to new concepts of childhood and adulthood.

One can see that this would have been regarded as a species of conservative ideology: whatever happens, it is all for the best, or a temporary stage on the way to long-term improvement. The extent to which this ideology is grounded in the Durkheimian tradition has made it much less popular in recent years than the various kinds of conflict or microinteractionist theory. Nevertheless I want to show now that the Durkheimian tradition is not exhausted by this macro-wing, with its implicit conservatism and its lack of real causal explanations. Although Parsons and Merton tended to take every institution at its most favorable social image, Durkheim himself was in a good position to explain how ideologies are generated. His microsociology of rituals gives a mechanism by which the social group—not some disembodied society-as-a-whole—produces religious and other beliefs that cloak its practices with legitimacy. Durkheim's society is more like an arena of witch doctors practicing their magic over people's minds than it is like the altruistic professions and public servants the functionalists like to depict. Durkheim's theory of rituals and symbols is more conducive to a realistic explanation of the inflation in educational credentials that characterized the student disillusionment with the educational system in the 1960s and 1970s, and the cynicism that went along with grade inflation in the 1980s, than Parsons's functionalist ideology.

The Second Wing: The Lineage of Social Anthropology

Durkheimian ideas have been especially powerful, not so much as applied to the structure of the entire society, but to particular group practices within it. It is this aspect of Durkheimian thought that has been so influential in social anthropology. It brought about an entire British school going by that name, led by A. R. Radcliffe-Brown. They were *social* anthropologists by contrast to either the Germans and Americans who concentrated on describing the culture, or the physical anthropologists who concentrated on measuring and classifying human races. Durkheim reinforced their interest in looking at the social structure as primary, and his theory of rituals gave the social anthropologists a method for explaining how cultural ideas and practices are determined. The Durkheimian lineage is even more obvious in French anthropology, where his nephew Marcel Mauss led the field after Durkheim's death, followed by Claude Lévi-Strauss in continuing this tradition.

Anthropology goes back before Durkheim, but it was only in his day that it was crystalizing into a discipline and acquiring a theoretical basis. Because explanatory theory thrives best on comparisons, it is not surprising that the early anthropological theorists were more likely to be library scholars than field workers. The latter were busy collecting curious facts around the world, but had little inclination to analyze them. The theoretical impulse came largely from classics scholars and historians who looked at the ancient myths and texts of the Greeks and Romans with new eyes, sharpened by the parallel examples of primitive tribes in Africa, the Americas, and the South Seas. Where previous Europeans had always seen the Greeks as white alabaster statues and philosophers of pure rationality, scholars like James Frazer, J. J. Bachofen, Friedrich Nietzsche, and Jane Harrison (the last of whom came a little later and was influenced by Durkheim) saw them as tribal people with their own rituals. Instead of pure rationality, one saw instead how much ancient civilizations were founded on ritual and religion.

In this respect, the anthropologists gave powerful new ammunition to the emerging sociological tradition. Society's claim for priority over the individual takes the form of the moral sentiments: strong and prerational attachments to religion, to the family, or to society itself. The emphasis on faith and loyalty can be found in Comte, especially in his later phase when his "Positive (i.e., scientific) Philosophy" was turning into the cult of Humanity, with Comte himself as High Priest. This was also the major theme of Louis De Bonald and Joseph De Maistre, reactionary aristocrats writing in the 1820s, whose antirevolutionary polemics took the form of a violent defense of the importance of the Established Church. What Durkheim did was to turn these ideological claims into a theory of how prerational solidarity is generated: the mechanism of ritual, most clearly exemplifed in religion, but that by extrapolation can be found underlying other areas of social life.[3]

FUSTEL DE COULANGES AND RITUAL CLASS WAR

It is from this point of view that the most neglected of Durk-heim's predecessors emerges into the light. This was his teacher at the École Normale Supérieure, the historian Numa Denis Fustel de Coulanges. Fustel in his great work on ancient Greece and Rome gave a detailed case study of how religious rituals can form an entire society. Durkheim was not merely speaking metaphorically when he claimed that society is a reli-gious phenomenon; he had in mind Fustel's analysis in *The Ancient City* (1864). Fustel showed that religion was the basis of social institutions, ranging from the family and property to war and politics. He also depicted the process of social change as springing from transformations in the nature of religion. Fustel was not a sociologist in the sense that Durkheim was to be-come one by raising Fustel's insights to the level of abstract generalizations, although Fustel declared strongly that history is a science, not merely an art. In the specifics of his model, Durkheim to a certain extent "stood Fustel on his head," ex-plaining religious ideas by society instead of vice versa. At the same time Fustel de Coulanges deserves attention for more than reasons of intellectual history. His analysis was only par-tially exploited by Durkheim, who took from Fustel the ele-ments of a theory of social solidarity but neglected the model of conflict that plays an equally prominent part in Fustel's *The Ancient City*. Fustel deserves to be restored to an honored place in the Durkheimian lineage of core ideas in sociology. More than anyone else, he shows us how ritual solidarity is not incompatible with conflict. More than that, it can be the basis of class struggle itself.

Fustel's *The Ancient City* shows us society emerging in-itially as a religious cult. On the basis of references in classical texts, he reconstructed the oldest religion of the Greeks and Romans, a religion he believed was also shared by the Aryan invaders of India in the Vedic period. Its center was a cult centered around the family fire. The hearth was the original altar; the principal ceremony took place as the family assem-bled for meals, which were accompanied by sacrifices, prayers, and hymns. This describes all the social ingredients that Durkheim was later to specify for a ritual: the presence of the group face to face, a common focus of attention and shared emotion, nonpractical actions carried out for symbolic ends. As with Durkheim, the successful ceremony constitutes the group and gives it a moral unity. Each family had its own ritual; indeed what made someone a member of a family was being admitted to its domestic rites.[4] Outsiders were excluded; thus, the ritual sharply marked the boundary between the group and the outside world. It also constituted domestic authority: the power of the family patriarch was due to the fact that he was the family priest, and he alone presided at rituals.

The city was also based on ritual. Originally the Greek and Latin cities were coalitions among various families. Only the patriarchs were citizens because they alone represented the family to the outside world. But a coalition could only form as itself a cult. Thus, each city was organized around a temple, a cult center in honor of a god or goddess (like Athena at Athens) or a heroic ancestor (like Romulus at Rome or Theseus at Thebes). Archeological research has confirmed that the original temples were built in the form of a dwelling with a hearth, the home of the god or alleged ancestral spirit. The citizens at first kept their homes outside the city walls and only retired there for political and religious assemblies and for military defense.

The first civic officials were priests of the civic cult itself. Ritual was the basis of politics. The early "kings" were actually ceremonial leaders. Later, struggles among social "classes" arose between those who were admitted into the privileges of religious (and therefore political) participation versus those who were excluded. Only full citizens had legal rights, because they alone could appear before the religious officials who were the judges. Religion was not only the basis of the law, but it set the form of legal punishments. The most severe punishment was exile because this meant exclusion from the cult. The cult alone guaranteed rights of property and physical protection. The exile was, therefore, a social outlaw, subject to anyone who could despoil him. Even war, the main business of the ancient state, was carried out in a ritual manner. The army assembled under religious auspices and with common sacrifices, and it marched into battle ceremonially invoking its gods with eerie shouts and the weird sounds of instruments. War between two cities was regarded as war between their gods. Hence, peace could only be established by an alliance on the religious plane; the cult of the foreign god would be established in each of the allying cities. This automatically gave an imperialist character to ancient alliances: allied cities could not remain mere externally cooperating partners, but were linked by participation in common rituals. The Romans in particular made a great point of inviting the gods of cities they were about to invade to leave, on the promise that they would be worshipped in Rome.

Ancient warfare was carried out with great ferocity towards its victims. The losers had no rights, and they and their families could be massacred or sold into slavery without a moral qualm. This was because the boundaries of morality were established by the religion itself; only those who shared the civic cult had moral (and legal) obligations to one another. Similarly the family cult established moral barriers to outsiders that prohibited no outrage against them, although strict obligations held among its members inside the family.[5] The ritual community was the basis of morality, a point Durkheim was to stress.

The structure Fustel describes was what Durkheim would call "mechanical solidarity," the small undifferentiated society with its localistic and repressive collective conscience. Under these conditions, moral beliefs were highly concrete rather than abstract and generalized. The formalities of correct ritual observance were more important than subjective belief. One had to follow all rituals to the letter, in order to guarantee their effects. A lawsuit was lost by incorrect recitation of the legal formulas rather than by the substantive merit of the case; in religious observances the attitude of the supplicant was less important than the correct form of the sacrifice. Durkheim later was to describe an evolution from this kind of concrete conscience and localized moralities to the universalistic morality of the society of an advanced division of labor. Fustel anticipated this theme of moral universalization. He attributed it to Christianity, which appeared in the ancient world as a force breaking down the isolation of families and cities, although one can see it even earlier in the cult of Zeus, a god of justice and protector of strangers.

Religion not only established the basic social groupings, but also their politics and moralities. It also shaped the economy. According to Fustel, property had its origin in the respect given to boundary stones endowed with religious significance. As indicated (see footnote 4), modern scholarship has not accepted Fustel's assertion that this was based on a practice of burying ancestors at one's own home. The use of ancestor cults as claims to property apparently came later. But it is true that property was tied up with the cult system. The main basis of the economy outside of self-supporting households was the cult centers. It is here that the first early stores of wealth were established, in the form of gifts to the gods. The earliest money—that is, a socially sanctioned and standardized unit of value, and later of exchange—developed out of the ceremonial tripods that were dedicated to temples. Later, temples became the first banks, places to store valuables, and, hence, centers for money lending. When Jesus threw the money changers out of the temple at Jerusalem, he was bringing to an end a connection between religion and money that went back to the origin of money.

Durkheim was to generalize each of these points into an abstract sociological theory against utilitarians like Spencer who regarded economic exchange as the basis of society. Durkheim used Fustel's lesson that the primary economic institutions themselves were at first moral and religious. One aspect of Fustel's account that he neglected, however, was his treatment of politics. Fustel devoted a great deal of space to the succession of revolutions that took place in the ancient city-states. Marx early in his life learned about class conflict from his studies of classical antiquity, and the very term "proletariat" comes from the disenfranchised class at Rome. For Fustel, though, politics was closely connected with ritual. Thus, Fustel opens the way to developing a still-missing aspect of the Durkheimian tradition, a theory of ritual as the basis of conflict.

It is already implicit in Fustel's account that ritual is a weapon of domination. It provided the basis for the authority of the family head; later, in the coalition that made up the city, the civic cult was an organizing device by which the aristocracy could monopolize political power. One might even speak of ritual as the "means of emotional production," parallel to Marx and Engels's "means of mental production," that ensured domination in the realm of ideas. Fustel also provides a useful corrective for the functionalist belief that ritual solidarity eliminates or at least greatly diminishes conflict. For if ritual is a weapon that results in domination, then at the same time it generates a split into a class of dominators and a class of dominated. The first class conflicts, then, are not organized on an economic basis per se, but on the possession of *ritual property:* on control over, or exclusion from, the means of emotional production.

Actually ritual property established more than two groups in ancient society. Fustel speaks of four great revolutions that altered religious participation and, hence, the entire social structure. *The first revolution* took place in the 600s B.C. as the aristocracy of family heads took away the power of the king. Both factions were defined by ritual: the aristocrats were priests of their own household cults, whereas the king was the priest of the coalition's cult. This revolution, which took place in various cities throughout Greece and Italy, left the king in a merely ceremonial position. This was in a sense the rise of the state because it established a political organ separate from a religious one.

The second revolution pitted the aristocrats against the clients. The latter group consisted of persons who lacked citizenship rights because they were merely subordinate members within some aristocrat's family cult. These might be members of younger branches of a family, servants, or outsiders or retainers who had been adopted into the family worship, but only as underlings. The battle to establish full political rights for the clients meant freeing them from obligations to their aristocratic masters, which were tied up with their subordinate religious status. Fustel believed that this involved the overthrowing of an original right of primogeniture, although modern evidence indicates that no such practice appears to have existed in early times.

The third revolution (which may not be so clearly distinguished from the second as both took place ca. 600–400 B.C.) involved the battle of the plebian class to enter the city. The plebians were aliens, persons who lacked family cults of their own, who lived outside the city walls. Without a family religion, they had no social honor, no legal rights, and no place in the political assembly of the city. Owing especially to shifts in weaponry, which made the plebians valuable as troops (a point that Weber also was to stress), the plebians achieved some citizenship rights. The process was not identical everywhere; at Athens a full (male) democracy was established; at Rome, the most conservative of the ancient cities, the plebians acquired only limited concessions. It was the victory of the plebians in Greece that ushered in the classical period of democracy. Only after this political revolution did class stratification based primarily on wealth arise. It is in this period that we find the plutocracy, denounced by conservatives like Plato and Aristotle.

Fustel describes the *fourth revolution* as flowing from this situation. The citizens were now divided into rich and poor, classes based on wealth rather than ritual distinctions. There also existed a conservative faction, the old-line aristocrats, who periodically plotted to overthrow democracy and reestablish the traditional oligarchy of limited participation in a civic cult. Amid these shifting political tides, popular tyrants arose who appealed to the poor against the reactionary aristocrats and against the new rich. The result was the final destruction of the ancient city-states. They were superceded by kingships, now no longer religious but purely political despotisms. Here again Rome held out longest against the trend, but finally the Republic gave way to an emperor, rising to power through demogogic appeals to the poor.

Fustel opens a path in the Durkheimian tradition that has scarcely been exploited. *The Ancient City* remains a secret weapon; even partially used, it was a key to Durkheim's strength. The general point that rituals create classes and class conflicts suggests a theory of politics and revolution yet to be created. But the Durkheimian tradition has been leaning in this direction, as we will see, in developing a theory of class cultures.

DURKHEIM'S THEORY OF MORALITY AND SYMBOLISM

Durkheim's system culminates in his last book, *The Elementary Forms of the Religious Life* (1912). The most powerful impact of the book is in its demonstration that the reality of religion is not transcendental and that the god is the symbol of the society and its moral power over individuals. Durkheim here brings together the religious and the scientific aspects of his own intellectual tradition. One line of thought, going back to De Maistre and other conservatives, had argued that religion is the moral foundation of society and that we cannot survive without respect for traditional Christianity. In Durkheim's own day, too, American pragmatists like William James were arguing that religion is deeper than mere rationality and science, and that we cannot give up the will to believe. Durkheim agreed there was one valid element in this line of argument. Society does not rest on a conscious and rational foundation, and religions could not have played an important role throughout the centuries if they were merely based on a mistake. Nevertheless Durkheim does not yield primacy from science to religion; instead, he produced a scientific theory of religion as a powerful moral force underlying the rest of society. Religion is produced by rituals, that is, by certain configurations of social interaction in the real world. This theory of ritual is capable of being extended to cover all the varieties of how moralities and ideas are socially produced.

Durkheim focused on the tribes of central Australia, which had just been described in anthropological reports. This left his analysis with certain weaknesses. It did not provide the kind of comparative analysis for which Durkheim's own methodological pronouncements called. Instead, Durkheim believed that by isolating the most primitive form of religion, he would have the elements out of which all others would later grow. This assumption rests on our accepting an evolutionary view of history, which is not so obvious today; it also assumes that Australian tribes are the most primitive social forms. In fact, although the material technology of these tribes is extremely simple—they have no houses, no pottery, and no tools other than very simple ones, and they live by hunting and gathering in the desert—nevertheless these tribes actually have one of the more complicated forms of social structure at the tribal level, consisting of complex marriage rules among different segments of society. Durkheim also picked out some quite untypical tribes within Australia, ignoring clans that did not have totems and other factors that did not fit his model.[6] Nevertheless Durkheim's theory has turned out to be stronger than his evidence for it. W. Lloyd Warner's firsthand anthropological study, *A Black Civilization, A Social Study of an Australian Tribe* (1937), supported Durkheim's general conclusions. Later, the sociologist Guy Swanson did a comparative analysis to show that indeed Durkheim was right and that the type of god did correspond to the type of society: belief in local spirits and totems is found in more fragmented tribal groups, whereas cults of powerful high gods exist in stratified societies with an impressive center of earthly power.

The Elementary Forms of the Religious Life has a twofold message. Part of its theory concerns the sociology of knowledge. It attempts to show that sociology can give a more powerful explanation of human ideas than can philosophy or psychology, either of the Kantian version or of the empiricist version. Kant argued that ideas exist a priori as categories through which experience enters the mind; Durkheim agreed, to the extent that ideas exist prior to any given individual. But the ideas of space, time, number, and other general categories are not universal and unchanging but take their form from the structure of society and change as the society changes. Similarly the empiricists are right to the extent that they believe in a material world existing prior to ideas. But people do not merely acquire ideas by generalizing their sensations. The crucial aspect of the material world is society itself. The way human bodies are spread out or come together produces the categories through which all other experience is filtered.

Rituals are the mechanism that produces ideas charged with social significance, and the content of ideas reflects the structure of society. Durkheim granted that ideas, once they were formed, have a partial autonomy. Later, Claude Lévi-Strauss shook symbols loose from their ritual base. He attempted to show how symbols, encapsulated in a society's myths, were shuffled about by history into new combinations, which the analyst had to decode. Eventually Lévi-Strauss lost interest in the social structure that produced the ideas originally; his "structuralist" method became a search for the basic symbol-forming laws inside the human mind.[7] Even here Lévi-Strauss was following up one of Durkheim's thoughts. Durkheim had suggested that if ideas are partially autonomous of their social origins, they nevertheless have their own laws of mutual attraction and repulsion. Durkheim envisioned a branch of sociological science that would be like electricity or chemistry, only applied to the "collective representations" that we call ideas. Presumably it would include laws of how ideas are charged with emotional force denoting social membership (because they are used in social rituals) as well as laws of how ideas combine on their own when society is not present. Something like this form of analysis is now becoming more possible with the progress made on conversational analysis as a chain of ritual interactions.

The second message of *The Elementary Forms* is its theory of rituals that launches the microportion of the Durkheimian tradition. Ritual theory is already implicit in Durkheim's earlier analysis of crime, for punishment is a ritual that reminds people of the law and reenacts their emotional commitment to it. In the anthropological materials, Durkheim pushed further to make the point that society does not merely manifest itself in a negative form, as a set of obligations that become visible mainly when they are violated. It is a positive force as well, and the way in which this is produced can be seen in rituals like those ceremonies that bring together a primitive tribe to celebrate its religious rites. Much of the work of mapping out these religious phenomena was done by two contributors to Durkheim's *Année Sociologique*, Marcel Mauss and Henri Hubert, in the 15 years preceding the actual publication of *The Elementary Forms*. Durkheim's last book summarizes the theoretical points towards which the whole group had been driving.

Apart from the impact of this theory on subsequent anthropologists interpreting tribal rituals, there is its long-term effects on the sociology of *modern* societies. It lets us see our own society through a new lens and discover the rituals that create our own beliefs and moral boundaries. These rituals are of course not the same as those of tribal societies because our social structure is different, the ultimate determining factor in the Durkheimian perspective. This influence of the Durkheimian tradition is not so well known, although it shows up clearly enough in the title of one of Erving Goffman's books, *Interaction Ritual* (1967). What is most important about the lineage of ritual analysis, I would argue, is the way it ties in with the central phenomenon of modern societies: stratification. This brings it onto the territory of conflict theory, and in this form, not as an enemy, but as a much-needed supplement.

THE RITUAL BASIS OF STRATIFICATION: W. LLOYD WARNER

Erving Goffman is an important figure in this development, but we must first start with his teacher, W. Lloyd Warner. Warner was originally an Australian anthropologist whose earliest field work was a vindication of Durkheim's analysis of aboriginal societies. He concluded that we knew more about tribal societies than we did about our own, and he then moved to the United States. He and his students proceeded to carry out a series of community studies, including a tradition-ridden city in Massachusetts ("Yankee City"), a middle-American town in the Midwest ("Jonesville"), Chicago's black section ("Bronzetown"), and a segregated county in Mississippi ("Deep South"). Warner also realized that the social structure of a complex society like the United States could not be captured by looking at the status system of separate communities, so he carried out studies of social mobility and inheritance in the national business elite as well as an even more macrostudy of the corporate economy. The scope of W. Lloyd Warner's work has rarely been properly appreciated. He was never part of the insiders' factions in American sociology, and his analysis of stratification was regarded as too cultural and insufficiently economic for the Marxian or conflict approach that was also being introduced at the time. Warner set off the study of stratification as a system of prestige and also as a set of distinct communities: as if his Australian tribes were ranked one on top of another like a totem pole. It has not been sufficiently appreciated how instrumental these approaches were in starting up the study of status stratification and of social networks, which have now progressed with quantitative methods far beyond Warner's qualitative descriptions.

One might ask why Warner moved so quickly from the study of tribal rituals to the study of stratification. The answer is that when one tries to deal with a modern society or even just a community within it, one fact immediately hits one in the face: stratification. There is not merely one culture, one social group, but a larger number of such groups. Searching for principles to relate them together, one quickly sees some form of ranking among them. "Classes," in at least a loose sense of the term, are the most obvious thing about the diversity of modern society. The era of large-scale empirical sociology began in the 1920s with a vogue of community studies and continued into the 1930s and 1940s.[8] Warner was part of this phase. So were Robert and Helen Lynd, anthropologists who decided to study a midwestern town ("Middletown") instead of the South Seas islanders. They, too, ended up discovering stratification as the primary reality; it is the same in virtually all community studies. There are no community studies that are not basically stratification studies.

Warner brought the Durkheimian perspective to modern stratified society by pointing up its rituals. We tend to regard modern society as secularized and rationalistic. Warner showed that we can look at ourselves through the anthropologist's eyes and find ritual everywhere. One set of rituals of course is religion. For Warner, Christianity is fair game for the same analysis one applies to tribal religion. The key to modern religion, as to every other, is the ceremonies by which it assembles the community and gives it a symbolic identity. The modern churchgoing congregation is reenacting its bond of moral solidarity every time it meets, every Sunday morning as well as at the other religious ceremonies throughout the year. Warner was particularly alive to the fact that these religious communities are part of the stratification of modern society. In "Yankee City" the major lines of status stratification were ethnic, and they divided the Anglo Protestants (who included most of the upper class) from the more recent immigrant

Catholics (who made up the bulk of the working class) and the Jews (who spread out across both the middle and the upper-middle classes, but who were sharply segregated from the WASPs).

Different religious doctrines not only symbolized different social groups, but also served to keep these groups separated and stratified. Religious rituals reproduce the class structure. They do this by affecting people's consciousness of moral and cultural differences and because they reinforce the structure of interpersonal associations and exclusions. The lived reality of stratification, for Warner, is the question of who associates with whom and on what terms of intimacy. Warner is the father of the network analysis of stratification, which in recent years has achieved considerable sophistication through the survey research of Edward Laumann and others. This has revealed the multiple dimensions of the web of stratification in which we live: hierarchies of social class further subdivided by ethnicity and other enclaves of personal acquaintanceship. Now the most intimate kinds of associations are those of the family. Ethnic and class patterns are powerfully enforced in everyday life by who marries whom.

Religions powerfully reinforce this basis of intimate associations because they are especially concerned with the maintainance of the family. Families belong to churches together; at least in devout families, religious ceremonies permeate family life. Saying prayers before going to bed, saying grace before dinner: these are ceremonies using the "ritual capital" of the church to reinforce the family unit. The father in the traditional family has his authority reinforced by the fact that he sits at the head of the table and presides at the saying of grace. The picture is not so different from that drawn of the ancient Greeks by Fustel de Coulanges. The major religious holidays moreover are elaborated into family rituals: Christmas (a family gift-exchange ritual), Thanksgiving (a family-assembling feast), Easter (Easter bunny games and candies for the children, together with the tradition of showing off one's community status by going to church in one's best clothes). Even Halloween, with its barely believed panoply of ghosts, is another children's gift festival, spun off from a traditional Christian commemoration of the dead. The church, in other words, surrounds the family with ceremonies designed to keep it together. Birth is consecrated by christening, adolescence by confirmation or bar mitzvah, marriage by the church wedding, death by the funeral.

Warner pointed out that the very symbols of modern religions reflect the family. Traditional Protestantism exalts the Father "who art in Heaven," who is stern, disciplining, and moralistic, just as it reinforced an authoritarian human father in each autonomous home. Catholicism places more emphasis on the way each human family is subject to a centralized church that mediates the power of God through a hierarchy of Pope, bishops, and priests as well as saints. The central family symbol of Catholicism is Mary, the mother, who is simultaneously the perfect woman because she is virgin: thus idealizing the family without the disrupting pressure of sexual drives. Given these major differences in the type of family structure symbolized by the religion, Warner notes, it is not surprising that the ethnic groups based on these religions should be so divided. He also argued that if the family structure were to change, the predominant religious conceptions would change also.

Warner also analyzed secular rituals, but always in relation to their effects on stratification. Patriotic ceremonies like the Fourth of July parade, Labor Day, and historical commemoratives are ceremonies designed to focus the community on itself as a unit. In "Yankee City," these parades and rituals made a point of incorporating virtually all community groups but under historical symbols that always exalted the role of the WASP aristocracy. George Washington and Abraham Lincoln are once-ordinary humans, now blown up into ideal images of the Protestant virtues. In celebrating them, one celebrates not only one's country, but also the implicit leadership of the latter-day WASPs who made a point of continuing this high-status ritual lifestyle. Patriotic ceremonies are ritual weapons of class domination; they suppress feelings of class conflict and dissension by emphasizing group unity, while implicitly conferring legitimacy on the class that leads the rituals and exemplifies the culture expressed in them. For the same reason the upper classes are particularly involved in taking care of the graves of their ancestors, because of the honor this "cult of the dead" confers on them, the living.[9]

ERVING GOFFMAN AND THE EVERYDAY CULT OF THE INDIVIDUAL

Warner thus introduced anthropological rituals into the analysis of modern everyday life. His research assistant at the University of Chicago around 1950 was Erving Goffman, who took the analysis one step further. Warner dealt with the obvious, formal rituals of our lives. Goffman found rituals of which we are not ordinarily aware as such, rituals that permeate every aspect of our social encounters. Of course not every aspect of our lives is equally ritualized, nor do all people participate in them equally. But this makes Goffman's "interaction ritual" especially useful because it sets up a stratification between different people and different situations.

The most clearly formulated of these rituals of everyday life are what we call politeness or good manners. In these, Goffman points out, we are presenting little idealizations of ourself and of other people. "How are you?" is not meant literally; it is a symbolic formula, showing that one accords the other person sufficient status to be treated as an individual (as opposed, for instance, to a purely businesslike situation in which one walks up to a ticket window and unceremoniously says "Two tickets for the late show"). Every such ritual—and there are many—both gives some deference to the other person and claims some status for oneself by showing that one is a person who knows how to carry out the "proper" formalities. Whole conversations can be ritualistic in this sense, as when two people at a cocktail party exchange information about their jobs or hometowns or the weather, which is of no interest to either of them as information; nevertheless the exchange can be completely satisfactory to both of them if it negotiates a ritual tie between two people who are sufficiently enamored of each other's status.

Goffman here is not being cynical, although he is often misinterpreted as such. He is explicitly following Durkheim's point that in differentiated modern society, the gods of isolated groups have given way to worship of the one "sacred object" we all have in common: the individual self.[10] At the same time Goffman sees that people do not give up their self-interest just because they are participating in rituals. Interaction rituals are weapons that people can use to score points: to make the right contacts, to embarrass or put down rivals, to assert one's social superiority. Sacred objects and beliefs are created by rituals: in tribal societies (or in our own churches) the ritual creates a god or spirit; in everyday encounters, the ritual creates the self. For Durkheim a ritual is a particular kind of configuration of human beings focusing their bodies, attentions, and emotions in a certain way. Goffman adds an even more materialist note: rituals are analogous to the theatre. They are performances that we put on, hence, they require real props: costumes, stages, places for the audience, and places for the performers to get their gear together. Hence, Goffman's famous distinction between "front-stages" and "backstages": the former is the storefront where the salesperson hustles the customer, the latter the backroom where the employees divide up their sales territories, establish their sales line, and let down their hair after the manipulation they have gone through. In another sphere, there is an analogous distinction between the cleaned-up livingroom and a carefully laid table where the ritual of a dinner party is to reaffirm status membership with one's guests, and the backstage of bathroom, kitchen, and bedroom before and afterwards, where emotional as well as physical garbage is disposed of.

Rituals, then, are performances. They not only have social consequences—creating ideal images of the self, negotiating social ties, controlling others—but they also require certain resources, both material properties and cultural skills. They hold society together, but they do it in a stratified way. Rituals are weapons upholding and renegotiating the class structure. They not only create the self, but they rank selves into different social classes.

INTERACTION RITUALS AND CLASS CULTURES: COLLINS, BERNSTEIN, AND DOUGLAS

Goffman himself did not explicitly stress the stratification that comes out of rituals, but his analysis has lent itself easily to this development. His own materials for the frontstage/backstage model all came out of stratified situations: studies of factory workers and managers, each putting on a performance in each other's presence, whereas their informal groups act in an entirely different manner;[11] studies of high-status professions (such as medical doctors) that raise their public image by carefully guarding any activities that would make them appear as less than fully authoritative and omniscient; studies of upperclass people who maintain an elaborate ritual front as compared to the lowest status people of all, inmates of mental institutions, people who have lost all resources of privacy from which to control their public images.

These analyses fit nicely with a great deal of other information about the cultural differences among social classes. The theory that emerges is that there are *two* major dimensions of difference among people. Both dimensions are related to the rituals in which people participate. Various aspects of this theory have been stated in recent years by myself and by the English sociologist Basil Bernstein and social anthropologist Mary Douglas.

One important dimension consists of what I call power rituals. Social classes are divided according to how much they give orders or take orders. This can be a continuum: some classes giving orders at the top of long chains of command in big organizations, others involved in passing along orders in the middle levels, and still others never giving orders but only taking them. This gives us a Goffmanian equivalent of Ralf Dahrendorf's version of conflict theory: the main dimension of stratification is organized power. This can be based on property, or on military or political control. Hence, we find the same general lineup of classes in capitalist and in socialist societies because private property is only one basis for giving orders. In both cases, those who give orders are in charge of the organizational rituals. They constitute the "official class," those who uphold the ideals of the organization and believe in its formalities. In Goffman's terms, they are "frontstage" personalities. At the opposite end, people who only takes orders (the workers, the rank and file) are alienated from the official ideals in whose name they are ordered around. Lacking control of "ritual property," they withdraw from the "frontstage" world and identify instead with the "backstage" world of their informal groups.

The second dimension of social class adds a horizontal complexity onto this vertical lineup of power. Apart from whether people control their rituals or are controlled by them, there is the question of the sheer number and kinds of rituals in which they participate. Some people are in the midst of large social networks, meeting people, wheeling and dealing right and left. Others remain in little local communities, interacting with the same individuals and living in the same space for years at a time. This is of course the same dimension that Durkheim used to compare different societies, only now it is applied to the position of different individuals within the same network. As Herbert Gans pointed out, working-class people in modern cities do not have the widespread professional contacts that members of the higher social classes do; they are more like little peasant villages set down in a modern metropolis. Because of this difference in local social structure, different social classes have their own distinctive mentalities.

Thus, the members of the higher social classes have a culture that is like the one Durkheim said corresponds to a complex division of labor: abstract ideas, individualism, thinking in terms of long-term consequences. The lower social classes, living in their little enclaves, have a culture like Durkheim's model of tribal societies: powerful pressure for social conformity, highly reified symbols, a habit of thinking in terms of particulars rather than abstractions. Basil Bernstein has shown that this Durkheimian model applies to the differences in language among social classes. The lower classes use what he calls a "restricted code," a form of talk that refers to particular people and things and assumes that the listener knows the local details of what is being talked about. The higher social classes use an "elaborated code," talk that deals more with abstractions and that communicates information without depending on the local context. At the extremes, this is the difference between gossip in a local slang and the technical speech of specialized professionals; the former holds together a small community and is virtually meaningless outside of it, the latter is a kind of money that is negotiable for making ties with expert groups of this sort around the world.[12]

We can see again another way that the Durkheimian theory of stratification fills out the conflict model. Engels and Marx's own model of politics stressed the advantage that the higher social classes have because they are mobilized, whereas the lower classes are not mobilized. Thus, a much smaller minority could dominate the more fragmented majority beneath them. The Durkheimian model developed by Bernstein and myself points out that these structural differences not only account for differences in political power, but also affect the cultural outlooks of the different classes. The degree and kind of participation of individuals in interaction rituals determines their class cultures.

The anthropologist Mary Douglas has given a strong statement of these two dimensions of culture. She shows that not only do these two aspects of social structure affect rituals and beliefs within modern societies, but also that they explain why there is such a variety of cultures among different tribal societies. Durkheim had set up a quite general comparison in *The Division of Labor in Society:* on the one hand there were all traditional societies (lumped together) that produced a highly repressive and particularistic collective conscience, on the other hand there were modern societies, with a high division of labor, that produced an abstract and individualistic collective conscience. As we have seen, the modern end of this comparison is overgeneralized because the higher social classes are one cultural type and the lower classes are another cultural type, one that resembles more the "traditional" type of structure. Douglas shows the same differences among traditional societies.[13] Some of these societies tightly restrict the individual with religions that ritualize every action of everyday life and give no leeway for choice under threat of taboos, pollution, and severe penalties for sin. Others are easygoing and individualistic, believing in benign rather than punitive spirits or even skeptical that spirits exist at all. Durkheim was mistaken in thinking there was a simple evolution from one social type to another, with repressive group consciousness as a characteristic of all tribal societies and secular and individualistic consciousness as a characteristic reserved for modern ones.

But the analysis of differences in social structure that Durkheim pioneered remains highly applicable, even if his types do not form a sequence in time. The tribal societies that have the most repressive rituals and punitive beliefs are those that fit the model of densely packed societies—which Douglas points out usually occur in environments with a great deal of concern for scarce resources; the tribal societies in which individualism is prominent are the ones in which the group boundaries are permeable, with people coming and going constantly and at will. There is also another dimension that cuts across different tribal societies: how unequal they are in power differences among their own members and, relatedly, how much conflict there is with outside groups. In essence this is the first dimension of the pair that I sketched out above, a dimension that determines the extent of an individual's participation in "power rituals." Thus, tribes vary not only in the amount of control over the individual by the group, but also in the degree of inner domination and implicit conflict. Tribal cultures (generally this means their religions) are spread out along two dimensions: (1) from the highly collectivized to the highly individualized and (2) from those with powerful chiefs to those with considerable equality among their members. Each type of society has its own particular form of symbolism.

Douglas's model is general enough to explain religious and secular cultures in all types of societies, including the variations within our own. She points out, for example, that the type of control people exert over their own body depends on the structure of the group they inhabit. In tribal societies, the contrast is between those groups in which religious trance is interpreted as a possession by spirits that brings beneficial powers to the group, as compared to those groups (much more authoritarian ones) in which any deviation from strict control of one's emotions and body is taken as a sign of sin and pollution. The contrast is found in our own society: highly ascetic and moralistic groups versus those that put a premium on self-expression and "doing your own thing."

Long-hairs versus crew-cuts; flowing clothes versus buttoned-up styles; different ways of organizing one's household furniture—all of these can be explained from this structural analysis of culture.

Douglas's scheme is resolutely multidimensional. Societies can differ from each other along two different continuums; hence, we cannot place everything in a single line but must see things as spread out across a two-dimensional grid. The same applies more generally to the theory of class cultures in our own society. Modern society is made up of many different "tribes," which we may glibly call "classes" for convenience but that actually shade away from each other in several directions. The place each individual occupies within this stratified space may well be unique because each individual participates in his or her personal combination of rituals. This is another reason why individualism is an overriding reality of modern society: no one is exactly like anyone else because the differentiated social structure exposes each person to a slightly different nexus of groups. Nevertheless individuals manage to deal with each other, even though they come to their encounters with somewhat different cultural outlooks. How this happens and how it even reproduces a stratified order of society is the subject of yet another application of the Durkheimian tradition.

Ritual Exchange Networks: The Micro/Macro Linkage

A crucial question for Durkheim—after he had written about law, crime, and suicide in the 1890s—was how the individual fitted in. His model showed society bearing down from the outside, exercising external constraints and creating collective sentiments and ideas. But each person is not always in the presence of others, nor completely guided by their pressures. How, then, do we explain this individual aspect of behavior? And because ideas, too, are used by individuals for their own thinking—in unique situations and in creative ways—how much can be attributed to a social base?

This is the issue of how the microlevel and macrolevel of

analysis are related, viewed from the side of the macrostructure. In the early 1900s, Mauss had already begun to work on the problem.[14] His materials were not the complex modern society where the individual reigns supreme, but the tribal settings where individuality supposedly counts for nothing against the power of the group. If individual actions and thoughts could be found here, the mechanism that produced them would be cast into sharp relief.

MARCEL MAUSS AND THE MAGIC OF SOCIAL EXCHANGE

Characteristically, Mauss found what he was looking for in the sphere of religion. The phenomenon of prayer seems to show us a type of action that is individual and private: indeed, showing that even rituals need not be social. But instead of undermining the basic Durkheimian theory, the explanation of prayer reinforces and extends it. For one thing, it is our modern conception that prayers are an inner experience: talking to God inside the privacy of one's own heart. Mauss argues that historically prayers were always vocalized and public; many societies even prohibited private prayers as a sacrilege. The private, individual prayer is an offshoot of public ceremonies, in which collective conceptions are carried about by individuals and lodged in their own inner consciousness. One could even say that the development of rituals such as prayers, which are verbal formulas rather than ceremonies, opens the way for individuals to appropriate them; it is by the internalization of collective formulas that modern individuals acquire their capacity for steering by an inner moral gyroscope and for thinking on their own.

Mauss makes a similar argument about an even more primitive practice, magic. Magic seems to escape the influence of society. Its nature is antithetical to that of religious rituals. Where religious rituals are almost always collective and official, magic is a private matter—often illicit—carried out by individual magicians for the benefit or harm of someone in particular, not for the benefit (or harm) of the community. Nevertheless Mauss and Henri Hubert pointed out that magic depends on the same kinds of things, ideas, and actions as religion. Magic is always a derivative of some religion; the demon-calling spells and black masses of medieval Europe are clearly a part of the Christian universe, just as the tribal shaman calls on forces that are continuous with the religious framework of his tribe. In fact the magic power that is invoked—whether to kill a victim, bring good fortune, make someone fall in love, or all the other traditional aims of magic—is a version of the general spiritual force that some Pacific island tribes call *mana*. But this spiritual force is itself social: it is the most general conception of the power of the society over individuals. The official religion uses it for its collective purposes, whereas the magician siphons it off for private ends.

For Durkheim and Mauss, religion is not an illusion. It symbolizes a real thing: the power of society. *Mana*, too, has a concrete reality. It is *emotional energy* that circulates among people and moves them, seemingly mysteriously, from out-side. Mauss claims that magic often worked, at least to a suffi-cient degree that people kept on regarding it as effective. Magi-cians, in social contexts where people believe in them, are not frauds; in fact it is because they sincerely believe in their own magic that they have an emotional force over other people. Magic is a real substance that circulates invisibly in the social atmosphere: an emotional contagion traveling on certain collec-tively charged ideas. For the tribal members who believe in it, to receive notice of a voodoo doll shaped after oneself is tanta-mount to death itself.

From the point of view of sociological theory, magic is not just a quaint custom. It reveals a general lesson: that a phenome-non, social in its origins, can become lodged in the individual consciousness, where it becomes part of one's personality and one's personal strategies in the struggle for social advantages. It also shows that social forces do not merely hang somewhere over a society like an invisible cloud, but they circulate among individuals. They are quantitative, forces that vary in intensity from one individual to another. The magician, feeling full of the force of magic she or he controls, has more self-confidence, power, and energy than others. The same thing is true for the above-ground, official distribution of *mana*. The tribal chief or "big man" is regarded as more sacred, more powerful, more exalted than ordinary people because he has more *mana*. He has, in short, captured more of the emotional energy released into social circulation by the "electrical generators": rituals. Mauss's analysis of magic and *mana* shows the mechanism underlying those exalted individuals whom Weber called charismatic. It reminds us that charisma does not just appear as a divine stroke, as it seems to do in Weber's exposition of it, but that it is part of a system of social stratification and of the distribution of socially generated energies and beliefs.

Thus far we have the individual interpreted as the bearer of forces that have their source in the macrostructure. Mauss's argument also cuts in the other direction to show what mechanisms make up the macrostructure itself. Mauss's most famous version of this is his 1925 article, "The Gift." Already in 1914, Mauss had proposed the theory that *mana*, when crystalized into material objects, constituted the primitive origins of what later became money. In other words, the economy was founded on religious belief in a fairly literal sense. For money is a medium of exchange, a universal standard and store of value that makes it possible to convert all other particular goods without the cumbersome process of barter. The monetary economy grew slowly and through many levels before it reached the easily convertible paper money and the even more easily manipulable stocks, futures options, and all the paraphernalia of modern capitalism. The tribal "money" on which Mauss focused is still relatively bulky and hard to manage. But it is social in that it has the prestige and the sacred quality that only society can bestow. And it inspires social confidence, which is the one thing money must have if it is to be universally acceptable. (Compare money to barter, where one does not accept a good unless one has need of it or a pretty sure idea of with whom it can be traded for something one does want.) Schematically one can say that money came out of magic, because magic is the individualized use of the collective *mana*.

The earliest "moneylike" objects were similar to jewels: extremely precious objects that are regarded as having an aesthetic quality that reaches out of the ordinary.[15] What makes these objects special is not merely their scarcity, but the social significance given to them: they consist of items charged with social confidence. Because of this, they are able to serve as links between one situation and another. They build up the larger social structure through a network of exchange.

The idea that society is an exchange system among its various parts is an old one, found in the early economists like Adam Smith as well as in utilitarians like Herbert Spencer. But Durkheim had sharply criticized these models, as long as they remained merely on the level of the exchange of material advantages. On that level an economy would not be possible, because utilitarian self-interest does not bring about exchange but fraud, deception, and the war of all against all. For this reason, Durkheim attempted to lay bare a moral, emotional foundation of "precontractual" solidarity. Mauss carries out the same idea but in a more dynamic fashion. His point is that the material economy quite literally was created on the basis of a system of ritual exchange. There are two levels of exchange: one operating beneath, and making possible, the other.

In his famous analysis *The Gift* (1925), Mauss describes the "kula ring" of the Trobriand islands. The chief of each island leads a trading expedition to the neighboring island. His expedition carries two kinds of goods: fish, coconuts, and so on (whatever is the produce of the island) to barter for the specialties of the next island. This is mundane economic trade. But it is preceded by another, symbolic form of trade: the visiting chiefs ritually offer gifts to the native chiefs—ornamental shells or armbands (equivalent to jewels)—and receive other such gifts in return. Thus, the fish or coconuts move among adjacent islands, and the "symbolic money" travels around the islands in a ring. The ritual gifts are a form of diplomacy. Until they are given and accepted, the two tribes are armed and suspicious. They cannot carry out the mundane economic trade until peace is guaranteed by the ritual trade of symbolic gifts.

The kula ring is a paradigm for economic structures in general. At their core: a *social* tie must always be negotiated before the bargaining for social advantage can take place. In modern terms one would say that Max Weber's point is vindicated: some religious or other status system must first organize the economy before it can operate. *Status groups* are more fundamental than classes, as the latter can emerge only on the basis of the former. Weber defined status groups as communities that associate together in a certain lifestyle and follow a certain code of honor. Whereas the marketplace has as its principle the cut-throat pursuit of self-interest, the mark of the status group is precisely *the absence of hard bargaining*. In other words, status group members give each other gifts in the same way that Mauss's Trobriand chiefs, only in the modern case these consist of the gifts of dinner parties, Christmas presents, and *all the ceremonial exchanges of everyday politeness that Goffman analyzed*.

Mauss describes various kinds of economies that can be sustained by gift exchanges. The kula ring is a relatively egalitarian form, with exchanges passing horizontally around the islands. Elsewhere in the South Pacific and New Guinea as well as in many other tribal societies, gifts take the form of hierarchical "redistribution". The chief receives gifts of food and other forms of wealth, which he in turn gives back to his followers at huge ceremonial feasts. This sounds like an exchange system in which everyone gets back more or less what he puts in to it, but an extra benefit does accrue to one person: the chief or "big man." He may periodically bankrupt himself with his largesse, but he gains socially and politically by being the ritual center of attention. These "redistribution" feasts are like political campaigns, with the highest status going to the person who collects the most followers. These followers make one powerful in warfare, too, as in the warfare practiced among head-hunting tribes.

Gift exchanges can also be extremely competitive. This is illustrated in the potlatch found among the wealthy coastal tribes of the Canadian Pacific, where different chiefs try to insult and overpower their rivals by showering gifts on them, gifts that their rivals cannot afford to repay. To receive a gift obligates one to give a gift of equal value in return or else suffer a loss in status. For this reason, Mauss implies, the status realm is also a realm of stratification. It binds together equals who can indeed afford to exchange valuable gifts among themselves; at the same time it implicitly excludes all those who cannot afford to keep up with the level of symbolic exchange. Gift exchange seems horizontal, but it has vertical consequences. We will see that this is true in the modern-day version of symbolic exchange, which is now being analyzed as a conversational marketplace for cultural capital.

LÉVI-STRAUSS AND ALLIANCE THEORY

The gift-exchange model has been influential in numerous directions. Lévi-Strauss developed a version of it to explain the entire structure of tribal societies: Mauss's two-level model applies, with symbolic gifts providing the basis for material exchange. In this case, what is being exchanged is not the jewel-like ornaments of the kula ring, but human beings themselves as sexual partners. The basic structure of the family is a network. Because of the incest taboo, no family may derive its sexual partners within its own ranks but must go outside the family. Marriages are exchanges much like gifts; a family does not usually receive a sexual partner back immediately when it gives one away; nevertheless there is an obligation to reciprocate in the long run. This giftlike quality of marriages creates moral obligations that can only be violated by a loss of status; marriages become the basis for tribal status politics. Moreover, following the principle that the symbolic level of exchange makes possible more material transactions, families that intermarry now become economic trading partners and military allies. It is hardly too much to say that the marriage exchange creates all the alliances that are the basis of tribal society.

Different types of tribal kinship systems have their distinctive structures of exchange; some link together two clans or groups by the constant interexchange of marriages, whereas others trade partners around in a long circle, something like the kula ring. Each of these has an implicit logic. As Durkheim pointed out in an early paper, Australian marriage systems are put together as if they were a problem in mathematics. Lévi-Strauss developed the formal implications of each system of who marries whom: some of these constitute "short cycles" that knit together several groups but leave them isolated from outsiders, whereas others make up "long cycles" that integrate large numbers of families though long-distance networks of exchange. Lévi-Strauss proposed that the earliest fate of societies depended on the strategies of marriage politics they pursued. Only those that took the greater risks of investing in the long cycles were able to amass larger alliances and, hence, acquire the political networks and the economic wealth that made possible the rise of the state. Lévi-Strauss's idea of the "kinship revolution" which initially broke down some tribal societies into a new form, has not been much followed up; in his subsequent work, Lévi-Strauss drifted away from the structural organization of societies into an effort to decode their myths into basic mental forms. Alliance theory, though, has become an important tool for the anthropological analysis of kinship politics, and it remains an important metaphor for understanding the logic of political exchange in more complex societies.

One application, for instance, has analyzed science as a gift-exchange system. Warren Hagstrom points out that what distinguishes science from commercial activities is that knowledge is supposed to be freely shared and treated as an end in itself; it carries with it the high honorific status of membership in the scientific community. Hence, there is a competitive aspect, as indeed in all gifts, but cloaked under the normative tones of "contributions." Scientists compete for recognition, attempting to have their gifts accepted by the community of their peers and legitimated as real knowledge. Scientists regard themselves and their ideas as "pure," untainted with ordinary motives other than intellectual curiosity. By the same token, they resist any application of sociological explanation to what they are doing. Science for them, as David Bloor points out, is a Durkheimian sacred object; it is constituted by rituals that mark off a self-contained community. But the Durkheimian perspective itself gives license to the sociology of science, as yet another application of the theory of how ideas reflect the social structure whose members created them. In this case, the community is the *network of scientists themselves*, not the surrounding society as a whole.

Although Hagstrom does not develop the point, the two-leveled model of exchange applies here as well. Scientists' symbolic exchanges constitute the moral core of the community, but once these are established, one's scientific status can be traded on for more crass material goods such as academic appointments and salaries, book sales, royalties for inventions, and the like. And to step outside the Durkheimian framework for a moment, the latter can be seen as the material means of mental production, which the conflict tradition uses to explain the content of ideas produced. Both of these levels interact: the ritual gift exchange of scientific ideas goes on in its own "sacred" realm of disinterested truth, but these ideas themselves become "intellectual property," a form of what the French sociologist Pierre Bourdieu calls "cultural capital." Scientists maneuver to invest their intellectual capital to gain further recognition and thereby get the positions and material resources that can be used to produce further scientific ideas. The cultural market and the economic market both operate to produce scientific ideas in a system marked both by ritual solidarity and by domination and conflict.

A THEORY OF INTERACTION RITUAL CHAINS

Notice that we have been sketching the connections between the microlevel and macrolevel of analysis. Durkheim's theory of rituals explains how certain configurations of people with their emotions and attentions constitute rituals that produce ties of social membership and the symbols to represent them. These "collective representations" now become lodged in individuals' minds and act as gyroscopes that steer individuals towards certain encounters and away from others. One microsituation leads to another in predictable and structured ways. Thus, the mechanism of microrituals adds up to a larger pattern, the entire society on the macrolevel. Mauss filled in this model in a crucial way by showing how gift-type exchanges create status claims and obligations to replay the exchange ritual. He also showed how the ritual charges physical objects with social significance—variously defined as magic, money, or perhaps other things—that can circulate as surrogates for a social presence. These symbolic objects tie together people and situations that are far apart and that may never actually see each other face to face. Out of this charging of objects with social energy comes the phenomenon of property. The Maussian perspective becomes a fundamental underpinning for Marx.

I have proposed the notion of *interaction ritual (IR) chains* to show how microinteractions add up to the larger class structure of modern society. Every interaction is a ritual in Goffman's sense. Greetings and other forms of politeness tie people together or else set them off as status unequals. The same operates nonverbally through the symbolic significance of the way we dress and groom ourselves. Even the words of ordinary conversation are charged with a hidden code, carrying with them connotations of membership in particular groups that they received in previous conversational encounters. Giving and taking orders is a Goffmanian ritual that produces order-giving classes and order-taking classes and their symbolic outlooks (as outlined earlier in our discussion of the theory of class cultures). The same occurs in the second dimension of stratification. People whose overall pattern of encounters are cosmopolitan or localistic also have their outlooks correspondingly affected. Every aspect of people's mental and cultural possessions becomes charged with significance as a marker of social membership. Only now, instead of Durkheim's vision of rituals creating membership in the whole society, we see society broken up into stratified groups, each of which implicitly recognizes its members from the bits and pieces of stratified symbolism they bring to their social encounters.

The entire society can be visualized as a long chain of interaction rituals, with people moving from one encounter to another. There need be nothing rigid about this structure. Any combination of people might come together in a face-to-face encounter. But once they are there, they are faced with negotiating some kind of relationship, some ritual conversation. How they do this depends on the cultural capital, the symbolically charged ideas they bring to the encounter. Various outcomes are possible, depending on how *each person's cultural capital* matches up with the *other person's cultural capital*. Through a marketlike process, individuals tend to make their most satisfying exchanges at their own level. Moreover cultural capital itself circulates through the network, so that new ideas with implicit group membership attached pass from one person to another. These symbolic resources tend to stay within stratified channels; the higher social classes reproduce their own type of symbolic capital, while the lower classes also circulate their own capital, but only within their localized group. Moreover rituals that bring together unequals—bosses with employees for instance—also tend to reinforce the different symbolic outlooks of each side, giving one side a continuing share of the emotional energy and self-confidence that keeps it dominant and putting the other side at an emotional deficit that keeps it from competing effectively. But eddies in the circulation of cultural capital can upset the smooth reproduction of social strata; this is the reason why there is social mobility, as well as the dramatic ups and downs in the careers of politicians and entrepreneurs in all walks of life.

The potential is now present, in my opinion, to build together the microanalysis of face-to-face interaction in all sorts of situations, into a theory of the macrostructure of the state, of organizations, and of classes, which have been the bulwarks of the conflict tradition. Interaction rituals constitute the cultures of different social classes, and the networks made out of such repeated ritual encounters make up the reality of the larger structures. What ties all this together is a theory of stratification: the paramount reality on both levels.

The Future of the Durkheimian Tradition

We see that the Durkheimian tradition has been a rich and prospering jungle, teeming with ideas and applications in many directions. It provides a theory of rituals in the minutest level of everyday life as well as a macrotheory of the largest and most abstract forms of social structure covering the landscape of the earth. It explains the production of ideas, both in the form of religions and myths, as well as potentially explaining science itself. Many of the Durkheimian tradition's most exotic aspects have not been touched on here—such as Bourdieu's notion of education as symbolic violence or his analysis of the tribal vendetta as a status game of "lending" and "returning" throats to be cut, in which having enemies is actually a way of showing off one's status and murder is a type of exchange of gifts.

Most central of all, I would argue, the Durkheimian tradition fills in the essential underpinnings of the conflict tradition. On the microlevel of interaction, it provides the conflict tradition with an explanatory theory of the varieties of class cultures, and it builds out of these interactions a stratified network that makes up the macrostructure of domination and power struggle in the whole society. Theories of the two-leveled exchange system—of the market for cultural capital in ritual interactions and the economic market that rides on this—should be important on the agenda for tying together these two traditions. The conflict tradition can be permeated with the deeper explanatory mechanisms revealed by the Durkheimians.

To be sure, not all of Durkheimian theory necessarily goes in this direction. Durkheim's theory of crime, for instance, has its own lineage of contributions. Kai Erickson, taking up the point that crime is functional for society, developed the theory that societies actually create deviance at times when they are undergoing a boundary-maintaining crisis. What is considered deviant is always relative to the society; somewhat pessimistically, this means that even a society of saints, as Durkheim himself stated, would create its own category of deviants by magnifying small faults into significant transgressions. Erikson applied this to a real society of would-be "saints," the Puritan settlers of New England. The craze of witchcraft accusations and the persecutions of the Quakers and other "heresies" all may be seen as ways in which the colonial society as a whole, rather than individual "deviants" within it, created periodic waves of crisis. More recently Donald Black has developed the Durkheimian perspective into a general theory of social control. In our own day outcries about "crime in the streets" and about the inequities of police violence need to be seen as part of a larger process in which crime *issues* are a "normal" part of ritual imposition of social order.

Ultimately these theories of crime will need to be integrated into a consistent framework with the model of the stratified society that has been emerging on the pages of this chapter and the preceding chapter. In the meantime these theories are instances of how much vitality there is in the Durkheimian tradition. In many ways the most profound and least obvious set of ideas in sociology, the Durkheimian tradition remains somewhat of a half-kept secret amidst the various empirical and theoretical proceedings of the field today. Its potential for pulling sociology together around a common core, in my opinion, remains even more powerful today than ever before.

NOTES

1. Montesquieu also had a third type of society, Oriental despotism: a society that is large and dense like the European monarchy but that lacks its internal separation of powers and its freedom of the individual. Montesquieu had no good explanation of why this type of society should arise and merely used it to raise fears that European monarchies might grow despotic and turn into the Oriental type. Durkheim, too, was unable to explain it and, instead, put it aside as a pathological type, whereas the organic solidarity type of division of labor was the normal type for large and dense societies. Throughout his career Durkheim combated this same problem. According to his model, modern differentiated societies ought to be healthy, well integrated, and supportive of individualism; hence, he had to regard capitalist class struggles as pathologies. Tendencies to despotism would be pathological too; unquestionably this would have been Durkheim's verdict on the Fascist regimes that appeared within decades after his death. In general the Durkheimian tradition has always had trouble dealing with conflict and domination as normal, all-too-present features of society.

2. The theory of sociological statistics actually goes back to the Belgium astronomer Adolphe Quetelet. In the 1830s he collected some of the same kinds of statistics that Durkheim was to use later; Quetelet argued that because the rates were stable from year to year, there must be some social laws producing them. But Quetelet came up with no actual laws determining the statistical patterns. This Durkheim believed he had done by applying the comparative method that Quetelet had neglected to use. Interestingly enough, Durkheim got many of his statistics from the French government statistical office,

whose head was Gabriel Tarde. Tarde was Durkheim's main oppo-
nent in the sociological theory of his day. Tarde was an extreme individual reductionist who declared that society is only a collection of
individuals. The uniformities of statistics, in Tarde's view, were to be
explained by a psychological process of imitation as individuals followed the example set by other individuals. Durkheim had relatively
little trouble in disposing of this as a naive form of psychology that
did not explain why actions occurred in the first place for others to
imitate. Nor does it show who is imitated, by whom, or when and
when not. Durkheim's ritual model in fact is able to make room for
imitation when it does happen to occur: by specifying that there is a
contagion of belief *if* individuals share a focus of attention and an
emotion within a group. Notice, though, that statistics lend themselves to diametrically opposing interpretations: indicators of individual processes *or* indications of the independence of social structures.
On statistics as a *theoretical* rather than methodological issue in sociology generally, see my "Mathematics Versus Words," in *Sociological
Theory 1984* (San Francisco: Jossey-Bass, 1984).

3. There is an interesting contrast here between Marx and Comte,
who were more or less contemporaries. Both existed in an intellectual
milieu in which the powerful established Church was finally being
challenged. Marx's reaction was to treat religion as an ideology, although he was still hung up on it to the extent that most of his early
works were spent fighting with the other Young Hegelians, who tried
to generate a liberalized form of Christianity. Marx's mentor, Bruno
Bauer, wrote a famous book entitled *The Essence of Christianity* (1841),
which Marx and Engels made fun of in 1844 in *The Holy Family*. In
1846, in *The German Ideology*, Marx was still satirizing his religious-
minded compatriots by calling them "Saint Bruno," "Saint Max," and
so on. Comte, on the other hand, took religion not so much as an
illusion an enemy but as an indicator of the place of moral sentiments
underlying the social order. He simply regarded the older supernatural religions as belonging to an earlier evolutionary stage. Some modern commentators such as Robert Nisbet have claimed that sociology
has conservative origins because Comte's ideas, which in turn came
from reactionaries like De Maistre, laid the basis for Durkheimian
sociology. But De Maistre was hardly a sociologist: he argued for
belief in the supernatural, not for analysis of it. Comte and Durkheim
took the insight about the moral order and made it an idea of scientific
analysis; and, incidentally, they detached it from conservative implications, even giving it a liberal slant.

4. Fustel believed the origins of the domestic cult was the worship of dead ancestors. He claimed the hearth was built over the bones of the family founder; and in fact that as late as the Christian period, families would assemble to eat a funeral meal upon the tomb itself. (See Peter Brown, *Society and the Holy in Late Antiquity*. Berkeley: University of California Press, 1982.) This theory allowed Fustel to bolster his picture of an aboriginal patriarchal family and of the early existence of private property, which was guarded by the family's perpetual possession of the land upon which the ancestor's tomb stood. Fustel's theory of ancestor worship is the most criticized part of his work. There is no evidence that the Greeks and Latins buried their dead in family tombs on their estates; tombs were usually placed alongside roads and virtually never inside a city (Arnaldo Momigliano, "Forward" to Fustel de Coulanges, *The Ancient City*: Baltimore: Johns Hopkins University Press, 1980: ix–xiv). In fact the cult worship of the bones of heroes and reputed ancestors comes rather late (around 700–500 B.C.). Such worship seems to have been used to bolster new claims to land ownership as cities expanded their territories (Anthony Snodgrass, *Archaic Greece*, Berkeley: University of California Press, 1980: 38–39). Tombs that proclaim family unity and continuity are from 300 B.C. and later; even then these tombs are in the minority (S.C. Humphries, "Forward, Part II" to Fustel de Coulanges, *The Ancient City*: Baltimore: Johns Hopkins University Press, 1980: xx). Durkheim criticized Fustel's ancestor-worship theory, but he pointed out that it is not necessary for the better attested picture of the family religion centered on the hearth and common meals and sacrifices nor for the theory of the origin of the city in a religious cult. Fustel's ideas also entered the anthropological tradition by their influence on V. W. Robertson Smith, whose *The Religion of the Semites* (1889) described the ancient Hebrew sacrificial cult as a communal meal, and its god as a divination of the clan. Durkheim was much impressed with this book and made it the basis of his own sociology of religion.

5. Fustel's picture of ancient morality, which Durkheim incorporated into his own comparative sociology, seems overdrawn. It is true that cities treated each other ferociously in war. It is also true, as Max Weber was later to stress, that kinship-based cults established moral barriers against outsiders that inhibited the development of the capitalist market economy. But it is an exaggeration to say that exiles had no rights; at least in the 400s B.C., a political exile like Thucydides could retire to his estate elsewhere in Greece and live a secure and prosperous life. Similarly, even in the archaic period, there seems to have been an external morality in the form of the ethic of hospitality.

Guests were welcomed into the home (although not into its domestic rites), and they were given gifts that bound one to the donor with expectations of reciprocity. Such extrafamilial alliances of good will were upheld by religious beliefs: for example, the theme that Zeus protects the stranger or by the numerous myths in which a god or goddess appears in the guise of a poor wanderer, an object of charity. At the same time Fustel does seem to have captured accurately the callousness and cruelty towards losers that was so characteristic of ancient Greece. Marcel Mauss, a later generation in the intellectual lineage of Fustel and Durkheim, was to add the missing piece of the puzzle by showing how reciprocal gift exchanges among groups established social ties on a ritual basis, but of a different type. Lévi-Strauss's theory of kinship even made this exchange structure the basis of tribal society in general.

6. Durkheim and Mauss, in their study *Primitive Classification* (1903), which was a preliminary version of the theory presented in *The Elementary Forms*, made similar mistakes with the empirical evidence, this time regarding Indian tribes in the American southwest. They failed to use sufficiently their own preferred method of concomitant variation and were too quick to focus only on certain evidence that fitted their theory that a society's forms of classifying objects in the world corresponds to the actual structure of the society. Nevertheless the line of analysis they opened up proved fruitful in later versions, as, for example, Lévi-Strauss's *La pensée sauvage* (*The Savage Mind*, Chicago: University of Chicago Press, 1962).

7. French structuralism should be distinguished from the way the term "structuralism" is commonly used in American sociology. The former deals with structures in the realm of mental forms, the latter with structures in the external society such as networks of people or organizations.

8. This research method began to be replaced in the 1950s by sample surveys, which allowed the application of more sophisticated statistical methods but in the process lost the sense of actual groups that the community studies had.

9. Warner goes on to point out that small towns are particularly fond of wars because of the opportunities they give for this kind of ritual politics. They generate a feeling of solidarity and exaltation of the individual into a larger order of things generally missing in isolated communities. Here Warner gives an explicitly Durkheimian explanation of the nationalistic conservatism that Marx had pointed out among the French peasants in *The Eighteenth Brumaire*.

10. It has often been claimed that Durkheim was hostile to the individual because he placed great emphasis on the controlling influence of society. Durkheim's model of social ritual borrows from the so-called "crowd psychologists" of his own day, such as Gustave Le Bon, who emphasized that the individual in a crowd becomes taken over by a collective emotion and no longer acts by their own rational choice. But Durkheim shared none of the hostility to "the mob" that these crowd-theorists used as an argument against democracy. Durkheim attempted to show that the society itself created the very concepts of thinking that are the instruments of rationality; moreover, the changing social structure itself produced the modern society with its complex division of labor and *this is what allowed the autonomous individual to emerge in the first place.* Goffman carries out Durkheim's insight in great detail, documenting the ways in which modern society, far from being antagonistic to individuals, actually gives them extensive ritual obeisance. This is not to say modern society is not full of the dangers of bureaucratic and political manipulation and even totalitarianism, but that just means there is a war between different parts of society—my point, incidentally, not Durkheim's or Goffman's. For all that, modern society is far more individualistic than any premodern society.

11. The most famous of these studies were those begun in the 1930s by Elton Mayo at the Hawthorne plant. Mayo was another Australian, like Lloyd Warner, and a follower of Durkheim. His discovery of the informal group underlying the formal structure of the organization is a direct application to modern life of Durkheim's point that a ritual and moral tie of solidarity underlies any purely practical, utilitarian interaction.

12. Of course professionals and the upper classes generally have their own form of local gossip. The major point is that the lower classes have only their own "restricted code" that keeps their local group tied together but isolated from other groups, even at the bottom level; the higher classes have their own in-groups and corresponding forms of "restricted code" gossip and slang, but they *also* have access to the "elaborated codes" that enable them to negotiate with people at long distance with whom they may never have met.

13. Durkheim's *The Division of Labor in Society,* like Montesquieu's *The Spirit of Laws* and Tönnies's *Gemeinschaft und Gesellschaft,* describes only two types of societies: a premodern type and a modern type. This is a tremendous oversimplification of history. Although Durk-

heim's evolutionism led him to believe that his mechanical solidarity type is most pronounced among tribal societies, in fact the characteristics Durkheim described, especially a repressive legal system, are most common in stratified agrarian states, which is a much more complex form of society.

14. Marcel Mauss did a great deal of background work for what eventually became Durkheim's *The Elementary Forms of the Religious Life*, and he took primary responsibility for writing the large number of analytical reviews on anthropological studies in the *Année*. It has not yet been properly appreciated how instrumental Mauss was in this enterprise, long before his uncle's death. Although he does not have quite the same importance that Engels did for the thought of Marx, it remains a considerable distortion to try to isolate "Durkheimian" thought without seeing how permeated it was by Mauss's influence in the latter part of Durkheim's career (from the late 1890s onwards).

15. Mining true precious stones was not technologically possible until the agrarian civilizations. But even in these relatively sophisticated economic systems, precious jewels were often regarded as having magical powers as well as being the emblems and prerogative of kings and high religious officials.

4: *The Microinteractionist Tradition*

Just as we say that a body is in motion, and not that motion is in a body we ought to say we are in thought, and not that thoughts are in us.
Charles Sanders Peirce, 1868

A Native American Sociology

We come now to the distinctively American tradition: the microinteractionist and interpretive sociology that extends from Charles Horton Cooley, W. I. Thomas, and George Herbert Mead through Harold Garfinkel and the ethnomethodologists. Not that this is the only kind of sociology we have ever done in the United States. The Durkheimian and the conflict traditions have been imported and have flourished on this side of the Atlantic. And there are other native traditions such as the evolutionism of Lester Ward or that of William Graham Sumner (who founded American sociology) or the statistical emphasis of the last several decades. Microinteractionism is not the only American tradition in sociology; my own claim is that it is our most original contribution to sociological thought. It is not *the* American tradition, but only what we do best.

It is of course not without foreign relatives and even ancestors. It is a tradition that concerns the human subject and builds the social world out of human consciousness and human agency. It opposes the hard, structural image of society put forward by the Durkheimians, as well as the materialism of conflict theory. Against the rigid predictableness of science, it upholds the fluidity and meaningfulness of humanism. Thus it ties to what is sometimes called the Romanticist tradition in German philosophy: the idealism of Immanuel Kant and especially the flowing historical streams of Georg Hegel, Arthur Schopenhauer, and Wilhelm Dilthey. One can see the contrast between this and the French tradition by comparing Émile Durkheim with Ferdinand Tönnies, who launched German sociology in the 1880s with his *Gemeinschaft und Gesellschaft* (*Community and Society*). The book rather parallels Durkheim's *The Division of Labor in Society*: both contrast a personalistic traditional type of society with the impersonal modern society. But where Durkheim's "mechanical" and "organic" solidarity are two different structural types, distinguished by population density and the extent of the division of labor, Tönnies's polar types are based on two kinds of human will: *Wesenwille*, which is a "natural" expression towards other human beings, and *Kürwille*, which is rational and calculating. One might say Tönnies psychologizes and subjectivizes society, making it into a projection of individual mental processes blown up to a large screen.

SOME MAIN POINTS OF THE MICROINTERACTIONIST TRADITION

1870–1900	American pragmatists:
	    Peirce, James
		German objectivists:
		    Brentano, Meinong	

1900–1930	Dewey	Cooley Thomas Mead	Husserl

1930–1960	symbolic interactionism:
	    Blumer
	theories of deviance,
	occupations and professions:
	    Hughes
		Schutz	existentialism:
			    Heidegger
			Sartre

1960–1990	role theory		ethnomethodology: Garfinkel conversational analysis cognitive sociology
		Goffman's frame analysis	

It is this type of theme that the American sociologists were following. The early American sociologists and philosophers all went to study in Germany, as was the fashion in the late nineteenth century. This was the time, we should recall, when the American colleges were being reformed into graduate research universities. German universities, which had undergone this revolution 75 years earlier, were the model. Thus, it is not surprising that the early American sociologists imported German ideas. Again, in the 1940s and 1950s, another wave of microsociology was set off in the United States by a German refugee, Alfred Schutz, who inspired Harold Garfinkel to create ethnomethodology. Garfinkel proceeded to bring in an additional set of German intellectual ancestors, especially the philosophers Edmund Husserl and Martin Heidegger.

Despite these German roots, American microinteractionism is much more than an imitation. In both the earlier wave that gave rise to symbolic interactionism and the later wave that resulted in ethnomethodology and phenomenology, the Americans profoundly transformed what they received. German philosophy was a stimulus, but it was the Americans who went on to create genuinely sociological theories. Where the Germans, so to speak, left the philosophical level of consciousness as something inviolable to which one must pay one's respects, the Americans took it apart and in the process created a social theory of mind.

In what follows, I will concentrate on these achievements in microsociology. That is not to say that theorists like Cooley and Mead wrote only about the mind and the self. They also spun out theories about the larger structure of society. But this was not their strength; the picture that emerges is comparatively naive and unsophisticated by comparison to the strengths of the Durkheimian and the conflict traditions. It has a kind of goody-goody quality about it that makes social institutions seem like a grade-school assembly. When Talcott Parsons came back from sojourning in Heidelberg and the London School of Economics in the 1920s, he had little trouble in sweeping this away before his more powerful imports of European macrosociology. What has maintained its strength in America is the part the Europeans lacked: a genuine microsociology of the self and the flux of situations that it immediately faces. It is to this we now turn.

PHILOSOPHY BECOMES A BATTLEGROUND
BETWEEN RELIGION AND SCIENCE

The American tradition arises at first, not within sociology but among American philosophers, in the form of pragmatism. The sociologists of the late 1800s were by and large concerned with social problems such as immigration and crime, and when they did raise theoretical issues they did so by invoking evolution, a macroconception. In philosophy, though, the time was one of major intellectual upheaval owing to the university revolution. The new research-oriented university was replacing a system of colleges that had provided religious instruction. The original mission of American colleges was largely to train ministers. The reason why the United States has so many hundreds of colleges goes back to the frontier days when every Protestant denomination felt it had to have its own college in every locality so that the Baptists could study good Baptist doctrine, the Methodists could study good Methodist doctrine, and so forth. But the new German-style universities no longer emphasized piety but rather science and scholarship. Even biblical studies had now been transformed into history and textual criticism. In the modern world, the old "unreformed" colleges and their religious instruction carried the sign: "Out-of-date."

This created a problem for the American profession of university professors; none felt it more acutely than the philosophers. Other specialized subjects might evade the issue of what to make of the old religious studies, but the philosophers had to meet it head on. Philosophy had been a major subject in the old colleges, but it took the form of a preliminary to theological studies. What could it now gracefully say about religion in a time when science was riding high? Darwin, Spencer, and the controversy about evolution had put religion on the defensive; at the same time a dazzling set of discoveries in physics and chemistry were changing the world with electricity, steel mills, and gasoline engines.

The same issue had to be faced in Europe as well. One

type of reaction was that of France. The French Revolution already at the time of Napoleon had abolished the old medieval university dominated by the theologians and replaced it with technical schools like the École Polytechnique and the École Normale Supérieure. France reacted to the new science by embracing it wholeheartedly and abolishing religion entirely from its official intellectual purview. The typical French intellectual, like Émile Durkheim, was an atheist who wished to replace religion with an entirely secular outlook.

In England and Germany, the old religious instruction was not replaced so abruptly. It was necessary to make some compromise between religion and the new secular scholarship. The form this took was Idealist philosophy: the generation of Kant and Hegel (around 1800) is the generation of the German university reform. Because the British reformed their universities much later (in the 1880s, at about the same time as the Americans), their wave of idealist philosophy came later, led by such thinkers as T. H. Green and F. H. Bradley. Idealist philosophy is a kind of intellectual compromise with religion: it declares that the world is a manifestation of Spirit and that there are transcendent values. Religion thus still has a place, but at the cost of abandoning the old literal interpretation of the Scriptures. The bulwark of faith is no longer the Bible, but a liberalized theology worked out by the reasoning of philosophers.

From the point of view of the orthodox believers, this was all rather heretical. The virgin birth, the miracles, the literal divinity of Jesus, even the stern punishments and Heavenly rewards of God the Father were being displaced by a reasoned argument for Spirit and the importance of social good works. In America, one philosopher declared that God's world was not a Kingdom but a Republic, and the Harvard philosopher Josiah Royce must have raised some eyebrows by his assertion that "it is the State, the Social Order, that is divine." Nevertheless, something had to be done to make religion more palatable in a secular world dominated by the obvious triumphs of science. From about 1880 to 1920, Idealism became the leading philosophy throughout American universities.

This by itself does not sound like a promising basis for a sociology of mind. But it opened the way for it. Part of its argument for the reality of spiritual factors in the universe was to point out the important role of consciousness in the material world. The most obvious "spiritual" institutions are such entities as art, literature, law, the history of thought. Royce and the young John Dewey went further and argued that social institutions like the state are not material, but are sets of ideals that people orient towards and by which people guide their conduct. Thus, the social world was interpreted as manifestations of human consciousness. Ideas were taken as objective— existing outside the individual human being—because one can actually see them out there. Our ideas are not invented by ourselves, the way the materialist philosophers had claimed. One does not get ideas by viewing things with one's senses and then forming mental associations that result in ideas like "chair," "red," and so forth. On the contrary, these ideas are passed to us ready-made in the form of language. The argument was made on a philosophical level as a way of defending the priority and objectivity of the Spiritual side of things over the material. But one can see that this argument opened the way for a sociological interpretation of the mind: the individual not as an isolated observer of the physical world abstracting from chairs and patches of color, but the individual as a participant in human society whose mind is filled up through the medium of language.

The Idealist philosophers opened the pathway, but they could not follow it. For them, the emphasis was too much on the objective side of the Spirit. Human beings were merely passive recipients of the Spirit, a kind of register for receiving a Divine message: God declaring himself in a secular world. To turn this into sociology, ideas had to be brought back down to earth and given their origins in real individuals. And those individuals had to be set in motion, made into active agents in the here and now of the real world. The thinkers who took this step were the pragmatists.

The Pragmatism of Charles Sanders Peirce

The most famous pragmatist was William James, the Harvard psychologist and philosopher. His basic argument was that ideas are not copies of external objects but rather that truth is simply a form of action, consisting of ideas that work, that bring about the consequences we desire. James was rather a lightweight philosopher, and the lack of objectivity in his system left him an easy target for his professional colleagues. Actually he was not really interested in questions of epistemology, but in using philosophy to defend religion. This was of course what the Idealists were doing too, but whereas they tried to find a Spiritual equivalent of God in the world around us, James took a more psychological approach to the sentiment of belief. For James, it is correct to believe in free will because one could not otherwise act morally; and it is correct to believe in God, even with the absence of convincing evidence, because *all* of our thoughts in fact are likewise based on faith rather than complete evidence. James ends up in effect endorsing any religion, without providing any means to ascertain what precise theology might be true. This was not very satisfactory to theologians, but it was as far as James wished to go.[1]

The real intellectual leader of pragmatism was James's friend, Charles Sanders Peirce. Peirce is probably the greatest philosopher ever produced in the United States. At the same time he was one of the most idiosyncratic. He never held a regular academic position (though he lectured at Harvard and Johns Hopkins) nor published a book. He left behind a jumble of manuscripts on all manner of topics, much of it confused and ill integrated. He was often deliberately esoteric, and he was fond of obscure expressions and of coining new ones: agapasticism, idioscopy, fallibilism (Peirce's term for his own philosophy), phaneron (for idea), pherneroscopy (for phenomenology), synechism, enthymene, illation, not to mention "the Chorisy, Cyclosy, Peripraxy, and Apeiry of Space." His own metaphysics divides the world into three aspects, which he infelicitously labeled Firstness, Secondness, and Thirdness. Psychology for Peirce was "psychognosy," geology was "geognosy." One suspects he was often joking at his colleagues' expense, such as when he objected to the way James had developed pragmatism and announced that he would use the word "pragmaticism" for his own doctrine because it was "ugly enough to be safe from kidnappers."

One might wonder how Peirce's ideas ever received any recognition. The answer is simple: Peirce was a genius, and he was right in the center of things. His father, Benjamin Peirce, was a Harvard professor and America's most famous mathematician. Charles Peirce lived in Cambridge and was regularly consulted by important intellectuals. Royce received what technical sophistication there is in his system from Peirce's suggestions; John Dewey, too, came under Peirce's influence. In the early 1870s, William James and other future luminaries (including the pioneering legal pragmatist and Chief Justice of the Massasetts Supreme Court, Oliver Wendell Holmes) used to meet for an informal seminar in Peirce's study and carried away his ideas, if only in a less sophisticated version.

One difference between Peirce and the later pragmatists was that he was much more deeply grounded in science and less favorable to religion than they were. Partly this may be accounted for by their backgrounds. William James's father, Henry James, Sr. (the junior Henry James, the novelist, was William's brother) was a well-known popular philosopher, a follower of the Swedish spiritualist Swedenborg. The Peirce family loyalty, by contrast, was first of all to science, and they were somewhat hostile to religion because of the obstacle its dogmas had been to the development of scientific truth. Charles Peirce took the approach that he would make philosophy into a science by expanding on the discipline of logic.

This was a visionary step. Logic in Peirce's day was a set of formal deductive exercises, going back to the medieval scholastics and beyond them to Aristotle. Various forms of thinking were classified into types of syllogisms, of which the most famous, referred to in student colloquialism as *Barbara*, ran:

(A) All men are mortal.
(B) All Greeks are men.
(C) Therefore, all Greeks are mortal.

Peirce objected to this version of logic as a hindrance to actual reasoning. Little of the way we actually think, he pointed out, takes this form. How does one arrive at the major premise (A) for example? It is here where most of science takes place, and indeed much of ordinary thinking. *Deduction* is much less important than *induction*, the process of arriving at such generalizations.

But Peirce goes even further. Induction is not simply a matter of looking at the evidence and automatically coming up with a conclusion. Unlike many of the "associationist" philosophers of his day, Peirce knew enough about scientific research to realize that generalizations do not just leap out of the facts. There is a whole strategy of investigation, not the least of which is a purely mental effort to frame one's hypotheses. This preliminary process of conjecture Peirce called *abduction*. It is nonrigorous and nonempirical, a mere guessing at relationships. But nevertheless it is a crucial aspect without which science could never accomplish anything. Moreover in Peirce's view abduction too, is a form of inference—of logic in the largest sense—by which one moves from one set of ideas to their conclusions in another set of ideas. At its basis, science is founded on processes of the human mind that are the same as those involved in common sense.

This gave Peirce a way of broadening the method of logic, not merely to include science and philosophy, but to become an entire theory of the mind in all its activities. Every form of thinking, he proposed, consists of some connection from one idea to another. These connections and their laws can be investigated empirically. The science that he founded to do this, he called "semiotics." Here at least the term stuck (although Peirce also used his own peculiar variants "semiosy" and "semiosis"), unlike his term "abduction," which never achieved popular usage.

Semiotics is the science of signs. In Peirce's view one never perceives or thinks about the world directly, but only through the mediation of a sign. Meaning is always a three-cornered relationship, between the *sign*, the *object* (but only in the aspect to which the sign refers), and the *internal referent* or thought. There is no direct connection—as the associationist philosophers like John Locke and his followers had believed—between the idea and the external object to which it supposedly refers. The sign is always there in the middle, exerting a controlling influence. For signs are not isolated. They are external to the individual and their essence is that they are equivalent for everyone who uses them. Thus, words (or visual symbols, noises, etc.) always intervene in the process of thinking and intrude an element of the universal and the social into the individual mind.

Moreover, in a second sense, signs are not isolated. Signs are used in chains, one after another; they connect not only to object and to inner thoughts, but also to each other. One sign carries connotations of other signs. Part of this connectiveness is in the sign's penumbra of meaning, as one word refers to other words into which it may be partly or wholly translated (what is now called *semantics*). Another part is the dynamic connection of words in a sentence or chain of thought (what is now called *syntax*, although Peirce had in mind a very broad conception of such thought sequences, far beyond the individual sentence). Logic, in Peirce's sense, consists of these connections of signs with each other, with all that this implies about their relation to thoughts and objects as well. Our logical inferences are mental habits; what we consider to be a valid belief is a habit of moving from one sign to another that is so well established that it takes place without any doubt at all.

Even emotions come into this scheme. Emotions have their own logic—an inference from one mental state to another—through the mediation of signs (and sometimes with reference to outside objects). Consciousness itself is a certain kind of emotion, usually very mild, attached to certain kinds of sign relations. Peirce, 20 years or more before Freud, was conceiving of mental processes as operating unconsciously as long as the habits of connection are firmly established and nothing happens to disturb the smooth flow of inference. On the other hand we become highly conscious of something, when we become emotionally aroused about it; in fact the emotion is simply the particular type of disturbance we are experiencing in the flow of inference.

From this vantage point, Peirce attacks the type of philosophy expressed by René Descartes, which attempts to reach certainty by doubting everything until there are only certain fundamentals left that cannot be doubted. Descartes' *"Cogito, ergo sum"* ("I think, therefore I am") is an impossibility, Peirce proclaims, because we cannot think at all without having signs, and the signs contain a reference to other signs and to other people who also use them. Thinking always takes place in a community, and indeed what we call truth is objective only because it is the mental habits towards which we as a group will inevitably tend as these mental habits enable all of us to operate in the world. Peirce's epistemology, thus, leaves room for an objective, material world in a way that James merely glossed over. At the same time it proposes an essentially social theory of mind. Man, said Peirce, is simply the sum total of his thoughts, and this sum is always a historical bundle of his society's experience. We never arrive at total certainty on anything in the sense of a rigorous logical proof; even in mathematics, it is possible to question the fine basis of connections from one idea to another. In fact we never do so; our working criterion of truth is simply the absence of doubt, a pragmatism that is working well enough at the time so that the ideas flow seemingly automatically. This is what we mistake for absolute truth.

Peirce was not explicitly a sociologist. He did not visualize the possibility of such a science, though he does include in his classification of the "Human Sciences" a branch called "Descriptive Psychics, or History." He had little conception of social structure. This was quite typical of most American thinkers of his generation and several generations thereafter. One of his pragmatist successors, John Dewey, wrote a great deal about questions of social philosophy, although this can hardly be considered a realistic contribution to sociology. Dewey was more concerned with the ideals of democracy than its actualities. He did a great deal of publicity work for "Progressive Education," the notion that schools should become part of a general course of life adjustment rather than a learning of traditional subjects. This served as an ideological justification for diluting the scholastic contents of schooling in a period of massive expansion of the school system in the early twentieth century; but neither Dewey nor any of the other followers of pragmatism had the detachment to see the struggles over social status that were involved in this nor the trend of credential inflation that they were setting in motion. As is typical with most philosophers who want to treat society without mastering any explanatory principles of sociology, their ideals of how things ought to be get in the way of seriously understanding why things are as they are and, hence, of having any realistic chance of putting their ideals into practice.

The pragmatists never dominated their home ground of American philosophy. During the heyday of Peirce, James, and Dewey—approximately 1870 to 1930 of their overlapping lifetimes—philosophy departments usually taught versions of Idealism, which could claim to be more genuinely philosophical than pragmatism in dealing with grand questions of metaphysics and more objective in its conception of truth. When Idealism finally collapsed in the secularism of the twentieth century, it was replaced in the 1930s and 1940s by logical positivism, which concentrated on a narrow technical set of rules of what was conceived to be the scientific method. Peirce's broader and more realistic conception of science was forgotten. It has only turned up again, in a somewhat different guise, in the echoes found recently in the sociology of science.

In general the sociologists ended up being the heirs to the pragmatist tradition. Not that they accepted everything. The pragmatist defense of religion, James's prime interest, was the first to go. Dewey's Progressive ideology, too, did not stand a chance once American sociologists began to import the more serious Durkheimian and conflict theories. Dewey did make a contribution, perhaps not yet sufficiently appreciated, to the sense of the fluidity of life as it emerges in an ongoing sequence of situations. The most important contribution of pragmatism though was to stimulate empirical sociologists to set forth an action-oriented and completely social theory of the nature of mind and self.

Society Is in the Mind: Cooley

Charles Horton Cooley was a colleague of John Dewey at the University of Michigan. But Cooley was a member of the newly founded sociology department, not a philosopher, and his theory is built up from empirical observations, if only a somewhat casual kind. The first significant statement of American micro-sociology came early in the twentieth century, in Cooley's *Human Nature and the Social Order* (1902).

Cooley begins with the commonplace observation that children often have imaginary playmates. Physically they may be alone, but in their imagination they are still in the presence of others. Cooley takes this as a clue to the development of the mind. Thinking, he proposes, consists of imaginary conversation, carried on silently inside. Children learn to think initially by learning to talk. Talking with imaginary playmates, then, is an intermediate stage as the child learns to internalize talk; here the talk is still carried on out loud, but with an imaginary partner.

Even for adults, Cooley continues, there is no essential difference between real and imaginery persons. Other people are real to us only because we imagine an inner life that we do not directly observe, but which we project into them. "All real persons are imaginery in this sense," Cooley declares. "My association with you evidently consists in the relation between my idea of you and the rest of my mind." Cooley thus proposes a kind of phenomenological empiricism. One only encounters one's ideas of other people, never the people themselves. Their physical bodies standing before us are important only because they provide a center around which to crystalize our sentiments. After all, asks Cooley, what can one learn from weighing or measuring people's physical traits that gives any clue to their true personality? The aim of sociology is to observe the true facts of society, and these consist of no more than the imaginations that people have of one another.

Society, then, must be studied primarily in the imagination. Physically real persons are not socially real unless someone actually imagines them. They cannot act upon us unless we become consciously aware of their social intentions towards us. If someone went into a strange country and hid himself so well that no one knew he was there, Cooley declares, he would have no social existence for the inhabitants. This seems to give a rather ethereal view of society, but Cooley makes this into a theoretical virtue. If persons are thought of as primarily physical, there is no way to explain how society exists. One observes only separate bodies, and society must be conceived of as some mysterious force added on from outside, called sociality, altruism, or the like. But there is no problem when one realizes that each person's mind is already social and that the social is the mind. Society is a relation among ideas. "In order to have society it is evidently necessary that persons should get together somewhere; and they get together only as personal ideas in the mind. Where else?" The human Mind (which Cooley now capitalizes) is a collective growth extending across the ages, and it is the locus of society in the broadest sense.

Cooley's view of society, as one can imagine, is extraordinarily benign. There is no real difference between selfishness and altruism, he declares, because the self and the other do not exist except in relation to each other. Altruism is not a special motive but is implied in all our sentiments; and one can never even think "I," except with an implicit reference to other persons. Conflict or domination can scarcely enter into such a scheme. Social problems are just a matter of misunderstanding and can be solved by a broader appreciation of the point of view of others. The naive American ideology is apparent here. Cooley's social idealism is so extreme that he sees no difference between fictional persons and really existing ones; Hamlet is just as socially real as the janitor downstairs—in fact probably more so because more people think about Hamlet. Cooley declares that the Russian nobleman who thinks of the serf as a mere animal is not socially affected by him because the serf does not act on his mind and conscience. The example is extremely ill chosen because the serf provides the material labor on which the nobleman's style of life depends, and indeed his very existence as a social class. Cooley writing in his middle-class study in Ann Arbor, Michigan, 15 years before the Russian revolution was lulled into a fanciful view of such things.

Nevertheless one cannot write off Cooley as a mere dreamer. His theory is next to worthless as a model of the larger structures of society. But it did open the way to a theory of microsociology as a process of mental interpretation. Cooley's example of Hamlet being more socially real than the people around us is a little foolish, but it becomes much less so if one substitutes an historical name like Jesus or Mohammed or the

contemporary name of some distant pop star who sets the ideal
for millions to emulate. "The imaginations which people have of
one another are the *solid facts* of society," Cooley declared. Not
the only solid facts, one should add, but solid and important
enough nevertheless.

George Herbert Mead's Sociology of Thinking

Where Cooley was suggestive but superficial, George Herbert
Mead developed this line of thought into a sophisticated theory
of the social mind. Mead was not a sociologist, but a philosopher who taught at the University of Chicago in the same
department as John Dewey (who had moved on from Michigan). He had studied at Harvard with Josiah Royce, the Idealist
philosopher mentioned earlier for his extravagant beliefs in the
divinity of the state. By comparison, Mead was a hard-nosed
empiricist, even a materialist. He called himself a social behaviorist and admired the psychologist John B. Watson who proposed to reduce the mind to the study of overt behavior and to
induct the laws of human behavior from experiments on animals. For Mead, however, the crucial behavior is always social
behavior. It is the interaction between biological organisms and
the internalization of this back-and-forth motion inside human
beings that constitutes the mind.

Mead takes his point of entry by distinguishing sharply
between the self and the body. The self is something that is
reflexive, that can be both a subject and an object, and that can
make an object of itself. Our bodily parts (e.g., the heart, the
digestive system) are capable of running along without our
conscious control, and they take what unity they have because
we make them belong to our self. When we are completely
absorbed in doing something, there is no self. Moreover there
are many experiences of the self without reference to a body: in
thinking, in imagination, or in memory.

Where, then, does this nonbodily self come from? The self
is a point of view. We can never see our body as whole, even
in a mirror. The individual experiences him/herself not by direct observation, but only indirectly from the standpoint of

others. This is what is distinctive about human communication as well; an animal makes noises that carry some significance to other members of their species, but the human's words are symbols that are directed not only to others, but also to oneself. Unlike Cooley, who had only a crude sense of the mind, Mead had assimilated the sophisticated three-pointed structure of Peirce's theory of meaning. The human being is distinguished from other animals because he/she can be an object for him/herself. It is this reflexivity, Mead declares, and not some supernatural entity like the Soul, that makes one uniquely human, thus breaking entirely from the religious sentiments of his own teacher Royce.

This self, which can be an object for itself, arises only in social experience. After one has acquired this social viewpoint, one can then become solitary and carry on one's internal thoughts, but not before. Thought is a conversation of gestures carried out with oneself. But even conversation with others has this self-referential quality. We are able to think of what words we are going to say next because we take the point of view of the other and assess the other's reaction to what we have said so far. This also applies in the internalized conversation that constitutes thought: we have to monitor ourselves continually as inner speaker by taking the standpoint of inner audience so that we can direct the flow of the subsequent parts of our thoughts.

Mead goes further than Cooley in yet another respect. Whereas Cooley had the commonsense notion of a unitary self, Mead pointed out that each individual has multiple selves. We have different relationships to different people and are one thing to one person and another thing to someone else. There are different selves for different kinds of social relationships and some parts of the self that exist only subjectively in relationship to oneself. Mead thus enters into the same kind of territory as Sigmund Freud, although with a rather different division of parts of the self. As we will see, this emphasis on multiple selves was especially followed up by Erving Goffman.

Mead was a pragmatist in his emphasis on meaning and belief as a form of action. He elaborates Peirce's semiotic triad of meaning: there is always a gesture (which might be a sound) made by one organism to another, a response by the other,

and the resulting act that responds to the gesture. Our thinking takes place by means of symbols charged with meaning in
this manner. Even something as mundane as a chair is symbolized by the gesture (verbal or possibly otherwise, such as the
physical act of sitting down) that enters into communication in
this way. Symbols are not part of the physical world around us
because that always consists of particular objects—*this* chair,
that corner of the room—whereas symbols are universals. They
call out the same response in everyone and, hence, cross over
innumerable particular situations. Even nonverbal language
depends on calling out the same response in others. "A person
who is saying something is saying to himself what he says to
others," declared Mead, "otherwise he does not know what he
is talking about."

Mead describes the development of the mind in childhood
in a fashion that takes off from Cooley's description of children's imaginary playmates. Mead broadens this to play in
general, whether alone or with other children. The earliest
form of play is a version of make-believe: being a mother, a
policeman, the driver of a toy car (or even the car itself), or
whatever. Small children play endlessly at these passtimes
because this is the first and simplest stage of "being another to
one's self." It is learning to take the role of the other, which is
crucial for being able to take an external stance on oneself.

The next stage, for older children, is organized games.
Whether it is hide-and-seek or baseball, there is now a new
structure to be mastered. The child must take the attitudes of
everyone involved in the game to play any one position. The
shortstop must know what the batter is doing as well as the
first-baseman to whom he or she is throwing the ball; the attitudes of all the others are intertwined in every position. At this
stage one's social self becomes further crystalized. Earlier the
small child switches rapidly from one role to another, from one
imaginery game to the next, and from one mood to its opposite. This rapid succession of roles, Mead points out, is both
the charm and the weakness of childhood. It explains both the
child's wonderful spontaneity and capacity to be absorbed in
things and also the volatility that will pitch him or her from
laughter to tears in a moment.

Organized games represent a more advanced stage of the organization of the self. One takes on roles more deliberately and stays in them as the social situation demands. Both the self and the surrounding network of roles become more solidly structured. It is for this reason that children begin to take an interest in rules and may become quite inflexible about the importance of following them exactly. The higher level of reflexivity in which the players realize that rules are invented and can be changed has not yet been reached. What these external-seeming rules represent is the attainment of a mental structure that Mead calls "the Generalized Other." This is not merely the taking of the stance of some particular other person upon oneself, but a permanent faculty of the mind that takes the attitude of the whole community. It is a kind of spectator's-eye view of the entire baseball team, with each role intermeshed into the others. "The Generalized Other" is the basis for the complex institutional cooperation that makes up the institution of society. Property, for example, is not merely one's relationship to some physical thing, but a recognition that one's right will be generally recognized by others.

"The Generalized Other" is also crucial for the individual's own mind. Only by taking the attitude of "the Generalized Other" towards one's self is it possible for the individual to think in those abstract symbols that constitute the rational, adult mind. Words are universals, which call out the same attitude in everyone; this implication of universality could not exist if there were not some mental structure that takes the attitude of everyone. It is a kind of global mirror off which each individual person bounces his or her own utterances to give them a general significance.

The other parts of the self are derived from this structure. Cooley spoke of "the looking-glass self," as a kind of self-image derived from outside. Mead pointed out that this is only part of the structure. There is an "I," a spontaneous action part of oneself that responds to the social situation and makes gestures to others. The self is *not* completely determined from outside, but it has an element of freedom and initiative. There is also the "Me," the self comprised by the attitudes taken by other people towards one. This is the self-image, the self as proud or humble, good or bad, ugly or beautiful. The "Me" is a derived self, which emerges only reflectively after one has made active gestures toward other people. Cooley's looking-glass self is reduced to a lesser position and, thus, the entire system is made more dynamic. In all of this the Generalized Other plays a pivotal role. The "looking-glass" is not merely outside, as Cooley had it; rather, it has to become a permanent fixture inside one's mind if one is to be able to glance one's thoughts off it and thus give them the general significance that makes them communicable. It is equally important even when one is alone. It is the Generalized Other that provides an abstract, nonspecific audience that can be used for the internal conversation that makes up one's thinking.

Mead thus provides a model of the mind as a set of interacting parts. It is socially anchored because "the Generalized Other" is its central reference point, though an invisible one. At the same time it is individual and fundamentally free because the "I" always negotiates with other people rather than accepts preexisting social demands. Yet again one's thinking is permeated by society because the counters that one moves around in one's mind as one plans out a course of action are aspects of the "Me," little images of oneself that one imagines in various situations as one mentally tries out various alternatives. One might say (though this is my metaphor, not Mead's) that the self is a kind of checkerboard on which the "Me" (really the *several* "Me's") are the checkers, the "I" is the player who makes the moves, and the "Generalized Other" is the light hanging over the board that makes the moves intelligible. Or to use another metaphor, the self is a series of mutually reflecting mirrors continually in motion.

Blumer Creates Symbolic Interactionism

One can see that there are several different directions in which Mead's system can be taken. One direction emphasizes the fluidity and negotiatedness of the social order. This is the direction taken by Herbert Blumer, reinforced by the tendency of the Chicago school of sociology. Another direction is exactly the opposite, to stress the embeddedness of the self in a set of social roles, which gives rise to so-called role theory. We will take up each of these in turn.

George Herbert Mead, as noted, was not a sociologist, nor did he publish more than a few sociological writings in his own lifetime. But his lectures at the University of Chicago were popular in the 1920s among sociology students. This was the time when American sociology was acquiring its first real research tradition, led by the Chicago sociologists W. I. Thomas and Robert E. Park. These sociologists were not particularly strong on theory, and their research interests tended to focus on social problems of the modern city and the assimilation of new immigrants into American society. What theories they did derive tended to be ecological and structural rather than micro-interactional. But W. I. Thomas, who had some training in German philosophy owing to his sojourn there around the turn of the century, did stress a voluntaristic element that fitted in well with the activist side of Mead. Lodged in the pages of a social problems tract called *The Child in America*, Thomas formulated a few brief sentences that have subsequently become famous as "the Thomas theorem." "If men define situations as real, they are real in their consequences," goes his leading point. Social life has the quality that what people think it is, it tends to become. If a certain behavior becomes defined as prestigeful, that will be what people will do; if it is defined as the reverse, it will become socially deviant and avoided by those who wish to be respectable.

This makes life highly fluid and capable of rapid changes. If the definition of a situation can be shifted, the behavior it elicits will switch, sometimes to startling extremes. It was this interpretation of Mead that was stressed by Herbert Blumer, at the time a young instructor in the University of Chicago's sociology department. After Mead's death in 1931, Blumer became his ardent spokesman. He coined the term "Symbolic Interactionism" to summarize Mead's position, which he claimed to be faithfully reiterating. It should be noted, though, that there has been considerable controversy over this point. Blumer's Symbolic Interactionism looks a good deal more like a development of Thomas's "definition of the situation" than it does like the side of Mead that follows the behaviorist Watson, and it is very different from the role theorists who attempted to crystalize Mead into a determinative set of explanatory laws.

There may also be an element of John Dewey's philosophy in Blumer's Symbolic Interactionism. Dewey had also been on the philosophy faculty at the University of Chicago before moving on to Columbia, and he could easily have been part of the intellectual atmosphere surrounding Blumer. Dewey had attacked the utilitarian model of the rational actor as someone who chooses means to achieve ends and thereby maximize one's rewards and minimize one's punishments. Dewey pointed out that means and ends are not really separated in the real world. In ordinary situations, one merely acts habitually, finding ends as one moves along at the same time as one finds means to reach them. One situation flows into another, and a rational calculating mentality does not ordinarily enter into it.

Blumer adopted this situational model and pushed it to an extreme. People do not simply find roles ready-made. They constantly create them and recreate them from one situation to the next. So-called social institutions—the state, the family, the economy—only exist as people actually come together in situations. We can act together because we construct actions together. This is done through the mechanism Mead had pointed out: each individual projects himself or herself (i.e., the "Me" aspect of the self) into various future possibilities; each one takes the role of the other in order to see what kind of reaction there will be to this action; as a result each aligns his or her own action in terms of the consequences he or she foresees in the other person's reactions. Society is not a structure, but a process. Definitions of situations emerge from this continuous negotiation of perspectives. Reality is socially constructed. If it takes on the same form over and over again, it is only because the parties to the negotiation have worked out the same resolution and because there is no guarantee that they cannot do it differently next time.

Blumer's version of Symbolic Interactionism places a premium on spontaneity and indeterminateness. Any institution can change; society can erupt into revolution. This never became the dominant position in American sociology. Even during Blumer's own career, the evolutionary and ecological approaches to structure gave way to Talcott Parsons' and Robert Merton's structural functionalism on the one hand and then increasingly to macroconflict theories on the other hand. But Blumer made Symbolic Interactionism into a powerful undercurrent and a vocal opposition. He vehemently critiqued all rival positions, which in his view reified the social structure and lost sight of the primary reality, the individual negotiating social situations. Functionalism, in Blumer's view, was an unreal playing with abstract categories. Survey research and the quantitative research methods in general (which became increasingly popular in one wing of sociology from the 1950s onwards) were equally condemned by Blumer as losing the essence of social life. Answers to a questionnaire about one's attitudes, Blumer stated, are completely unrealistic because they abstract out the real situations in which people act. To ask someone their attitudes about race relations, for example, is merely showing how people act in the situation of talking to an interviewer and has nothing to do with how they behave in various situations when they actually deal with black or white persons. Blumer's negative comments stung his opponents, one of whom charged him with being "the grave-digger of sociological research."

Nevertheless Blumer exerted considerable influence. He held forth at the University of Chicago for 20 years and edited the prestigeous *American Journal of Sociology;* then in the 1950s, he moved to the West Coast to organize a famous sociology department at the University of California, Berkeley. Symbolic Interactionism did not remain merely a critique of other sociologies, but created its own tradition of research. Building on the strength of the Chicago School in participant observation, it developed a theory of occupations and professions in which these become not entities but processes: forms of interaction negotiated by the participants themselves. Under the guidance of Blumer's Chicago colleague Everett Hughes, the symbolic interactionist approach to professions saw doctors, lawyers, and janitors alike as maneuvering to hide their dirty work and manipulate their public image. [The empirical influence of this on Erving Goffman has already become obvious, although

Goffman brought his theoretical interpretations from a different (Durkheimian) tradition.] The picture that emerges is far
from the official, laudatory view of the professions held by the
functionalists; instead, it is a kind of exposé of the hidden
politics of professions.

The other stronghold of Symbolic Interactionism has been
the field of deviance. Such researchers as Alfred Lindesmith,
Howard Becker, and Edwin Schur took an "insider's" approach to the situations and outlooks of delinquents, alcohol-
ics, drug users, and other violaters of society's standards rather
than accepting the official viewpoint of the social control
agencies. They pointed out how "deviants" go through their
own careers and arrive at an interpretation of themselves that
makes them pursue a path contrary to the "straight" or
"square" world. From this perspective, "deviance" itself is not
a category to be taken for granted; the standards that are violated are not an objective entity, but are themselves politically
negotiated. Edwin Schur describes the creation of "crimes
without victims," such as drug use, gambling, or abortion, and
Howard Becker created the concept of "moral entrepreneurs"
to analyze the manuevers of persons on the official side who
attempt to create categories of deviance to impose on others.

Symbolic Interactionism has taken an underdog slant that
contrasts sharply with the benign and official platitudes about
society that Cooley used to endorse. The trajectory of the last
70 or 80 years has been from the superstraight into the underground, with Blumer's critique of official sociology as the turning point. In recent years Symbolic Interactionism has even
become allied, at least for some sociologists, with a Marxian
conflict approach. This is not true of all forms of conflict theory, especially the more hard-nosed materialist variety, but
Symbolic Interactionism has been made to fit fairly well with
an antipositivist, antiscience version of Marxism that speaks of
the transitoriness and arbitrary features of the capitalist social
order. There is even a deep intellectual logic to this convergence because both traditions have remote ancestors in the
German idealist and historicist philosophies such as those of
Hegel and Dilthey.

Not all of Mead's followers have gone in this direction,

however. There remains another branch, which also calls itself Symbolic Interactionism—though sometimes also called "role theory"—which attempts to work out a general scientific theory of the self in relation to the social structure. For this line of analysis, social institutions are made up of roles into which individuals fit. The family has roles of father, mother, children, sibling, and so on. These roles are preexisting rather than negotiated by the participants. This theory links up with the functionalist view of society, especially when it describes the roles as being made up out of institutionalized norms and values. This may be somewhat empty categorizing, but one part of the theory attempts to deal with empirically discernable differences in individual behavior. The most elaborate part of the theory deals with multiple roles that an individual may have in their "role set" (a term created by Robert Merton, who integrated role theory into his functionalist analysis). Thus, one individual can be simultaneously wife (to her husband), mother (to her children), daughter (to her own parents), employee (to her boss at work), leader (of a PTA committee), and so on. The question then becomes: How do individuals deal with possible conflicts among different parts of their role set? In the most refined part of the theory, developed by Ralph Turner, a set of propositions is offered that attempts to predict in what roles the individual is most likely to lodge himself or herself: that is to say, which roles will the individual most identify with as "truly" himself or herself and which roles will the individual see as the most superficial?

There is a considerable difference in tone between the two branches of Symbolic Interactionism. Role theorists like the kind of banal and homey illustrations given above (the PTA mother and so forth), as compared to "underground" topics preferred by the more radical Blumerian situationalists. The role theorists have resolutely plodded ahead in creating a scientific theory, while the situationalists have generally attacked abstract theorizing in favor of being true to the fluidity and spontaneity of real life. Nevertheless the tradition may have run itself into the ground theoretically. The situationalists have tended to abandon theory for the examination of particular social problems, thus returning to the atheoretical stance that dominated in the early years of the century. Role theory continues to work towards an advancing scientific model, but it has cut down its scope to the fairly narrow question of how the self is embedded in social roles. This not only loses the dynamic side of the individual, which Mead had stressed, but also it becomes only a partial theory of the self. For Mead had produced a model of the mind, specifying the internal apparatus of consciousness—the internal conversation of "I," "Me," and "the Generalized Other" that makes up a sociological theory of thinking. Role theory loses focus on this internal structure and merely points to ways in which the self becomes attached to one or another part of society. In Mead's terms, this is really only a theory of the "Me."

In my opinion the Meadian theory of the mind has not been exhausted. In fact it has scarcely been touched. Both the situationalist and the role-theory versions of Symbolic Interactionism have taken attention away from Mead's most important contribution, a genuinely sociological theory of thought. Perhaps this is one reason why the theoretical impetus in microsociology has been taken over in recent years by another line of theory, one that does not come from the American roots in Peirce, Cooley, and Mead at all. This is an entirely different approach to the sociology of consciousness, sailing under the flags of ethnomethodology or phenomenology.

The Sociology of Consciousness: Husserl, Schutz, and Garfinkel

In 1966, Peter Berger and Thomas Luckmann published a book with the revealing title, *The Social Construction of Reality*. The authors, an American and a German, had been students of theology and philosophy, and their argument brought a shock to the mainstream of sociology, which was used to regarding the world as objective and independent of the human beings within it. A year later came an even more radical statement, Harold Garfinkel's *Studies in Ethnomethodology*. Garfinkel's book was a collection of previous papers, which had already been extensively studied by a group of his ardent followers meeting in private. With the publication of the book, this "underground" movement was suddenly cast into the spotlight. Sociology was being challenged at its core by a group of epistemological radicals who declared that sociology was naive, ungrounded, and needed to be replaced by a new discipline called "ethnomethodology."

Needless to say this did not happen, but it did make everyone aware that the old sociological Establishment was no longer commanding allegiance everywhere and that among the contending factions of the new intellectual scene was one that was explicitly revolutionary. The "ethnos," as they came to be called, were not necessarily revolutionary in the political sense; for most of them Marxism was just as much a part of the old way of thinking that had to be overthrown.

What were they demanding? Many people were not quite sure. Garfinkel and his followers tended to write in a convoluted language with a private terminology, and they usually met in private and made little effort to introduce the rest of the field into their province of understanding. Many sociologists simply regarded them as a cult. Part of the issue was that the ethnomethodologists were making two radical innovations at once. On the one hand, they were making sociology much more philosophical than it had been for 60 years or more, and on the other hand, the philosophy that they were introducing was a hitherto unfamiliar strain going back to German phenomenology. But if the ethnos had been merely philosophical, they would have been easier to dismiss. But they also claimed to be much more empirical than conventional sociology. In fact one of their main grounds for dismissing existing sociology was the charge that it has not gotten to the real bedrock of facts that we ought to be observing. Survey research merely asked questions and mistook the answers for the real ways people handled their lives; historical sociology was based on documents even more remote from social reality. Symbolic interactionists like Blumer had made some of these criticisms, but the ethnos turned the same weapon on them. Symbolic interactionists merely glossed over the surface of interaction; they constructed interpretations of it but did not get to the heart of it because they failed to examine it closely enough.

Not surprisingly the symbolic interactionists were usually

outraged by this attack. For years they had been holding out against the hard, cold positivism of American sociology, pointing to the definition of the situation and the fluidity of social relationships. Now they were attacked from the flank where they least expected it and were told they were not radical enough and even that they were part of the same Establishment. Many symbolic interactionists reacted by claiming that the ethnos were nothing new: that the symbolic interactionists had said it all before themselves and also (a little inconsistently) that the ethnos had gone too far and destroyed social reality entirely.

With a little more detachment from the furor, it is possible to see that the ethnomethodologists were doing something different. Their philosophical and theoretical claims came from quite a different direction than anything stated in American sociology before, and their empiricism, too, was of a radically new kind.

Let us take up the philosophical lineage first. Garfinkel as well as Berger and Luckmann at one stroke had made the intellectual history of sociology much more complex. Both went back to the German philosopher Edmund Husserl, who had previously not been considered part of the sociological tradition at all, neither by himself nor anyone else. Husserl had been a contemporary of Cooley and Mead, and his works spanned the 1890s through the 1930s. His most famous disciples had been the existentialist philosophers Martin Heidegger and Jean-Paul Sartre. Now suddenly history was redefined so that these thinkers were now part of the sociological tradition. This was the social construction—or reconstruction—of reality for sure! And yet there was some logic to it. For another of Husserl's students had been Alfred Schutz, who fled the Nazis in the 1930s and ended up teaching at the New School for Social Research in New York City, an institution founded around emigré German intellectuals. At the New School in the 1950s, both Berger and Garfinkel had heard Schutz's lectures. Thus, when ethnomethodology and social phenomenology surfaced in the late 1960s, Schutz, too, was resurrected, his collected papers published, and he himself installed in the historical pantheon.

What, then, is the significance of Husserl for sociology? Husserl was an extremely ambitious philosopher who wished to dismiss all previous philosophy as unfounded and reestablish everything on a basis of absolute certainty. Husserl had begun as a mathematician, and his ideal was that philosophy should become as certain as mathematics was supposed to be: though even here, he regarded mathematics as not certain enough—even that science would have to be placed on a new foundation. Because Husserl regarded philosophy as the basis of all knowledge, none of the sciences could be considered secure until he had successfully carried out his work. We can see here why Garfinkel has taken the attitude he has about sociology: for its foundations, too, are insecure until ethnomethodology has done its work of applying Husserl's phenomenological method.

Why are the empirical sciences insecure? Because they rely on the naturalistic method. They assume there is a world out there, one which we can observe and from which we induct generalizations. But no amount of induction from empirical particulars ever gives completely secure knowledge: we know that something has occurred in a number of cases previously enumerated but that is no guarantee that it will happen in the next case or for every case into the infinite future. Similarly working out the rules of logic in the conventional manner does not yield valid rules for all reasoning because it does not give its own grounds for why the rules should be as they are. A true logic would have to be much more universal and cover not just particular kinds of reasoning but *every possible* kind of reasoning. We can see that Husserl has a very high standard of knowledge and that everything that falls short of this is to be rejected. He prefers, instead, to start over again with a new method that yields absolutely certain results in every case. This method he calls phenomenology.

The basic principle of phenomenology is that it is possible to get to the true essence of things without having to rely on any empirical evidence at all. No experiment or scientific observation, including psychology, could ever disprove (or prove) these essences, for they are prior to all experience. These essences are found, nevertheless, by observing them, though in a peculiar way. What one does is practice the method Husserl called *epoché* or "bracketing": one takes the contents of consciousness as they come, but suspends judgment as to whether it is true or false. It other words one takes experience not as experience but simply as a pure form of consciousness. Husserl was convinced moreover that these experiences contained the pure forms or essences. For one constantly sees things as *universals*, whereas empirical reality always comes in the form of *particulars*. When one sees two objects that are both red, for instance, one knows that they are the same color, although there is no way that this could be inducted from experience. For experience is aways of some particular object, and one would not be able to make the comparison and recognize both objects as red unless one already had a general, universal conception of red to apply to both of them.

Husserl thus set out to inventory all the pure essences that make up the absolute structure of the universe. Although he rejected the method of empiricism in the ordinary sense nevertheless he proceeded, so to speak, "empirically." The philosopher does not know in advance what these essences are; he or she must find them out by bracketing one form of experience after another and inventorying what one finds there. One, thus, comes out with laws that are supposed to be absolutely valid everywhere and under all circumstances. Applying this method to the study of time, for instance, Husserl offers such principles as "temporal relations are asymmetrical."

From time to time, however, Husserl was assailed by doubts as to whether he had probed deeply enough, whether the principles he proposed were sufficiently universal to be the absolute structure of the universe. And we might question, too, whether a German examining the "bracketed" forms of his own consciousness in the year 1910 would necessarily come up with the same things as, say, a Buddhist monk in India in the year 400 B.C. Nevertheless Husserl's method gave a tremendous impetus to subsequent generations of followers. It set off a search for the essence of things, for the laws, if not of the whole universe, at least for the universe as strained through human experience in various realms. Husserl's most famous student, Martin Heidegger, set off modern existentialism by searching for the essence of the human being. He came to a dramatic conclusion: human existence takes place quintessentially in time, and its ultimate essence is "being-towards-death." The essence of the human being is that he or she has no essence; he or she is logically unfounded: there is no reason why he or she should exist in the first place rather than nothing at all. The human being is merely "thrown into the world," with no ultimate reason. This is mirrored in the way time is the fundamental category of existence. The logical unfoundedness of existence finally comes due at its end in the form of death. In the 1940s, Jean-Paul Sartre made an even sharper formulation of this: human existence is sheer negation, and the flow of our lives is an endless series of acts of Nothingness carving out the blank future from the dead blocks of the past.

A dramatic set of ideas to be sure; but how do we get from here to ethnomethodology? Actually there is a more direct route through another of Husserl's students, Schutz. But the existentialists should not be forgotten, because the underlying tone in Garfinkel is much more like Heidegger than it is like either Husserl or Schutz. Garfinkel introduces a dramatic flair into sociology as well as an impassioned intensity that is something like the existentialist *angst* (anxiety) that Heidegger declared was the essential human emotion. If for Heidegger and Sartre human life is unfounded and hovering on the edge of oblivion, for Garfinkel the same unfoundedness characterizes society itself.

But let us take for a moment the safer path, through the social phenomenology introduced by Alfred Schutz. Schutz set out to investigate what essences could be found in a particular type of experience, people's experience of the social world. In this, he was simply applying Husserl's method to yet another specialized area. (He also conceived himself to be tracing out in detail what Max Weber should have done in following up his method of *verstehen*.) Schutz came up with a series of purported laws, among them: the principle that social consciousness has a specific tension, that of being wide awake; that social consciousness involves the suspension of doubt—we accept the reality of what is presented to us; that we assume a reciprocity of perspectives—the world presumably looks the same to you as it does to me; that our prevalent attitude is that of working towards some goal, and that we experience our self as our working self.

Now these may or may not be valid laws. Erving Goffman, for one, thought that they were not, and argued (as we shall see) that his own investigations turned up a much more complex and sophisticated version of the attitudes of everyday life. Certainly the notion that each person's self is experienced as the self working towards some goal is an undue generalization from Schutz's examination of his own personality (for many years he worked in a bank, unable to get an academic job). Garfinkel accepted some of Schutz's principles but only after he had examined the whole subject afresh. What for Schutz had remained an armchair phenomenology, Garfinkel turned back into an empirical investigation, although of a novel or even bizarre kind. In the process Garfinkel came up with some new discoveries that went far beyond what either Husserl or Schutz had seen.

Garfinkel has been the most famous of the sociological followers of Husserl's phenomenology, and deservedly so. Berger and Luckmann introduced the general notion of "the social construction of reality," but the phenomenological world that they spell out looks a great deal like the ordinary mundane world. It is subjectively—or rather intersubjectively—constructed, but it is pretty much the same straight world of ordinary belief, not unlike the idealized Boy Scout world described by Cooley. Garfinkel is in a different universe. His world sits over an abyss. It is socially constructed, mundane, and taken for granted: but not because it is really so. On the contrary. For Garfinkel the real world is unutterable and untouchable. It is there, but as a mysterious "X-factor" that we gloss over with social interpretations. Our strongest social principle is to leave the interpretations alone, lest we see how flimsy they are and reveal the unfoundedness beneath.

I said that Garfinkel is a radical empiricist. This is true in the sense that he holds one cannot make inferences about the world based on any kind of report. One must go and look oneself, and one must include oneself in the observation. In fact one's own methods of making sense out of experiences are the prime object of investigation. The term "ethnomethodology" itself refers to this focus: "ethno" or "ethnography," the observational study of; "methodology," the methods that people use to make sense out of experience.

Garfinkel was famous, at one point in his career, for sending his UCLA students out to do "experiments" that involved "breaching" the taken-for-granted surface of everyday life. Students would be sent home to act like strangers in their own houses, politely asking if they could use the bathroom, and so forth. Or other students would be told to go into a store, pick out a 99-cent tube of toothpaste and see if they could bargain the clerk into taking 25 cents for it. The point of this is not the particular social customs that happened to prevail in the home or the store, which were thrown into sharp contrast by violating them (all that is "bracketed" in the Husserlian manner). What is at issue, instead, is the general structure of the "natural attitude": how people expect everyday life to be organized. Garfinkel's method was perhaps more a teaching device than an experiment for a scientific audience. The object of studying phenomenology is to learn about the structures of one's own consciousness. Doing these experiments, as Garfinkel would say, is "good for one's soul."

Nevertheless Garfinkel has tended to vacillate on the issue of whether these experiences are generalizable and reportable. On one side, he still adheres to Husserl's program: to arrive at absolute certainty and show the most general, universal structures of experience; hence, it should be possible to report them in scientific discourse and write them up in books. On the other side, though, there is Garfinkel's own major discovery: that the world does not lend itself to being generalized in this manner. To report on it inevitably distorts its true nature. It is because of this insight that Garfinkel has apparently felt the only way truly to convey his principles is to his immediate students by having them go through the research experiences themselves. It is this intellectual stance more than anything else that has given ethnomethodology the reputation for being a cult.

It is still possible, though, for an outsider to convey something from ethnomethodology, laying stress on Husserl's own

aim of formulating general knowledge. In his later terminology, Garfinkel speaks of the world of "*Lebenswelt* objects" being turned into "signed objects." *Lebenswelt*, a term of the German phenomenologists, is literally "life-world," the world we
live in as we actually experience it. "Signed objects," on the
other hand, are the world as we talk about it or refer to it
socially. This seems like the same thing, but with a sharp difference: the sofa over there, the typewriter on the table, the car
parked out in the street—they are one kind of thing as we
simply take them for granted, use them, live with them, and
ignore them, but something else again when we refer to them
by our verbal signs. Moreover, we are caught in our signs. We
cannot jump out of our verbal skins. As soon as we start paying attention to things, we have made them into signed objects
and lost them as *Lebenswelt* objects. For us, as Garfinkel puts it,
the objects of the world are constituted by what makes them
accountable; they are what they are to us socially because of
the symbolic structure we use to account for them to other
people.

Garfinkel's world, then, is multileveled. There is the world
itself, and then there is the world as we reflect on it. The
reflection inalterably transforms what the world is for us; we
cannot know what the world is like without our reflecting on
it, any more than we can see what things are like when we are
not looking at them. In truth they do not "look" like anything.
All that we can say is that they are and that the world has this
dual structure. This last statement, then, is the fundamental
Husserlian law in Garfinkel's updated version of the system.

What are the sociological implications of this discovery?
Sociology, in Garfinkel's view, merely deals with "signed objects." It does not get to the reality of things, to the true *lebenswelt*. Even the symbolic interactionists are fooling themselves
in thinking that they are getting to the bedrock of social life in
their situations and role-takings. They, too, are merely producing yet another set of "signed objects," which stand in the way
of actual life as it is experienced.

Is there any way out of this? Garfinkel recommends that
sociologists start over again and get as close as they can to the
actual experiences that make up the moment-by-moment detail

of social life. Of course they cannot report the *Lebenswelt* itself because that is impossible; but they can get at the actual methods by which people turn their various *Lebenswelt* objects into the particular "signed objects" by which they believe they are surrounded. Thus, ethnomethodology turns into an elaborate and ultradetailed program of research. Ethnomethodologists, for example, have invaded the realm of the sociology of science. Garfinkel himself examined in great detail a tape recording of astronomers while they made an "inexplicable" discovery in the night sky and, then, gradually turned it into a "signed object" to which they gave the structure of a "pulsar." Science, like everything else, is socially produced by people who make interpretative statements that in turn become the allegedly objective knowledge itself.

Other ethnomethodologists have studied mathematics as it is actually produced, taking the real-life struggles of mathematicians to construct arguments and showing how these give rise to a set of theorems and proofs that are taken to have universal validity. Once the mathematical proof is created, all the real-life thinking that went into creating it is cleared away and the published formula gives a mistaken image of existing objectively, untouched by human hands. The entire world of work is examined in the same way. In every instance the crucial point is the "local production" of something that is then socially believed to be repeatable, accountable, and generalizable. A person constructs the occupation of being a "plumber" by certain local practices in very specific situations: by putting a social interpretation on what is being done that transcends the situations themselves. The *Lebenswelt* underneath the sink is transformed into the allegedly thinglike social "role" of being a "plumber."

In a certain sense, then, society is full of illusions. But they are necessary illusions. We cannot do without signed objects; we cannot live without turning specific situations into instances of general rules and roles, even though the latter exist only in our system of accounts. As the early "breaching" experiments revealed, when people are forced to question the taken-for-granted nature of their conventionally assigned meanings, they become upset. They realize intuitively that if things are recognized as arbitrary, there is nowhere to stop. Everything can crumble if we refuse to accept the conventional interpretations. Social reality is flimsy. Paradoxically its strength comes mainly from its flimsiness. People are fundamentally conservative, not in a political but in a cognitive sense, because they intuitively feel the social world is a set of arbitrary constructions built over an abyss. These constructions remain in place because we do not question them, and we resist questioning lest the whole thing fall down.

THE SOCIOLOGY OF LANGUAGE AND COGNITION

There is another route forward from Garfinkel's ethnomethodology. The program analyzing local production leads to extremely detailed accounts of how social events are constructed, but to no generalizations. Its message in fact is that all generalizations can be reduced back to the local situation that produced them. Nevertheless in the background there is Husserl's ideal of science: universal, absolutely valid knowledge. Garfinkel gave this an ultraempirical push, and modern research technologies have taken it even further. About the same time *Studies in Ethnomethodology* was published in the late 1960s, portable cassette tape recorders began to be available. They made possible a new degree of precision in research on everyday life. Whereas previously the "participant observer" had to take things in with his or her bare eyeballs and eardrums and occasionally rush off to the bathroom to write down notes, now the tape recorder could do the job of capturing every word that was said. And not only every word, but every intonation, pause, false start, and all the other details that make up the *actual* sounds of real-life talk.

Garfinkel's followers, notably Harvey Sacks and Emanuel Schegloff, quickly exploited the new technology and created the empirical research field of conversational analysis. They developed a transcript with special signs to indicate all the ways in which spoken speech differs from the cleaned-up version we see on the printed page. And they began to induct laws—general principles—about the organization of talk. No area of social life was ever studied in such precise detail before.

With the introduction of portable videotape machines a few years later, the field of empirical detail was broadened still further to include the nonverbal context as well as the spoken part. (As yet video analysis has not been developed as far as that of audio recordings.)

This impressive amount of detail was not merely to be another research specialty among others. Sacks proposed that the entire social structure is present, actually embodied in the language practices themselves. Where else could it be found if not in real people in real, empirically observable interaction? Schegloff and his colleagues stressed that their method was the truly scientific one, dealing with the only absolutely primary data and from it building up generalizations about the speech practices that constitute society. In a different direction, Aaron Cicourel proposed that the modern social structure is largely made up by the accumulation of written records. It is these that comprise the bureaucracies of government and business and that channel one's career through the school system or downwards into the criminal-processing agencies of delinquency and crime. Cicourel broadens the study of language to include the interplay between face-to-face talk and the seemingly "objective," thinglike written records of modern bureaucracy. On both sides society is made up of particular ways that thought is constrained by the verbal and written channels through which it passes. Cicourel proposes that the main topic is really the sociology of cognition in all its socially embodied forms.

Erving Goffman's Counterattack

Erving Goffman has already been discussed in a different intellectual lineage. His forte is microsociology, but his theoretical apparatus was the Durkheimian theory of rituals rather than the American tradition of symbolic interaction. Goffman always stressed that social structure comes first and subjective consciousness is secondary and derivative; even his theory of the presentation of the self is essentially a model of the self as a modern-day myth that people are forced to enact rather than a subjective entity that people privately possess. The symbolic

interactionists—whom Goffman certainly knew from his student days at Chicago and with whom he was frequently
classed by undiscerning outsiders—were never regarded by
Goffman as intellectually very serious. He scarcely mentioned
them in his earlier works, even to bother to criticize them.

But the ethnomethodologists were something else again.
They came on the scene after Goffman had established himself
with his major empirical works on everyday life and microin-
teraction. But now they were intruding on his turf with an
entirely alien philosophy and even claiming that he had not
even done his own work well! By the standards of Garfinkel's
ultradetailed examination of social cognition and the precision
of tape recordings of conversation, Goffman's studies fade into
a vague blur of casual observations, almost reconstructed armchair sociology. Not only that, but the younger "second generation" ethnomethodologists such as Sacks and Schegloff
were actually Berkeley Ph.D.s under Goffman's own sponsor-
ship. In the late 1960s, Goffman had the experience of seeing
his own field grow up and move beyond him, away from the
concern with interaction ritual and the nature of the social self
and into more philosophical questions of epistemology and
cognition.

Hence, a turn takes place in Goffman's last major books,
Frame Analysis (1974), and *Forms of Talk* (1981). He reenters
microsociology as if it were an alien territory, taking on the
new ethnomethodological themes and entering into the close
analysis of tape-recorded talk. And not only the ethnomethodologists, but all the rest of language studies become his target.
The 1960s and 1970s had become a modern Golden Age of
linguistic analysis. In formal linguistics itself, Noam Chomsky
had set off a revolution by producing a method for analyzing
the "deep structure" of grammar. Anglo-American philosophy
had long since forsaken metaphysics and was burrowing more
and more deeply into the nature of "speech acts"; French post-
structuralists and German philosophical Marxists like Jurgen
Habermas were searching for the basic cognitive code or analyzing society into acts of communication. Goffman took them
all on, mounting an offensive to reconquer his own turf.

Frame Analysis is partly directed against Garfinkel's ethnomethodology, partly a cleaning up of old business by critiquing Blumer and the symbolic interactionists. Schutz had declared that everyday life had certain qualities: the reciprocity of perspectives, an immersion in the self as worker, and so forth. To which Goffman replies: Why should we take his word for it? In fact there are plenty of situations in which one person's frontstage is not the perspective of the person to whom it is directed, and the other points in Schutz's list ought to be treated just as dubiously. The same approach, Goffman insinuates, ought to be taken with Garfinkel and his followers. Their "experiments" and observations are sometimes precise, sometimes merely fragmentary; we should not be carried away by their dramatics or by their high-sounding analysis into assuming that their interpretation is necessarily the right one.

Goffman proposes an alternative conception, pulling together his earlier work around a device that he now calls "frames." The metaphor evokes a picture with a frame around it; one can then put another frame around that, and then step back and repeat the process still further; or one can descend inside the inner frame and place a still smaller frame there, and so forth. (Goffman, who never sticks to his metaphors very long, also calls this "keying," in the sense that one can transpose the same melody on the piano into another key.) The notion is partly a reply to Garfinkel's claim that social cognition is characterized by reflexivity and the danger of infinite regress. For Garfinkel social reality is merely the methods that we use to account for it; hence, we are always stuck on the level of the "signed object" and can never get to the "*Lebenswelt* object" beneath. This is the meaning of "reflexivity," as if we are caught in an endless circle of trying to pull ourselves up by our own bootstraps. Garfinkel had also drawn the conclusion that people implicitly realize they should not question the arbitrariness of their social constructions for fear that they will fall into an infinite regress of questioning everything—with nowhere to stop.

Goffman rejects this as abstract philosophy, not real social practice. In actual fact people deal with the arbitrariness of social life quite readily, and we have devices that everyone uses for moving from one level of frame to another. In principle the number of levels may be endless but, as a practical matter, we never take it that far. We are capable of embedding quite a few frames around frames and still knowing where we are.

For example, people often play games, go through ceremonies, or sit in a theatre watching make-believe. These are all transformations of primary reality: not a real room but a room on a TV set, not an ordinary field of grass but a football game, and so forth. Upon these can be created yet other levels: a practice session for a game, for instance, or an exhibition game, or children pretending to play a game. Then we add the world of talk onto this and we see that conversation has its own level of conventions and rules, not to mention the times when it adds superimposed commentary onto some game or ceremony that is talked about. Talk also can comment on itself in various ways. When we add frontstages and backstages, which make up so much of the work world (and also the world of staged sociability such as parties), we can see that people are able to deal with multiple levels of reality as a matter of course. We are by no means confined to the surface, the way Garfinkel seems to imply.

Frame Analysis can also be regarded as a criticism of symbolic interactionism. It deals with the *definition of the situation*, the answer to the question, "What is going on here?" But whereas the symbolic interactionists deal with this from the point of view of the individual, whose behavior is supposedly determined by the prevailing definition, Goffman points out the structure that encompasses the viewpoints of all parties and all possible vantage points. This is the dress rehearsal for a wedding ceremony that will itself constitute a frontstage display of social status; it is a backstage conversation among lawyers out of sight of their clients, but they are talking about their children's football game. The outermost layer of definition is not necessarily the controlling one. Goffman is not merely doing tricks with mirrors, and social life is not an endless flux. If necessary, we can peel off the layers quickly and drop back to the core.

What is the core, the primary frame, as Goffman puts it? It is the real physical world and the real social presence of human

bodies within it. "Defining situations as real certainly has consequences," Goffman says, "but these may contribute very
marginally to the events in progress. . . . All the world is not a
stage—certainly the theatre isn't entirely. (Whether you organize a theatre or an aircraft factory, you need to find places for
cars to park and coats to be checked, and these had better be
real places, which incidentally, had better carry real insurance
against theft.)" We are back at Durkheim's vision of a real
material world in which human bodies come together, rituals
are carried out, and collective mental representations are
thereby created. Goffman adds layer on layer of how these
ceremonies and mental definitions can play off each other, but
the material world of human bodies is still basic. When a fire
breaks out in a theatre, all the other games are off.

Goffman's last book, *Forms of Talk*, takes this model of
multiple frames and applies it to conversation. He is critical of
the ethnomethodological approach of Sacks and Schegloff as
well as of linguists like Chomsky or philosophers like John
Austin and John Searle. For the constraints on how one speaks
and replies are not in the formalities of language, but in the
realm of social relationships, that is, in how one must display
oneself with respect to others. Speech is embedded in ritual.
The units of language are not grammatical (the sentence), nor
the turns people take (how long one has the floor for one
utterance), but social moves in some situation, which may take
either a good deal longer or a good deal less than a turn. Social
action is more basic than talk.

To buttress his point, Goffman offers a collection of evidence that only he would have noticed: the kinds of cries,
mutterings, and so forth, that people utter in the presence of
others but without being in conversation with them. This "self-
talk," as Goffman calls it, shows that a social situation is based
on the *physical copresence* of people, not necessarily on their
subjective and intersubjective awareness. Self-talk is embar-
rassing because it violates the demand that we should show
ourselves as competent and self-controlled persons. The
blurted sounds we make are not mere biological grunts, cries of
pain, or other sheer asocial expressions. On the contrary, they
arise following some action that others will notice, and they

invite other people's attention into our interiors, "not a flooding of emotion outward, but a flooding of relevance in." We
gasp or swear when we stumble on the sidewalk, not because
it is an involuntary physiological response, but because we are
thereby signaling to other people that we, too, regard it as a
clumsy accident. The cry serves to distance our social self from
our biological self. It is a kind of tiny ritual repair of the competent self-image we feel obliged to maintain.

Another thing this reveals is that the social situation is
larger and more fundamental than a focused conversation.
"Even when nothing eventful is occuring," Goffman sums up,
"persons in one another's presence are still nonetheless track-
ing one another and acting so as to make themselves track-
able." Beneath our human roles, we still do the same things as
other animals, that is, check for possible threats and allies. For
this reason, the sociolinguists' method of dividing talk into that
of "speaker" and "hearer" is not basic enough. Bystanders in
visual and aural range are also part of a conversational situation, although linguists would not recognize them as such. The
situation may break up into three parts: speaker/addressed
recipient/unaddressed recipient. It is this complexity that allows for "collusion," "byplay," "crossplay," and other modes
of communication (such as a knowing wink from the speaker
to an onlooker, etc.). And there are other kinds of talk besides
a conversation: public ceremonies, collective singing, lectures,
speeches. These are different kinds of Durkheimian rituals, not
just because of the different numbers of people involved in
them, but because of the different frames they involve and,
hence, the ways they channel people's attention. In effect they
are creating quite different kinds of "sacred objects."

Social life is a series of embeddings. There is human talk,
with all the levels of game playing and pretence to which it is
subject. The talk is part of a larger social situation among the
people involved, and this social situation is itself embedded in
an ethnological situation and in a sheer physical one. Often the
way talk arises or takes on meaning comes from the relationship of participants to some event or task in the physical realm
around them. The talk that occurs when individuals are repair-
ing a car ("There's the problem") or playing cards ("Spades.")

is not understandable unless one knows what is being done physically, and often this may require being right there on the spot and looking under the hood of the car from the same angle as the speaker. As Goffman says, the basis of language is not some primal intersubjectivity, but rather a common focus on a physical scene of action.

In addition to these series of embeddings, our distinctively human capacity for still further framing and frame breaking builds up the familiar multileveled world in which we live. Social sophistication consists largely in how easily one can move among frames and either fit them together smoothly with other people's frames or else deliberately manipulate frames to mislead other people about what we are doing. Although Goffman does not mention it, it seems likely that the invisible barriers among the cultures of different social classes have to do with these differences in framing techniques. He does show that the difference between frontstage and back-stage can be stated more precisely in terms of the amount of freedom one has to break one's own frame and shift to another one.

From Goffman's viewpoint, then, the efforts of Chomsky and other formal linguists to find a single deep structure underlying all talk is a foolish quest. Language is inherently part of a multileveled situation. It is language's capacity for endlessly distancing oneself from, and redoing, more primary situations that constitutes the key. Far from being a code programmed inside the brain, language is built up by a series of social actions, each reflexively referred back to the last. At the opposite extreme, the abyss of relativity expounded by the ethnomethodologists is equally unreal. The world is capable of being quite fluid, but the fluidity is rarely out of control. Whenever it gets carried too far away—or for that matter whenever something more important intervenes—we can quickly parachute back to ground zero, the physical world we are standing in and the posture of the human bodies around us. The world can become very complicated, but it is built up by repeating a small number of reflexive mechanisms. Scientific generalizations are possible because we can describe the mechanism.

A Summing Up

Of all the intellectual traditions we have surveyed, the lineage of ideas described in this chapter is probably the most chaotic. All the positions reviewed here still have their adherents today; hardly anyone would agree that there is a progression, that is, that more recent theories are advances that build on the older one theories. There are at least four great outposts that have never been taken in the endless skirmishes of the microsociology wars: Peirce, Mead, Garfinkel, and Goffman. For convenience we might reduce these to three because Peirce was primarily a philosopher with broad interests rather than a sociologist, and the most relevant part of his philosophy—his theory of semiotics—is largely incorporated in Mead's system. In the same way and only stretching things a bit, we may say that Goffman incorporates and extends Durkheim's ritual theory of microsociology.

Now what of these three? If not a progression, can we decide among them on the various points at issue? In some ways this is surprisingly premature. Although a good deal of empirical work has come out of (and sometimes gone into) the three theories, not much of it has tried actually to test the core theories themselves. Symbolic interactionists have usually just assumed Mead's and Blumer's theories and used them to interpret various pieces of description about deviance, the professions, and so on. The ethnomethodologists have used their evidence more to illustrate arguments than to support them in any careful showdown against countertheories. Although the various theories have inhabited the same arena for decades, they have done little more than shadowbox. Only Goffman has made any pointed attacks on their points of difference, and these have been mostly buried in the form of veiled allusions.

But let us see what might be ventured. First, Mead versus Garfinkel. This is a confrontation between two quite different philosophies, the pragmatists on one side versus the phenomenology of Husserl. Husserl set out to do exactly what Peirce said it was unnatural for the human mind to do, namely, to doubt everything and to suspend one's sense of belief. For the pragmatists, on the contrary, the "will to believe" without sufficient evidence is the most fundamental quality of the human mind. Not only that, but the pragmatists confidently believed that people are right enough of the time (as things work out in practice) so that this loose-edged procedure is quite satisfactory. For Mead and the pragmatists, there is no problem of how society is put together; we simply work it out.

The ethnomethodologists could hardly be farther away from this simple confidence. Human cognitive capacity has its strict limits and we can only hold things together because we shy away from questioning our conventional understandings very far. Society holds together as well as it does, not because we have worked out any common understandings nor because it is a pragmatically efficient instrument for achieving our collective purposes, but merely because we assume things are normal until they break down so badly we cannot avoid making some kind of repair. On this point I would say that the greater realism goes to the ethnomethodologists. The optimism of Mead and the pragmatists sounds like a philosophical version of conventional ideology, whereas Garfinkel's model fits more realistically with the macroevidence amassed by conflict theory.

The same thing can be said on a more detailed level. Mead had proposed that social order is fitted together in each situation as the participants each take the role of the other and mutually align what they are trying to do. But Garfinkel makes us aware of the infinite regress that lurks here. If you are trying to take account of my reactions as you plan your moves and I take account of your reactions as I plan my moves, each of us is going to have to take account of the next level of monitoring the other, and so on. Human cognition is just not capable of dealing with that level of endless reflexivity. Rather than really taking the role of the other, more likely we do what Garfinkel says: we simply assume the most normal, conventional understanding and go ahead with what we were going to do. People do not have to understand each other to interact, and they do not even have to worry about whether their understanding is true, unless things get so far out of line that the situations break down; even then, people tend to make only the minimal repair to restore a sense of normality.

Next, Goffman versus Mead. Goffman is critical of many aspects of symbolic interactionism. The "I," the "Me," and the "Generalized Other" are far too simple to capture the actual selves that one fluctuates in and out of, sometimes within minutes or even fragments of seconds. When someone is giving a lecture, for example—bear in mind that Goffman was saying this from a lecture platform, delivering a lecture entitled "The Lecture"—there are "multiple selves in which the self of the speaker can appear." There is the self who enunciates what it actually believes or wants, but also the self as a figure within the talk, and also the self as animator—the self who delivers a performance in that situation (the lecturer as lecturer). Furthermore one can break frame (say by stumbling over one's words and, then, apologizing in one's capacity as the person who is trying to be a lecturer); then again one can get into some personal byplay offstage; or one can stop to make one's further commentary on what one has said. In Mead's terms, one would have to say that all these are actions of the "I" trying out various "Me's" against the backdrop of a "Generalized Other." But the "Me" and the "Generalized Other" in each of Goffman's examples is on a different level of analysis and located in a different social space. There is no unitary "Generalized Other" inside one's head, Goffman seems to imply. What takes its place is often outside us, in the social situation, and also in some sense in our immediate past, as each self plays off the frame that was just set in previous moments.

Goffman criticizes, too, the developmental model by which the small child is supposed to have acquired this mental equipment. He comments that adults talk to small babies in a complex, not a simple way: they imitate a babyish tone of voice and speak *for* the child, not to it. ("Does baby want a nice teddy bear?") This is an embedding of social roles. The child is not simply acquiring a "Me" and a "Generalized Other," but is learning a fairly complex process of how to decode and perform embeddings. Baby talk may involve a simplified grammar and vocabulary, but "its laminative features are anything but childlike." Although the analysis has not yet been carried out, Goffman is suggesting an entirely new way to approach both the study of language and child psychology generally.

For all this, I would judge that Goffman here is making progress on the path started by Mead rather than turning in an entirely new direction. Mead and the symbolic interactionists are not very good at how social organization is put together, but their real strength is Mead's theory of thought. The criticisms I have just sketched coming from Goffman are no more than suggestions, not a systematic model, because Goffman never built a system. Mead still provides the basic outlines of a theory of thinking as an internalized social process, which remains the best building block available. Goffman points out that we need a much more refined and complicated picture of the components of the self and a more dynamic and multileveled view of how the components of the self interact with ongoing social situations. But this can be used to build onto Mead's framework. The only drawback is that we have not been used to building on it or for that matter on anything else. Our social psychology, as I have already said, has largely ignored Mead's theory of thinking in favor of an external application to social problems and social roles. And we are more used to debating and knocking down each other's positions than to building on what is useful progress within them. Nevertheless the potential is here for a sophisticated sociological theory of the mind.

Finally Goffman versus Garfinkel. Goffman attacks the ethnomethodologists fairly severely. He accepts their ultraempiricism but not their theoretical conclusions. The ethnos are too radical epistemologically. They insist that everything is locally produced, that there are no general laws at all (in Garfinkel's version of the unapproachable *Lebenswelt*), or that the laws are simply those of conversation itself (in Sacks and Schegloff's version). Goffman denies it. There is an overall social structure and we can make valid generalizations about it. Even within any situation, the talk and the cognitive constructions are not primary, but only part of a set of embedded frames. The largest frame is the physical world and the bodies of the people interacting in it performing Durkheimian rituals.

My own predilection is to side with Goffman on this point. The physical world is not as mysterious as Garfinkel makes it out to be, even though it is perfectly true that no one can ever capture in words all that might possibly enter into any particular situation in which one finds oneself. But interestingly enough there is a way in which Garfinkel and Durkheim— Goffman's lineage chief—converge on this basic point. Garfinkel is constantly arguing that human cognition is limited, and that it does not provide its own foundation. That is his big discovery as he carried out Husserl's injunction to go explore the fundamental structures of human experience, in this case in the social world. Underneath the world of "signed objects," there is always the *"Lebenswelt"* looming darkly and never reducible to what we say about it. But this is another version, on the cognitive plane, of what Durkheim had said about social solidarity in disproving the utilitarian social contract. Society cannot be held together by rational agreement, Durkheim argued, because that would lead to an infinite regress of necessarily prior agreements to live up to one's agreement.

Garfinkel and Durkheim both come to the same point. There is a large "X-factor" underlying society that is not part of our own rational agreements. Durkheim called it "precontractual solidarity"; Garfinkel described it as our preference not to question what holds things together. But in fact the "X-factor" may be exactly the same thing on both angles of approach. It is the *emotional* relationships among human beings that inevitably arise whenever human bodies are in the same place. It is this that provides whatever implicit understandings we have in any situation. Where the emotion is curtailed, negative, or distrustful and we have to fall back on common rational understandings, we find ourselves in exactly the infinite regress of arguments and misunderstandings that Garfinkel suggested is always potentially there.

Garfinkel, then, is partly right, at least on a crucial point of how society is held together. It is not held together by rational agreement or mutual understanding, and whenever it is reduced to that, the structure is bound to fail. But to the extent that it is held together, it is because there is something else going on. Garfinkel is too self-limiting in his unwillingness to explore the "X-factor" and come out with any general characterization of what lies inside. For what is inside the "X-factor" is exactly what Durkheim saw: emotional solidarity. It is not automatic; Durkheim and some of his followers went too far in assuming that society is inevitably integrated in almost every situation. Emotional solidarity is a matter of degree, and it is produced by quite observable conditions of physical interaction that make up rituals.

Goffman never succeeded in integrating his earlier theories of interaction rituals in everyday life with his later analysis of frames and talk. But the outline of how they fit together is clear enough. The bedrock of social interaction, the outmost frame around all the laminations of social situation and self-reflexive conversation, is always the physical copresence of people warily attending to each other. This, too, is where the basic ingredients of Durkheimian rituals are found. The talk embedded within becomes in various degrees a sacred object loaded with some emotional significance, large or small, that makes it a symbol for membership in some particular group. Goffman's later analyses give us an enormous range of possible groups of which one can be a member, many of them situational groups of only the most fleeting duration. And this, I would say, is scientific progress. The complexity of social life is slowly being brought into the purview of a general theory of extremely wide application.

NOTES

1. As a psychologist James does not greatly concern us here, although there are some elements of his psychology that foreshadowed Charles Horton Cooley and George Herbert Mead's theory of the self. James was typical of the early generation of experimental psychologists still working within philosophy departments who combined a description of the physiology of the brain with analyses of various mental functions. James's famous *Principles of Psychology* (1890) thus contains chapters on sight, hearing, attention, memory, habit, instinct, and so on. Among these topics he treats the stream of consciousness and the self as a center within this stream. One aspect of the self is the Social Self, the "Me" as an image seen from the point of view of others. Here we already have Cooley's discovery, one might exclaim! The judgment would be a little hasty. James's Social Self is only one part of

a hierarchy of selves, including the Bodily Self and the Spiritual Self; the alleged unity of all these into one Self is James's argument for the reality of the Soul. James was still preaching religion, even in his psychology. In a way James was the American equivalent of Wilhelm Wundt, the founder of experimental psychology in Germany; both were medical scientists who went into philosophy and established laboratories for the experimental study of the mind. But Wundt, operating in a more scientific atmosphere, took a much more extreme position and broke psychology free from philosophy; James, instead, lapsed from experimental psychology back into a religious philosophy. Hence, the founders of American psychology were students of Wundt, not of James. (These intellectual networks are treated in Ben-David and Collins, 1966).

The ways in which James foreshadowed the sociological theory of the self, in my opinion, are not very significant because James's line of thought would never have lead to a purely socially grounded self. Moreover his cardinal principle of a unified self is one of the main points that gives way under sociological analysis. We will see the most extreme form of this in Goffman's theory of multiple selves.

Epilogue

And now? Do the four traditions still exist in the sociological world of the 1990s? To a certain extent, we should admit, they have been merely convenient fictions, ways of describing the history of the field to bring out continuity and to try to display scientific progress where one can find it. There are thousands of sociologists in the world today, and—following the sociological principle of numbers producing specialization—they have created all sorts of intellectual niches for themselves. Our mentality today tends to be that of the specialist who can see only a small part of the field and usually tries to make each segment as autonomous from the others as possible. To counter this, it is worthwhile mounting to a certain height of abstraction to try to get an overview on what has been happening and whether anything has been accomplished in the last 100 years since the discipline has been alive.

Not everything in the field, to be sure, fits in one or another of these four traditions. There are a great many specialized empirical and social problem areas that have their own local theoretical traditions—or sometimes try to do without theories at all. My only claim is that the four traditions I have picked out are undeniably major, longstanding lines of thought in sociology, and that their arguments and accomplishments are a fair measure of the central tendency of sociological knowledge.

Even within each tradition, as we have abundantly seen, there are major disagreements. Although the conflict tradition has an underlying continuity between Marx/Engels and Weber, in my opinion the partisans of these classic thinkers for the most part have not seen it that way. The debates between Marxists and Weberians and among further subfactions of each camp have been, and remain, an important part of the intellectual action in that field. And the microinteractionist tradition, as we have just seen, is more unified by the kinds of problems it deals with than in any agreement on how to approach them or what counts as a valid solution. The Durkheimians probably have the greatest unity of the four traditions, although there is a serious enough split between those who followed the functionalist path and those who developed the more materialist analysis of ritual and collective symbolism.

For all that, the four traditions have not been hard to pick out as they wended their ways over the last century and a half. Part of the reason is that they have been fairly clearly localized geographically. The conflict tradition was founded by historically oriented Germans, and it has only been in the last 40 years that it has made significant inroads outside of Germany, with many important practitioners in the United States. The Durkheimian tradition is just as clearly French, although it tended to cross the English channel back and forth a bit. John Stuart Mill and Herbert Spencer got into the line of transmission between Auguste Comte and Émile Durkheim (although Durkheim felt he had to throw the English accretions of utilitarianism out). Again in the twentieth century, it was British social anthropologists who first picked up the Durkheimian message, and prominent recent Durkheimians like Basil Bernstein and Mary Douglas are again English. Here, too, there was a crossing of the Atlantic, this time starting in the 1930s with the version of Durkheimian functionalism imported by Parsons and Merton. The utilitarians are the core British tradition, however, until the 1950s when it was revived and expanded in the United States. And the microinteractionist tradition is resolutely American, founded and led by American sociologists from Peirce's generation to Goffman's and Garfinkel's. (I would maintain this is true, even considering the role that Husserl and his disciple Schutz were retrospectively given once Garfinkel had created ethnomethodology.)

These national boundaries, though, do seem to be breaking down in the last few years. The United States has become a mixture of all the traditions. Various alliances have appeared among the different lineages: the microtradition with the conflict tradition (especially its Marxian wing); the ritual part of the Durk-heimian tradition with the conflict tradition via the analysis of class cultures; even the Durkheimian tradition with the mi-crointeractionist (mainly through the activities of Erving Goff-man). The functionalists, who for several decades more or less monopolized the identity of the Durkheimian tradition, have now all but faded from active intellectual life in the United States. This was probably a prerequisite for the Durkheimian ideas on ritual to pull free and join with the opposing conflict and microtraditions. But in a surprising development for many observers, functionalism has found a new home, of all places, in Germany. German theorists like Habermas have also been active in importing the microsociology of Mead and the ethnomethod-ologists: the first time that this American sociological lineage has ever gone abroad. At the same time the native German conflict tradition seems to have lost its original homeland and migrated almost completely abroad, most notably to the United States. Conversely, the rational/utilitarian analysis now has a consider-able following in Germany as well as the Netherlands and Scan-dinavia. France seems to remain truest to its old intellectual tradition. The Durkheimians in their various wings continue to be strong there, either as post-Lévi-Straussian structuralists or in the amalgamation between Durkheim and conflict theory fos-tered by Bourdieu. But even here, one would have to say that France has experienced a long successful invasion of German philosophical ideas. Around the time of World War II, French intellectuals went to existentialism, which is an import from Germany based on Husserl and Heidegger; by the 1960s and 1970s, the popular positions were another set of German theo-ries, derived from Marx and Freud. In the 1980s, the leading Parisian intellectuals grew disillusioned with Marxism and criti-cized all such "foundationalist" positions from the point of view of Postmodernism. But Postmodernism again is largely within the traditions of German philosophy, especially historicism and cultural relativism, combined with a return to some of the nihilis-tic and antimodernist themes of the existentialists.

In chapter 2, I used the analogy between an intellectual tradition and a stream of water flowing across a broad plane—

sometimes as a narrow side current beside the main riverbed, sometimes as a flood that joins the rivulets together into a huge sheet of water. All four traditions can be seen as river systems of this sort, sometimes divided into their own patterns of brooks and canals, sometimes flooding over their banks and submerging their rivals. It is difficult to visualize the the four traditions in this way while staying true to the facts of real-life geography; but imagine, for the sake of clarity, that each of the four streams has a different color: perhaps blood-red for the conflict tradition, pale icy blue for the rational/utilitarians, jungle green water for the Durkheimians, full of tropical plants, and a steamy white mist for the microinteractionists. Over the past two or three hundred years, the different colored streams have ebbed and flowed, widened or diminished.

One might say, in the later decades of the twentieth century, the four streams have been lapping across the edges of each other's channels in various places. Rational choice theory has recently been combining with the Marxian and materialist aspects of conflict theory; on another side, in struggling with the paradoxes of rationality, those theorists have come perilously close to some of the classic antiutilitarian principles of the Durkheimians. (The clear blue water is becoming clouded with greenish tentacles from the emotionalist jungle.) And Durkheimian theory of rituals and emotional solidarity have mingled with conflict theories about class cultures and the means of mental production. I have suggested, too, that Goffman began to blend Durkheimian ritual theory with the microinteractionist tradition of cognitive theory, and that ethnomethodology has an affinity with Durkheimian emotionality, and even with the model of bounded rationality.

And the future? One might be tempted to predict that the separate rivers will blend into one great tide of rainbow-colored water, although two things make me doubt it. One is that in recent years there has been an increasingly sharp conflict between the relativistic, cognitively elusive philosophies that were at the basis of the microinteractionist tradition, and the other intellectual camps. At opposite ends of the terrain are the Postmodernists and the rational/utilitarians; although in between the extreme positions, the waters are blending together into various pastel hues. The second point, more in the vein of a sociology of sociologists, is that sociologists seem to cherish their separate identities, and get much of their intellectual energy from fighting against the other traditions. Hence even if some of these traditions were to merge, very likely further splits would occur to take their place.

Rather than speculate about what is likely to happen to the four traditions in the future, I would prefer to retreat to the safer terrain of what I hope will take place intellectually. The fact that the sociological traditions have overflowed from their original homes and have become somewhat mixed together is in my opinion a good thing. It is by the mutual confrontation of ideas that progress is made towards a wider truth. The weaknesses of one set of ideas can be discarded, and its strong points built up and integrated with the strong points from elsewhere. I have already given indications of where I think this has been happening. Hopefully, the future will show us even more of the same.

Bibliography

My general approach to the sociology of social science follows that of Joseph Ben-David, *The Scientist's Role in Society* (Englewood Cliffs, N.J.: Prentice-Hall, 1971). This was specifically applied to psychology in Joseph Ben-David and Randall Collins, "Social Factors in the Origins of a New Science: The Case of Psychology," *American Sociological Review* 31 (1966): 451–65. More abstract results of a comparison of six social sciences are found in my *Conflict Sociology: Toward Explanatory Science* chapter 9 (New York: Academic Press, 1975). An overview of the cyclical rise and decline of the medieval and early modern university system is contained in my "Crises and Declines in Credential Systems," in *Sociology Since Midcentury* (New York: Academic Press, 1981). The foregoing contain more detailed historical references for the material in this prologue.

Chapter 1. The Conflict Tradition

Hegel's most important work is *The Phenomenology of Mind* (New York: Harper, 1963; originally published 1807). The reference on p. 52 to history as a "slaughterbench" is from his *The Philosophy of History* on p. 21 (New York: Dover, 1956; original lectures ca. 1822). Among the best commentaries on Hegel are Walter A. Kaufman, *Hegel: A Reinterpretation* (Garden City, N.Y.: Doubleday, 1965); and Herbert Marcuse, *Reason and Revolution* (New York: Humanities Press, 1954; originally published 1941). Engels himself tells the story of the development of Marxism out of the Young Hegelians in *Ludwig Feuerbach and the End of Classical German Philosophy* (1888). [There are numerous editions of the works on Marx and Engels; among the better collections are Lewis

Feuer, *Marx and Engels, Basic Writings on Politics and Philosophy* (Garden City, N.Y.: Doubleday, 1959); and Eugene Kamenka, *The Portable Karl Marx* (Baltimore: Penguin, 1983). The latter contains a great deal of biographical material.] A modern biography of Marx is David McLellan's *Karl Marx* (New York: Random House 1973); the classic biography is Franz Mehring, *Karl Marx* (New York: Corvici, Friede, 1935), from which the quotation (p. 57) regarding Marx following in Engels's footsteps is on p. 260. Mehring also notes (p. 123) "Engels was much too modest about his own contributions." The standard biography of Engels is Gustav Mayer, *Friedrich Engels* (The Hague: Mouton, 1934); a recent biography is William Otto Henderson, *The Life of Friedrich Engels* (1976). A typically biased effort to heroize Marx and denigrate Engels is Norman Levine, *The Tragic Deception: Marx Contra Engels* (Oxford: Clio Press, 1975); pp. 232–39, which however, does give information on Marx's sexism and social snobbery and on Engels's greater personal liberalism. One of the few appreciations of Engels's superiority as a historical sociologist is Leonard Krieger's "Introduction," pp. ix–xlvi to Friedrich Engels, *The German Revolutions* [containing *The Peasant War in Germany* (1850) and *Germany: Revolution and Counter-revolution* (1851–1852)] (Chicago: University of Chicago Press, 1967). The major sociological writings, in addition to the preceding, are the *Communist Manifesto* (1848) and *The German Ideology,* (1846) written jointly by Engels and Marx; Marx's *The Eighteenth Brumaire of Louis Bonaparte,* (1852) and *The Class Struggles in France* (1850); Engels's *Condition of the Working Class in England* (1845), and *The Origin of the Family, Private Property, and the State* (1884).

A classic application of the "means of intellectual production" is Arnold Hauser, *The Social History of Art* (New York: Knopf, 1951). Also in this lineage is Karl Mannheim, *Ideology and Utopia* (New York: Harcourt, 1936; originally published 1929). The nested organizational model is developed in my *Conflict Sociology: Toward an Explanatory Science,* chapter 9 (New York: Academic Press, 1975). Sex-stratification theory is developed in chapter 5 of that book and in a more Marxian vein both by Karen Sacks, *Sisters and Wives* (Westport, Conn.: Greenwood Press, 1979); and by Rae Lesser Blumberg, "A General Theory of Gender Stratification," in *Sociological Theory 1984* (San Francisco: Jossey-Bass, 1984); see also Peggy Sanday, *Female Power and Male Dominance* (Cambridge: Cambridge University Press, 1981). Alliance theory is overviewed in Marvin Harris, *Cultural Materialism* (New York: Random House, 1979). The most systematic statements are Janet Saltzman Chafetz, *Sex and Advantage. A Comparative Macro-Structural Theory of Sexual Stratification* (Totowa, N.J.: Rowman and Allanheld, 1984), and

Chafetz's *Gender Equity. An Integrated Theory of Stability and Change* (Newbury Park, CA: Sage, 1990).

Max Weber's major works are *Economy and Society* (Berkeley: University of California Press, 1978; originally published 1922); General Economic History (Brunswick: Transaction Books, 1981; originally published 1923); *The Religion of China:* (Glencoe, Ill.: Free Press, 1951; originally published 1916); *The Religion of India* (Glencoe, Ill.: Free Press, 1958; originally published 1916–1917); and *Ancient Judaism (Glencoe, Ill.: Free Press, 1952* [originally published 1917–1919). A famous collection was made by Hans Gerth and C. Wright Mills: *From Max Weber: Essays in Sociology* (New York: Oxford University Press, 1946). Recent German commentaries stressing the rationalistic/idealistic side of Weber are summarized in Stephen Kalberg, "The Search for Thematic Orientations in a Fragmented Oeuvre: The Discussion of Max Weber in Recent German Sociological Literature," *Sociology 13* (1979): 127–39; see also Kalberg, "Max Weber's Types of Rationality," *American Journal of Sociology 85* (1980): 1145–79. Alan Sica, *Weber, Irrationality and Social Order* (Berkeley: University of California Press, 1988), critiques the emphasis on rationality in Weber and proposes the challenging thesis that Weber has difficulty dealing with irrationality.

Conflict themes from Weber are developed in my *Conflict Sociology* (New York: Academic Press, 1975) and my *Weberian Sociological Theory* (Cambridge and New York: Cambridge University Press, 1986). Jurgen Habermas develops another version in *Legitimation Crisis* (Boston: Beacon Press, 1975); compare the more economic theory of James O'Connor, *The Fiscal Crisis of the State* (New York: St. Martin's Press, 1973). Norbert Wiley makes some of the most penetrating uses of Weber as a theorist of class conflict in "America's Unique Class Politics: The Interplay of the Labor, Credit, and Commodity Markets," *American Sociological Review 32* (1967): 529–40; also in "The Convergence of Weber and Keynes," *Sociological Theory 1983* (San Francisco: Jossey-Bass, 1983).

Organizational theory as power struggle comes from Robert Michels, *Political Parties: A Sociological Study of Oligarchical Tendencies of Modern Democracy* (New York: Collier, 1962; originally published 1911); and this theory is further developed by Philip Selznick in *TVA and the Grassroots* (Berkeley: University of California Press, 1949); Alvin Gouldner in *Patterns of Industrial Bureaucracy* (Glencoe, Ill.: Free Press, 1954); and Melville Dalton in *Men Who Manage* (New York: Wiley, 1959). Theoretical synthesis is discussed in Amitai Etzioni, *A Comparative Analysis of Complex Organizations* (New York: Free Press, 1961); in my *Conflict Sociology* chapter 6 (New York: Academic Press, 1975); and in Samuel B. Bacharach and Edward J. Lawler, *Power and Politics in Organizations* (San

Francisco: Jossey-Bass, 1980). the ecological approach is represented by Howard Aldrich, *Organizations and Environments* (Englewood Cliffs, N.J.: Prentice-Hall, 1979). Harrison White's theory of markets is cited in the bibliography to chapter 3. Recent organizational theory, bringing it into connection with the bounded rationality approach, is represented by Arthur L. Stinchcombe, *Information and Organizations* (Berkeley: University of California Press, 1990).

Modern conflict theory was enunciated by Ralf Dahrendorf, *Class and Class Conflict in Industrial Society* (Stanford, Calif.: Stanford University Press, 1958); and by Gerhard E. Lenski, *Power and Privilege: A Theory of Social Stratification* (New York: McGraw-Hill, 1966). C. Wright Mills's most important book was *The Power Elite* (New York: Oxford University Press, 1956), which is heavily influenced by Karl Mannheim's *Man and Society in an Age of Reconstruction* (London: Rutledge & Kegan Paul 1935). Also well worth reading for the intellectual battles of the time is Mills's *The Sociological Imagination* (New York: Oxford University Press, 1959). A recent biography of Mills is that of Irving Louis Horowitz, *C. Wrights Mills* (New York: Free Press, 1983). Class theory of politics was set forth by Seymour Martin Lipset, *Political Man* (Garden City, N.Y.: Doubleday, 1960). Resource mobilization is stated by Charles Tilly in *From Mobilization to Revolution* (Reading, Mass.: Addison-Wesley, 1978); and by Anthony Oberschall in *Social Conflicts and Social Movements* (Englewood Cliffs, N.J.: Prentice-Hall, 1973). Historical views of the effects of economics on political mobilization are found in Arthur L. Stinchcombe, "Agricultural Enterprise and Rural Class Relations," *American Journal of Sociology* 67 (1961): 165–76; Barrington Moore, Jr., *Social Origins of Dictatorship and Democracy* (Boston: Beacon Press, 1966); Jeffrey M. Paige, *Agrarian Revolution* (New York: Free Press, 1975); and Craig Calhoun, *The Question of Class Struggle. Social Foundations of Popular Radicalism During the Industrial Revolution* (Chicago: University of Chicago Press, 1982).

An important neoMarxian historical interpretation is Perry Anderson, *Lineages of the Absolutist State* (London: New Left Books, 1974). Three volumes of Immanuel Wallerstein's *The Modern World System* New York: Academic Press, 1974, 1980, 1989) have so far appeared. World-system theory is systematically presented in Christopher Chase-Dunn, *Global Formation. Structures of the World-Economy* (Oxford: Blackwell, 1989). The state breakdown theory of revolutions was developed by Theda Skocpol, *States and Social Revolutions* (New York: Cambridge University Press, 1979), and given a new twist by Jack A. Goldstone, *Revolution and Rebellion in the Early Modern World* (Berkeley: University of California Press, 1991). The geopolitical theory of state expansion and state breakdown is given by Randall Collins, "Long-term Social Change and the Territorial Power of States" in Louis Kriesberg (ed.), *Research in Social Movements, Conflicts, and Change* , Vol. 1. (Greenwich, Conn.: JAI Press, 1978, 1–34, and applied to the Soviet breakdown in "The Future Decline of the Russian Empire," pp. 186–209 in Randall Collins, *Weberian Sociological Theory* (Cambridge: Cambridge University Press, 1986). The most important study of the determinants of revolutionary ideologies is Robert Wuthnow, *Communities of Discourse. Ideology and Social Structure in the Reformation, the Enlightenment, and European Socialism* (Cambridge, Mass.: Harvard University Press, 1989).

Georg Simmel's classic work is translated in Kurt H. Wolff (ed.), *The Sociology of Georg Simmel* (Glencoe, Ill.: Free Press, 1950), and *Conflict and the Web of Group-Affiliations* (Glencoe, Ill.: Free Press, 1955). Lewis A. Coser's functionalist conflict theory is found in *The Functions of Social Conflict* (Glencoe, Ill.: Free Press, 1956).

Chapter 2. The Rational/Utilitarian Tradition

A classic overview of the Utilitarian tradition is Elie Halévy, *The Growth of Philosophical Radicalism* (London: Farber, 1928). See also Charles Camic, "The Utilitarians Revisited," *American Journal of Sociology* 85 (1979): 516–50. The culminating work of the classic Utilitarians was John Stuart Mill, *Utilitarianism* (1863). The downfall of utilitarian ethics was precipitated by criticism by F.H. Bradley, *Ethical Studies* (Oxford University Press, 1876), and by G. E. Moore, *Principia Ethica* (Cambridge University Press, 1903). The reduction of ethics to language was carried out by Charles L. Stevenson, *Ethics and Language* (New Haven: Yale University Press, 1944).

Adam Smith's contribution to the utilitarian tradition of ethics was his *Theory of Moral Sentiments* (1759). His great work of economics is *The Wealth of Nations* (1776). The development of economic theory is presented in masterful fashion in Joseph A. Schumpeter, *History of Economic Analysis* (New York: Oxford University Press, 1954), perhaps the greatest intellectual history written on any social discipline. The reintroduction of economics into the social sciences in the late twentieth century is represented by Gary Becker, *The Economic Approach to Human Behavior* (Chicago: University of Chicago Press, 1976). On the other hand, the problems that economics has had with making general equilibrium theory into a useful predictive science are lucidly presented in Alexander Rosenberg, *Economics: Mathematical Politics or Science of Diminishing Returns?* (Chicago: University of Chicago Press, 1992). Recent efforts to analyze Marxism from a rational choice viewpoint are found in John Roemer,

Analytical Marxism (New York: Cambridge University Press, 1986), and Jon Elster, *Making Sense of Marx* (New York: Cambridge University Press, 1985); also Elster's more general work on problems of rationality, *Ulysses and the Sirens: Studies in Rationality and Irrationality.* (New York: Cambridge University Press, 1979). Harrison White's network theory of markets was given first in "Where Do Markets Come From?" *American Journal of Sociology* 87 (1981): 517–47, and developed into a general theory in *Identity and Control. A Structural Theory of Social Action* (Princeton: Princeton University Press, 1992).

The explicit concern for exchange theory is sociology was developed by George C. Homans, *The Human Group* (New York: Harcourt, Brace, 1950) and *Social Behavior: Its Elementary Forms* (New York: Harcourt, Brace, 1961). Homans launched the famous micro/macro debate in his presidential address to the American Sociological Association in 1964: "Bringing Men Back In," *American Sociological Review* 29 (1964): 809–18. Exchange theory was subsequently developed by Peter M. Blau, *Exchange and Power in Social Life* (New York: Wiley, 1964). Experimental evidence in exchange theories of power are represented by Karen S. Cook, Richard M. Emerson, Mary R. Gillmore, and Toshio Yamagishi, "The Distribution of Power in Exchange Networks," *American Journal of Sociology* 89 (1983): 275–305. David Willer presents his Elementary Theory in David Willer and Bo Anderson (eds), *Networks, Exchange, and Coercion* (New York: Elsevier/Greenwood, 1981) and David Willer, *Theory and the Experimental Investigation of Social Structures* (New York: Gordon and Breach, 1987). The theory of equity or distributive justice is advanced by Guillermina Jasso, "A New Theory of Distributive Justice," *American Sociological Review* 45 (1980): 3–32; and "Principles of Theoretical Analysis," *Sociological Theory* 6 (1988): 1–20.

Sexual and marriage markets were first described in sociology by Willard Waller, "The Rating and Dating Complex," *American Sociological Review* 2 (1937): 727–34; and more recently by Hugh Carter and Paul C. Glick, *Marriage and Divorce: A Social and Economic Study* (Cambridge: Harvard University Press, 1976). The effects of relative economic power on domestic power has been analyzed by Robert O. Blood, Jr., and Donald M. Wolfe, *Husbands and Wives* (New York: Free Press, 1960), and Maximiliane Szinovacz, "Family Power," in Marvin B. Sussman and Susan K. Steinmetz (eds.) *Handbook of Marriage and the Family* (New York: Plenum, 1987). Historical changes in men's and women's sexual behavior due to changes in their economic positions are analyzed by Randall Collins, "A Conflict Theory of Sexual Stratification," *Social Problems* 19 (1971): 3–21; more recent patterns of sexual bargaining, including both homosexual and heterosexual couples, are analyzed in Philip Blumstein and Pepper Schwartz, *American Couples* (New York: William Morrow, 1983). Arlie Hochschild's theory of how men's and women's emotion work is affected by their position in marriage markets was first presented in "Attending to, Codifying and Managing Feelings: Sex Differences in Love" (paper presented at the Annual Meeting of the American Sociological Association, San Francisco, 1975).

The inflationary market for educational credentials is analyzed in Randall Collins, *The Credential Society: An Historical Sociology of Education and Stratification* (New York: Academic Press, 1979); in Pierre Bourdieu and Jean-Claude Passeron, *Reproduction: in Education, Society, and Culture* (Beverly Hills: Sage Publications, 1970/1977); and in Pierre Bourdieu, *Homo Academicus* (Stanford: Stanford University Press, 1988). Edna Bonacich developed her theory of the split labor market in "A Theory of Ethnic Antagonism: The Split Labor Market," *American Sociological Review* 37 (1972): 547–59. The economic theory of crime and illegal markets was put forward by Thomas C. Schelling, "Economic Analysis of Organized Crime," in *Task Force Report: Organized Crime* (Washington DC: Government Printing Office, 1967).

The neo-rationalist theory of "satisficing" rather than "maximizing" was developed by Herbert A. Simon, *Models of Man* (New York: Wiley, 1957) and James G. March and Herbert A. Simon, *Organizations* (New York: Wiley, 1958). The "free rider problem" was formulated by Mancur Olson, *The Logic of Collective Action* (Cambridge, Mass.: Harvard University Press, 1965). The "prisoner's dilemma" is described in Robert D. Luce and Howard Raiffa, *Games and Decisions* (New York: Wiley, 1957), and developed for sociology by Douglas Heckathorn, "Collective Sanctions and the Emergence of Prisoner's Dilemma Norms," *American Journal of Sociology* 94 (1988): 535–62. For iterated games see Martin Shubik, *Game Theory in the Social Sciences* (Cambridge, Mass.: M.I.T. Press, 1984). Paradoxes and heuristics of people's actual decision-making are presented in Amos Tversky and David Kahneman, "Judgment under Uncertainty: Heuristics and Biases," *Science* 1974, 185: 1124–31); in Robin M. Hogarth and Melvin W. Reder, *Rational Choice: The Contrast between Economics and Psychology* (Chicago: University of Chicago Press, 1987); and in Richard H. Thaler, *The Winner's Curse: Paradoxes and Anomalies of Economic Life* (New York: Free Press, 1992). A theoretical overview of paradoxes is Thomas C. Schelling, *Micromotives and Macrobehavior* (New York: Norton, 1978); Schelling developed his theory of coercive coalitions in *The Strategy of Conflict* (Cambridge: Harvard University Press, 1962).

The rational theory of social solidarity is presented by Michael Hechter, *Principles of Group Solidarity* (Berkeley: University of California Press, 1987); and James S. Coleman, *Foundations of Social Theory* (Cambridge: Harvard University Press, 1990), which also contains Coleman's theory of corporate organizations and his policy principles for controlling their self-interested pursuits.

The modern utilitarian approach to the state was developed by Anthony Downs, *An Economic Theory of Democracy* (New York: Harper and Row, 1957). The "minimum winning coalition" is described in William H. Riker, *The Theory of Political Coalitions* (New Haven: Yale University Press, 1962). The theory of the state as extracting "protection rent" is presented by Frederic C. Lane, *Profits from Power: Readings in Protection Rent and Violence-Controlling Enterprises* (Albany: State University of New York Press, 1979). The economic resources involved in the rise of the state are analyzed in Charles Tilly, *Coercion, Capital, and European States. AD 990–1990* (Oxford: Blackwell, 1991); resource strains producing state breakdowns are shown in the works by Theda Skocpol and Jack Goldstone cited in chapter 1. The fiscal self-aggrandizement of government agencies is analyzed in William A. Niskanen, *Bureaucracy and Representative Government* (Chicago: Aldine, 1971).

Modern philosophies of rational public policy include John Rawls, *A Theory of Justice* (Cambridge, Mass.: Harvard University Press, 1971); James M. Buchanan and Gordon Tullock, *The Calculus of Consent* (Ann Arbor: University of Michigan Press, 1962); James Buchanan, *The Limits of Liberty* (Chicago: University of Chicago Press, 1975); James Buchanan and Richard E. Wagner, *Democracy in Deficit* (New York: Academic Press, 1977); as well as James Coleman's *Foundations of Social Theory* (cited above).

Chapter 3. The Durkheimian Tradition

Probably the best intellectual biography of any figure in the history of the social sciences is by Steven Lukes, *Émile Durkheim, His Life and Work* (New York: Allen Lane, 1973). The organizational politics of the French academic world of Durkheim's day are analyzed in Terry N. Clark, *Prophets and Patrons: The French University and the Emergence of the Social Sicences* (Cambridge: Harvard University Press, 1973). Jeffrey C. Alexander in *The Antinomies of Classical Thought: Marx and Durkheim* (Berkeley: University of California Press, 1982) gives a thorough treatment of Durkheim's intellectual development and of some of his French followers, and cites much of the secondary literature. Alexander, though, is mainly concerned with philosophical presuppositions and omits most of the substantive contributions the Durkheimians made to explanatory theory.

Translations of Durkheim's major works include *The Division of Labor in Society* (New York: Free Press, 1964; originally published in 1893); *The Rules of Sociological Method* (New York: Macmillan, 1982; originally published 1895); *Suicide* (New York: Free Press, 1966; originally published 1897); *Moral Education* (New York: Free Press, 1961); *Sociology and Philosophy* (New York: Free Press, 1974); and *The Elementary Forms of the Religious Life* (New York: Macmillan, 1961; originally published 1912). Durkheim analyzed his own intellectual predecessors in *Montesquieu and Rousseau* (Ann Arbor: University of Michigan Press, 1960); and in *Socialism and Saint-Simon* (New York: Collier, 1962). Excerpts from Comte's lengthy *Course of Positive Philosophy* are in George Simpson (ed.), *Auguste Comte: Sire of Sociology* (New York: Crowell, 1969). Herbert Spencer's major contribution is his *Principles of Sociology* (New York: Appleton, 1884).

The functionalist branch is represented by Robert K. Merton, *Social Theory and Social Structure* (New York: Free Press, 1957); and Talcott Parsons, *The Social System* (Glencoe, Ill.: Free Press, 1951); *Toward a General Theory of Action*—with Edward Shils and others—(Cambridge: Harvard University Press, 1951); and *Societies: Comparative and Evolutionary Perspectives* (Englewood Cliffs, N.J.: Prentice-Hall, 1966). Parson's interpretation of the Nazis is in his *Essays in Sociological Theory* (Glencoe: Free Press, 1949). An application of the Parsonian version of Durkheimian theory to modern culture in Winston White, *Beyond Conformity* (New York: Free Press, 1961). Kingsley Davis and Wilbert Moore's functional theory of stratification together with the debate it set off are reprinted in Reinhard Bendix and Seymour Martin Lipset (eds.), *Class, Status, and Power* (New York: Free Press, 1966). A critique of the functionalist theory of education and of the professions is in my *The Credential Society* (New York: Academic Press, 1979). The recent upsurge of functionalist theory in Germany is described by Jeffrey C. Alexander, "The Parsons Revival in German Sociology," in *Sociological Theory 1984* (San Francisco: Jossey-Bass, 1984).

A recent edition of Numa Denis Fustel de Coulanges's *The Ancient City* together with current scholarship regarding ancient Greece are cited in footnote 4, Chapter 3. Guy E. Swanson's comparative test of Durkheim's sociology of religion is found in *The Birth of the Gods* (Ann Arbor: University of Michigan Press, 1962).

W. Lloyd Warner's first book was *A Black Civilization. A Social Study of an Australian Tribe* (New York: Harper, 1937). It was followed by his "Yankee City" series: Warner and Paul S. Lunt, *The Social Life of a Modern Community* (New Haven, Conn.: Yale University Press, 1941); and several subsequent volumes, including his Durkheimian analysis of modern ritual in *The Living and the Dead* (New Haven, Conn.: Yale

University Press, 1959) of which the paperback edition, abridged and supplemented, was entitled *The Family of God* (New Haven, Conn,: Yale University Press, 1961). Warner's midwestern study, dedicated "To the Memory of Émile Durkheim," is *Democracy in Jonesville* (New York: Harper & Row, 1949). Other studies of the Warner group were Allison Davis, Burleigh B. Gardner, and Mary R. Gardner, *Deep South* (Chicago: University of Chicago Press, 1941); and St. Clair Drake and Horace R. Cayton, *Black Metropolis*, (New York: Harcourt, 1945). A work in the Warner tradition that deals with stratified social networks is Edward O. Laumann, *The Bonds of Pluralism* (New York: Wiley, 1973).

Erving Goffman's major works in the Durkheimian tradition are *The Presentation of Self in Everyday Life* (Garden City, N.Y.: Doubleday, 1959); *Asylums* (Garden City, N.Y.: Doubleday, 1961); *Encounters* (Indianapolis: Bobbs-Merrill, 1961); *Interaction Ritual* (Garden City, N.Y.: Doubleday, 1967); and *Relations in Public* (New York: Basic Books, 1971), the last was dedicated to the memory of the social anthropologist Radcliffe-Brown. Interpretive essays on Goffman as well as on Lévi-Strauss, Bourdieu, and other recent intellectual figures are found in my *Sociology Since Mid-century* (New York: Academic Press, 1981); this book also contains my theory of interaction ritual chains (originally published in the *American Journal of Sociology* 86 (March 1981), 984–1014. An effort to combine IR chains with the rational choice theory of markets is Randall Collins, "Emotional Energy as the Common Denominator of Rational Choice," *Rationality and Society* 5 (1993): 203–30. The recent development of the sociology of emotions as a link to the Durkheimian tradition is presented in Thomas Scheff, *Microsociology. Discourse, Emotion and Social Structure* (Chicago: University of Chicago Press, 1990), and Theodore D. Kemper (ed.), *Research Agendas in the Sociology of Emotions* (Albany: State University of New York Press, 1990).

Durkheimian/Goffmanian theory of class cultures is presented in my *Conflict Sociology: Toward an Explanatory Science* (New York: Academic Press, 1975), chapter 2, and further developed in my *Theoretical Sociology* (San Diego: Harcourt, Brace, Jovanovich, 1988), chapter 6. Herbert Gans analyzes working-class culture and sees it as being like that of peasant villages in his *The Urban Villagers* (New York: Free Press, 1962). Language differences in class cultures are analyzed by Basil Bernstein, *Class, Codes, and Control* which is in three volumes (London: Routledge & Kegan Paul, 1971–1975). Mary Douglas's comparative theory of cultures is found in her *Natural Symbols* (London: Routledge & Kegan Paul, 1970).

Much of the work of Marcel Mauss and his collaborators remains untranslated into English. Among the important pieces cited in the text are Henri Hubert and Marcel Mauss, "Introduction à l'analyse de quelques phénomènes religieux," (1906); Marcel Mauss, "La prière et les rites oraux," (1909); and "Valeur magique et valeur d'échange," (1914), in Marcel Mauss, *Oeuvres,* (Paris: Editions de Minuit, 1968); also Marcel Mauss, *A General Theory of Magic* (New York: Norton, 1972; originally published with Henri Hubert in 1902); *The Gift: Forms and Functions of Exchange in Archaic Societies* (New York: Norton, 1967; originally published 1925); Émile Durkheim and Marcel Mauss, *Primitive Classification* (Chicago: University of Chicago Press, 1963; originally published 1903). Max Weber's characterization of status groups as the absence of hard bargaining is in *Economy and Society* (Berkeley: University of California Press, 1978) p. 937. The gift-exchange theory of kinship of Claude Lévi-Strauss in found in *The Elementary Structures of Kinship* (Boston: Beacon Press, 1969; originally published 1949). Durkheim foreshadowed this notion that tribal kinship could be worked out like a problem in mathematics in his "Sur l'organisation matrimoniale des sociétés australiennes," *L'Année Sociologique* 8 (1905). Lévi-Strauss's later mentalist structuralism is developed in *The Savage Mind* (Chicago: University of Chicago Press, 1966; originally published 1962); and in *The Origin of Table Manners* (New York: Harper, 1978; originally published 1968). Warren O. Hagstrom applied the ritualexchange theory to science in *The Scientific Community* (New York: Basic Books, 1965). An even more Durkheimian theory of science as a modern-day sacred object is David Bloor, *Knowledge and Social Imagery* (London: Routledge & Kegan Paul, 1976). Pierre Bourdieu's theories of cultural capital and symbolic violence are translated in his *Outline of a Theory of Practice* (New York: Cambridge University Press, 1977), and applied to class cultures in *Distinction. A Social Critique of the Judgement of Taste* (Cambridge: Harvard University Press, 1979/1984). A critique and further development of this line of analysis is Michele Lamont, *Morals, Money and Manners: Symbolic Boundaries in the French and American Upper-Middle Class* (University of Chicago Press, 1992). The Durkheimian theory of crime as social ritual is developed in Kai Erickson, *Wayward Puritans* (New York: Wiley, 1966); as well as in Donald Black, *The Behavior of Law* (New York: Academic Press, 1976); and Donald Black (ed.), *Toward a General Theory of Social Control* (New York: Academic Press, 1984).

Chapter 4. The Microinteractionist Tradition

The social background and moral interests of American sociologists are vividly analyzed in Arthur J. Vidich and Stanford M. Lyman, *American*

Sociology. Worldly Rejections of Religion and Their Directions (New Haven, Conn.: Yale University Press, 1984). The philosophical background is nicely covered in Herbert W. Schneider, *A History of American Philosophy* (New York: Columbia University Press, 1963) and in John Passmore, *A Hundred Years of Philosophy* (Baltimore: Penguin, 1968). The quote from Josiah Royce (p. 184) is cited in Schneider, p. 416. Peirce's main writings are collected in Justus Buchler (ed.), *Philosophical Writings of Peirce* (New York: Dover, 1955); the quote on p. 186 is from Buchler, p. 255. A magnificent intellectual biography of William James is Ralph Barton Perry, *The Thought and Character of William James* (Boston, 1935). John Dewey's most influential book for sociology was *Human Nature and Conduct* (New York: Holt, 1922). On the sociology of the Progressive movement in education of which Dewey was a part, see my *The Credential Society* (New York: Academic Press, 1979).

The quotations from Charles Horton Cooley on pp. 254–5 are from *Human Nature and the Social Order* (New York: Schocken, 1964: 119, 121; originally published 1902). George Herbert Mead's sociological lectures were collected posthumously by Charles W. Morris (ed.), *Mind, Self, and Society* (Chicago: University of Chicago Press, 1934; paperback edition, 1967); the quotations on pp. are from Morris p. 147. Another selection of Mead's papers and lectures is Anselm Strauss (ed.), *George Herbert Mead on Social Psychology* (Chicago: University of Chicago Press, 1964). Mead's philosophy, of which his sociology was only a part, is better expressed in his *The Philosophy of the Act* (Chicago: University of Chicago Press, 1938); *The Philosophy of the Present* (La Salle, Ill.: Open Court Publishing Co., 1932); and *Movements of Thought in the Nineteenth Century* (Chicago: University of Chicago Press, 1936). The differences between Mead's thought and the Chicago school in general are stressed by J. David Lewis and Richard L. Smith, *American Sociology and Pragmatism: Mead, Chicago Sociology, and Symbolic Interaction* (Chicago: University of Chicago Press, 1980).

The scattered theoretical writings of W. I. Thomas are collected in Morris Janowitz (ed.), *W. I. Thomas on Social Organization and Personality* (Chicago: University of Chicago Press, 1966). His collaboration with the Polish sociologist, Florian Znaniecki, is described by Robert Bierstedt, *American Sociological Theory, A Critical History* (New York: Academic Press, 1981). Bierstedt lucidly presents most of what is worth remembering of American sociology, from the early evolutionists Williams Graham Sumner and Lester Frank Ward up through the sociologists of the 1930s and 1940s such as Robert MacIver and George Lundberg. Herbert Blumer's collected papers are in his *Symbolic Interactionism* (Englewood Cliffs, N.J.: Prentice-Hall, 1969). Representative works in this tradition are Alfred Lindesmith, *Opiate Addiction*, (Bloomington, Ind.: Principia,

1947); Howard S. Becker, *Outsiders: Studies in the Sociology of Deviance* (Glencoe Free Press, 1963); Edwin M. Schur, *Crimes Without Victims: Deviant Behavior and Public Policy* (Englewood Cliffs, N.J.: Prentice-Hall, 1965). Role theory is overviewed by Sheldon Stryker, *Symbolic Interactionism: A Social Structural Version*, (Menlo Park, Calif.: Cummings, 1980).

The phenomenological background of ethnomethodology can be sampled in English in Edmund Husserl, *Ideas: General Introduction to Pure Phenomenology* (New York: Macmillan, 1975); *Cartesian Meditations* (The Hague: Nijhoff, 1960); *Phenomenology and the Crisis of Philosophy* (New York: Harper, 1965). The existentialist classics are Martin Heidegger, *Being and Time* (New York: Harper, 1960; German original published 1927); and Jean-Paul Sartre, *Being and Nothingness* (New York: Washington Square Press, 1971; French original published 1943). Husserl was developed for sociology by Alfred Schutz, *Collected Papers* (The Hague: Nijhoff, 1962–1966), and by Peter Berger and Thomas Luckmann, *The Social Construction of Reality* (New York: Doubleday, 1966). Harold Garfinkel's collection of papers is *Studies in Ethnomethodology* (Englewood Cliffs, N.J.: Prentice-Hall, 1967). His later work includes Harold Garfinkel, Michael Lynch, and Eric Livingston, "The Work of Discovering Science Construed from Materials from the Optically Discovered Pulsar," *Philosophy of the Social Sciences*, 11 (1981): 131–38; Michael Lynch, Eric Livingston, and Harold Garfinkel, "Temporal Order in Laboratory Work," in Karin Knorr and Michael Mulkay (eds.), *Science Observed*, (Beverly Hills, Calif.: Sage, 1983). Developments in the sociology of language and cognition are represented by Aaron Cicourel, *Cognitive Sociology* (Baltimore: Penguin, 1973), and Harvey Sacks, Emanuel Schegloff, and Gail Jefferson, "A Simplest Systematics for the Organization of Turn-taking in Conversation," *Language* 50 (1974): 696–735. Erving Goffman's counterattack is in his *Frame Analysis* (New York: Harper, 1974); (the quotation of p. 281 is from p. 1 of this book); and *Forms of Talk*, (Philadelphia: University of Pennsylvania Press, 1981) (quotations on p. 282 are from p. 121 and p. 103; quotations on p. 286 are from p. 173 and p. 151). The ongoing development of conversation analysis may be seen in J. Maxwell Atkinson and John Heritage, *Structures of Social Action. Studies in Conversation Analysis* (New York: Cambridge University Press, 1984); Allen Grimshaw, *Conflict Talk* (New York: Cambridge University Press, 1990); and Deirdre Boden and Don H. Zimmerman (eds.), *Talk and Social Structure. Studies in Ethnomethodology and Conversation Analysis* (Berkeley: University of California Press, 1991).

A comprehensive model that attempts to synthesize the various aspects of microinteractionist theories is Jonathan H. Turner, *A Theory of Social Interaction* (Stanford: Stanford University Press, 1988).

Index